Applying Political Theory

D1256620

Applying Political Theory

Issues and Debates

Katherine Smits

First published 2009 by
PALGRAVE MACMILLAN

Palgrave Macmillan in the UK is an imprint of Macmillan Publishers Limited,
registered in England, company number 785998, of Houndmills, Basingstoke,
Hampshire RG21 6XS.

Palgrave Macmillan in the US is a division of St Martin's Press LLC,
175 Fifth Avenue, New York, NY 10010.

Palgrave Macmillan is the global academic imprint of the above companies
and has companies and representatives throughout the world.

Palgrave® and Macmillan® are registered trademarks in the United States,
the United Kingdom, Europe and other countries.

ISBN: 978–0–230–55508–2   hardback
ISBN: 978–0–230–55509–9   paperback

This book is printed on paper suitable for recycling and made from fully
managed and sustained forest sources. Logging, pulping and manufacturing
processes are expected to conform to the environmental regulations of the
country of origin.

A catalogue record for this book is available from the British Library.

A catalog record for this book is available from the Library of Congress.

10 9 8 7 6 5 4 3 2 1
18 17 16 15 14 13 12 11 10 09

Printed and bound in Great Britain by
CPI Anthony Rowe, Chippenham and Eastbourne

For Marty, Julia and Sophie

Contents

List of Boxes and Tables

Boxes

Tables

Preface

Although there is now an expanding literature on political theory, including several texts aiming to introduce the field to students, there are surprisingly few volumes that focus centrally on the applicability and application of political theory to key problems in contemporary politics. This book is intended to fill that gap. It offers a concise and accessible account of the contribution that political theory can make across a very wide range of pressing and controversial political issues.

With this in mind, I have made a conscious decision not to try to duplicate the excellent introductions to modern political theory already in print (for example, Heywood, 2004) or the history of political thought (such as Morrow, 2005). I sketch a brief overview of contemporary political theory in the Introduction, but focus in subsequent chapters on political ideas as they relate to, explain and illuminate each specific issue. This book is designed to be used in one of two ways: first, as a freestanding single text for courses specifically focused on issues, whether at a first level introduction or pitched at a more advanced level and building on a first level course covering theories and concepts. Second, it may be used in conjunction with texts such as those of Andrew Heywood and John Morrow for courses in which applications of theory are a smaller element.

I have been inspired to write this book by the many politics students I have taught in New Zealand and the United States who wanted to know how abstract political ideas were relevant to the real world. I am indebted especially to students in my modern political thought and social justice classes at the University of Auckland, who in their questions, comments and essays have challenged me to think about the relationship between political theory and the issues and controversies of the day, both local and global.

I wish to acknowledge the Faculty of Arts at the University of Auckland, which granted me research and study leave in which to work on this book. I am grateful for research assistance to Laura Murray, Cameron Pritchard and Bella Waugh. Thanks to my colleagues in the Department of Political Studies at Auckland, Steve Winter and Anita Lacey, who read drafts of chapters and provided insightful and thought-provoking comments and suggestions. Steven Kennedy at Palgrave Macmillan has been a constant source of encouragement and canny advice, and just the right degree of flexibility with deadlines. My husband Marty Wechselblatt has been, as ever, my most helpful critic and adviser, reading drafts of every chapter, and prompting me to write in a clear and accessible style. I am grateful always for his unfailing support, and for that of my daughters, Julia and Sophie, and I dedicate this book to them.

KATHERINE SMITS

Chapter 1

Introduction

Despite the billion-dollar bail-out packages hastily put together by governments, the recession into which the world economy had slipped by late 2008 led to soaring prices and collapsing house values and savings, even in developed countries. Global growth slowed, but as World Bank President Robert Zoellick pointed out, the human cost of the crisis was particularly high in the developing world. The Bank predicted that 100 million people would be added to the ranks of the world's poor, as a result of increases in fuel and food prices.

The global financial crisis that precipitated the recession and its wider social effects raises many of the most fundamental questions we ask in politics. Some of these are practical: How did this economic crisis come about? How can it be solved? But normative questions – those that address whether principles, policies and legislation are right, just or fair – are just as crucial. These include: How should the world's resources be apportioned? Should wealth be redistributed within nations, to reduce inequality? What, if any, are the obligations of people in developed and rich nations to the poor in the developing world? Should we conserve and protect scarce resources for future generations?

These questions preoccupy students of politics and political theory in the western tradition. Of course, the global recession is not the only pressing practical political problem that raises normative issues. Since the September 11 terrorist attacks in 2001, many nations have passed legislation designed to identify terrorists and prevent attacks. Critics have protested that these laws are unjustifiable encroachments on the civil liberties that define liberal democracies:

- Is it acceptable to tap phones if a government authority thinks that doing so might identify people planning terrorist attacks?
- Can we justify holding people for long periods without warrants and evidence, in defiance of the traditional protection of habeas corpus?
- Should we think of 'balancing' liberty with security?

Or, to ask one of the most central questions of modern politics: How extensive should the reach of state power be?

These are some of the questions that we consider in this book. But we also examine from a normative perspective other policy issues that, while not so

1

immediately pressing, have led to deep and widespread public controversy that has become embedded in public life. Many of these issues have a long history, but the lively debate around them in our own time reflects both the ethical and philosophical pluralism, and the participatory politics of modern liberal democracies:

- Should abortion and euthanasia be legal?
- How much power should the state have to regulate people's decisions about the beginning and end of life?
- Should prostitution and pornography be legal?
- What are their implications for the equality of women?
- Should people be allowed to make free decisions that might run counter to community morality, or that might indirectly allow the exploitation of others to continue?

Then there are other issues that arise from the cultural, social and ethical diversity of many modern states:

- Should minority cultures be protected with special rights?
- Should people be allowed to say whatever they choose about other cultures and groups?
- Should we try to compensate for historical injustices to minorities with affirmative action?
- Should institutions such as marriage be extended to same-sex couples?

These are the kinds of questions that political theory can help us to grapple with, and it is the purpose of this book to explore the ways in which political theorists and philosophers have approached some of these particularly important and controversial policy problems. Political theory, especially normative theory, is sometimes imagined as being a separate field of enquiry from politics or political science. It is deceptively easy to think of theory as being divorced from reality, as dealing with utopian ideals rather than the 'real world' of empirical facts. This distinction between facts and values was formulated by the nineteenth-century German sociologist Max Weber, who argued that social scientific analysis could never establish the truth of values or normative claims (Weber, 1946). Without disagreeing with Weber, we will see in the chapters that follow that political theory can help us to understand the principles and assumptions that underlie political arguments and claims, and also to see that the empirical world of politics looks very different from different theoretical perspectives. Our theoretical concepts and paradigms guide us in making political judgements, but they also help us to sort and make sense of the political world.

Approaches to political theory

Political theory is as old as the study of politics itself; in fact, until the Enlightenment, scholars did not distinguish between the analytical description of politics and prescriptions for good government. Today, we distinguish between the study of past political thought as a strand in the history of ideas on the one hand, and contemporary political theory or philosophy on the other. This does not mean that contemporary theory does not make reference to the ideas of philosophers in the past; in this book we will often refer to the ideas of historical thinkers. But we will consider the arguments they raise, and the concepts they explain, not in their original historical context but, rather, as ideas and arguments that influence our own thinking today. (For a more detailed discussion of key thinkers in the history of political thought, see Morrow, 2005.)

Contemporary political theory – and here we include authors writing from the twentieth century onwards – is often used to describe, as it has here, normative political theory. Normative theory is concerned with the way politics ought to work – as a branch of practical philosophy it tells us what we ought to do. But political theory can also be used to mean empirical or descriptive theory. This usage of the term is closer to that intended by those who study, say, sociological or economic theory. Empirical or descriptive theory sets out to explain the way political phenomena work, by exploring the ideas that shape and structure political processes, institutions and practices. The division between these categories, as we shall see, is not always clear-cut. In the past two decades, European political and social theory has become more influential in the English-speaking world, and so we might add to our two categories 'critical theory', which pays particular attention to the way ideology and culture reflect and maintain hierarchies of power, and 'postmodernism', which examines what lies behind the apparently fundamental principles, values and structures of our political lives. (See Heywood, 2004, for a more detailed discussion of these schools of thinking.) Some lamented the 'death of political philosophy' in the 1950s (Laslett, 1956) but, since the 1970s, political theorists have focused again on examining the ethical problems of public life, and normative theory has re-emerged as a vital field. This has meant a revival of interest in questions of justice, sparked largely by the publication of John Rawls' *A Theory of Justice* in 1971. Rawls' work makes a contribution to most of the debates that we consider in this book.

It is important not to overstate the distinction between these sub-categories of political theory. Every normative theoretical framework rests upon and assumes an analysis of how the political system works, what constitutes human nature, and how individuals and groups behave in public life. Feminism, for example, incorporates both an analysis of gendered power relations, and a prescription for a more just and gender-equal society. Marxism comprises a critique of how economics and ideology function under capitalism, and a prescription for a more just and classless society. Both of these could also be described as critical theories, as they are concerned with the relationship between ideology and the exercise of social power. In this book, we will concentrate on normative political theory, because our aim is to see how theory can help us to answer the crucial questions about how our public lives together should be organized. Most of the chapters here begin with 'should', and are answered by considering different ideas about what is good and right. Normative political theory is concerned with the relations between individuals, groups and institutions in civil society and governments. It asks:

- How much power should the state have over individuals and groups?
- Where should the boundaries between public and private life be drawn?
- How should individuals and groups treat each other in their interactions?

Normative political theory aims to identify, establish and defend principles and values that guide answers to these questions.

We will mainly use the term 'political theory' in this book, but most theorists and philosophers treat it as interchangeable with 'political philosophy'. Distinctions are sometimes drawn between them, but these vary and, in fact, any real difference tends to reflect institutional factors, particularly the way that the discipline of politics or political science has developed as an academic discourse, rather than any fundamental difference in their concerns. The academic authors whom we will discuss generally come from the wider study of political science, in which case they tend to describe their work as political theory, or from philosophy, in which case they might refer to their work as political philosophy. However, they address the same problems, using the same theoretical concepts and frameworks (see pp. 6–10 and 10–16). We will also discuss work by legal and social theorists, when they address political problems using the same normative concepts.

So far, we have used the term 'political theory' to describe a field of study. But it is also commonly used to refer to particular theories that establish frameworks linking normative values and explanatory concepts. Liberalism, conservatism, feminism and socialism are often referred to as political theories, though they are perhaps more often studied as ideologies that underpin and justify political movements and systems of government. Our primary interest here is in the way they operate as explanatory frameworks or paradigms systematically linking concepts and values. I outline these frameworks on pp. 10–16. As we shall see, however, their boundaries are often not very clearly defined and, in many cases, there is considerable internal variation within each, and overlap between them.

Liberalism is a case in point. As a theoretical framework of ideas, liberalism emerged in the late seventeenth century in response to religious pluralism, the development of capitalism and the modern state, and the idea of the individual. As a set of ideas, it has developed in many different directions over the subsequent three hundred years. In contemporary politics, liberalism might be associated with state regulation and intervention designed to achieve equality, or with laissez-faire free-market policies. It is impossible to pin down one liberal position on many issues, as we shall see in this book. Similarly, feminists might be found on either side, even with regard to issues that directly concern women, such as pornography and prostitution. The reason for this is that the values around which these frameworks centre can be interpreted in different ways. Liberalism, for example, is built around the key norm of individual freedom. But which freedom is more important: that of a person to do as he or she chooses with his or her own property, or that of someone to be able to develop his or her talents and achieve according to his or her potential? These freedoms are not necessarily compatible, as debates over redistribution show (Chapters 2 and 10).

At the same time, theoretical frameworks do not take particular positions on all issues. They developed to address particular sets of questions, and are not always equipped to answer others. So, we find that Marxism, for example, does not address some contemporary social issues such as same-sex marriage or abortion, as these do not fit easily into the economic analysis with which it is primarily concerned. Other frameworks, such as liberalism, have developed to deal with a wider range of issues.

For these reasons, this book does not focus on the theoretical frameworks themselves. We will refer to them, as they are relevant and helpful in organizing groups of thinkers on particular values, but with respect to some issues, such as humanitarian intervention, we will make only occasional reference to them. Our focus throughout will be on the concepts and values around which theoretical frameworks are organized. Because we are applying normative theory, to help us judge what we should do with respect to political problems, we will concentrate on political values: ideas about what is good, right and important in political life. The key values that appear in these chapters include liberty, autonomy, equality, justice, the role of the state, and the common good. These can all be interpreted in many ways, and the different interpretations of what they mean, and the different weights assigned to them, shape a range of theoretical frameworks.

This book applies the values and theoretical frameworks of political theory to real world political issues. But we should remember that these concepts, values and frameworks emerged in the first place as a result of thinkers wrestling with these issues. Feminism developed because women confronted the reality of their subordination to men – and this included issues such as abortion, prostitution and pornography. Liberalism developed because people were concerned about the power of a centralizing state over their freedom of speech and civil liberties. We aim here to shift the focus of these theoretical frameworks back to the real world problems out of which they emerged.

Normative concepts and values

Much of the debate over the issues we address in this book turns on different interpretations and weights assigned to some key values. We now look at these in more detail. The first two concepts we consider are very broad – it is the subsequent, more specific values that provoke much of the controversy in normative political theory.

Justice

Justice is one of the oldest concepts in western political theory – Plato's *Republic*, written in the fourth century BCE (Plato, 1981), is an extended discussion of the question: What is justice? Aristotle divided the subject into corrective and distributive justice (Aristotle, 1981) – the first is a matter for the criminal justice system, the second, for political philosophy. Justice also encompasses both the way individuals treat each other and the laws and institutions that structure society. In both these respects, justice is understood today as fairness. What makes a just society is one of the main concerns of normative political theory, and includes the principles by which social goods are distributed (distributive justice), and those that regulate the ways in which both state and individual citizens treat individuals and groups. All of the theoretical frameworks we refer to here address one, if not both of these categories. Justice is expressed or embodied in laws, in economic structures, and in social and political attitudes and practices.

Rights

Rights can be defined as our entitlements to act or to be treated in a particular way (Heywood, 2004). Individuals assert their rights against the state (these claims are often expressed as liberties) or against other people. Rights are derived from law (positive rights), or from claims to a higher authority, such as nature or God (natural rights). (We discuss the natural law tradition in Chapters 6 and 7.) Human rights are a modern and usually secular development of the idea of natural rights. The distinction between positive and natural rights maps onto one dealing with the scope of rights: positive rights are specific to particular political communities, while natural rights apply to all universally. (We consider questions of the scope of universal rights in Chapter 7, on abortion, and Chapter 12, on justice for future generations.)

Liberty and autonomy

Political theory is concerned with the liberty or freedom of individuals from state action, and in relation to other people. Liberty is an ancient concept, and individual freedom has been a fundamental concern of liberal political philosophy since seventeenth- and eighteenth-century theorists first explicitly defended individual freedoms against the state and the Church. The twentieth-century political philosopher Isaiah Berlin (Berlin, 1969) distinguished two different forms of liberty: 'negative' liberty and 'positive' liberty. Negative liberty refers to the freedom of individuals from restraints – usually the laws of the state, but including the pressures of public opinion. 'Positive liberty' refers to the freedom of individuals to develop their capacities, to act autonomously – that is, under no one's direction but their own – and to maximize their individual potential. Positive liberty includes our freedom to participate in making our own laws, and to govern ourselves.

Autonomy here means literally self-rule, and refers to people's abilities to make their own decisions and shape their own lives. Autonomy entails positive liberty, but we might also argue that it requires a range of options to choose from, a range provided by the intact cultural context in which individuals are embedded (see Chapter 3). Autonomy may also apply to whole societies, in which case it is bound up with the concept of sovereignty (see Chapter 11).

Certain more recent philosophers have suggested that Berlin's distinction between positive and negative liberty is an artificial one, as all liberties imply that one must be free of some restraint, in order to do or become something (Swift, 2001). Nevertheless, as we shall see, many of the debates over policy that we consider in this book involve different interpretations of liberty: some focusing on law as a restraint, and others on the way state action allows people to exercise their autonomy.

All the theoretical frameworks we discuss here share a concern for liberty, but they differ with respect to the relationship they prescribe between individual liberty and other values. Feminists, for example, think that individual liberty must be assessed in the context of a social, cultural and economic system that systematically represents male interests and privileges men. Libertarians, or classical liberals, see individual negative liberty as the determining value in politics. It is important to note that whichever conception of liberty is used, no political theory defends absolute liberty for individuals – it must, at a minimum, be compatible with the liberties of others. But there is a wide range of views among political theorists on whether – and how much – liberty should be restricted to allow for other social goods, such as national security or equality.

Equality

As with liberty, equality is an idea that is fundamental to modern political theory. It emerged with the Enlightenment reaction to the structuring of society on hierarchical lines. Modern liberal democracies all embrace equality before the law and – at least, in positive legal terms – equal liberties and equal rights for all. Some liberals argue that the state is required only to go this far – to enshrine equal liberties and rights in law. Any subsequent inequalities, they conclude, are due to the natural inequalities between different people's talents and abilities. Others have been more concerned with the way in which equal treatment by law affects people differently as a result of other social, economic and cultural circumstances. As Anatole France remarked: 'The law, in its majestic equality, forbids rich and poor alike to sleep under bridges, to beg in the streets and to steal their bread' (France, 1910). Egalitarian thinkers emphasize equality of opportunity, and the need to ensure that circumstances outside their control do not prevent people from taking opportunities. This second approach recognizes that laws are not the only impediments to equality; structures of social, economic and cultural power are also influential. Feminists argue that the system of patriarchy prevents women from being equal, even if they are assured equality before the law. In the United States, African Americans were assured formal constitutional equality under segregation, but the doctrine of 'separate but equal' clearly did not grant them equality with the white population.

Economic equality or equality of resources introduces more complications. Marxism and socialism are often seen as egalitarian philosophies but, in fact, Marx does not argue that resources should be distributed to everyone equally – rather, they should be owned in common and apportioned in accordance with people's needs. This raises a question for all egalitarian theoretical frameworks: Does 'equal' mean 'the same'? Does it require all people to be treated in the same way? In practice, equal treatment could result in very unequal outcomes. Two state pensions of the same amount paid to different people, one of whom is healthy and able-bodied, and the other is chronically ill with a disease that is expensive to treat, will produce inequality between them. Aristotle famously wrote in the fourth century BCE that 'like' people should be treated alike, or equally (Aristotle, 1981) but this merely begs the question: How do we determine whether people are 'alike'?

In any case, equality must be balanced with other political values, particularly liberty. Should individual freedom be limited in order to ensure that all are equal, however this is defined? This tension is one of the most important in modern political theory, and we will see it demonstrated in several of the issues we consider in this book.

Private property

As with liberty and equality, private property emerged as a key political value in the seventeenth century. Before then, philosophers believed that economic relations and the accumulation and distribution of wealth should be subordinated to the moral and ethical purposes of government. But capitalism and classical liberalism are based upon the right of individuals to private property, and later versions of liberalism, Marxism and socialism are structured around the question of how to balance rights to private property with equality, with positive liberty and autonomy, and with the common good. We discuss this in Chapter 2, where we ask:

- Can the state take property and redistribute it to others in need?
- Are collective purposes more important than the right of individuals to their property?
- Does such a right exist independently of the social good?

Marxism argues that private property reflects and perpetuates fundamental inequality in the economic system. It has no inherent value.

The common good

Students of politics have seen human beings as fundamentally social creatures since Aristotle described us as 'political animals' (Aristotle, 1981). Human beings cannot live the kind of lives for which they are meant – good lives – outside of society. But some important modern political thinking juxtaposes the interests of individuals to the common good. Classical liberals argue that if a conflict should arise between the claims of the community and the rights of the individual, the latter must prevail. They define communities as aggregates of individuals, which do have moral value in themselves. Others have followed the argument of Jean-Jacques Rousseau in the eighteenth century, that the rights and freedoms of the individual are compatible with the 'higher' common good (Rousseau, 1973 [1762]).

The situation becomes more complex when we consider the nature of the relevant community. We must decide whether we mean to take into account the good of the nation-state community, or sub-state communities such as racial or ethnic groups, or whether we should take into account the good of the world's population as a whole. National society in liberal democracies is often seen as a scheme of shared cooperation, which generates mutual obligations among citizens. We must then ask ourselves:

- What are our obligations across state borders to those in need?
- Do these moral obligations stem from our shared nature as human beings,

or do they stem from the relationships of reciprocity that exist within national borders?
- What are the implications of sub-state national communities for these?

Sovereignty

Considerations of the common good inevitably raise questions about the role of governments in representing and protecting that good. The fundamental normative justification of government is the protection of citizens, and the pursuit of their interests and goods. But this obligation must be considered in the context of the principle of sovereignty. The modern concept of sovereignty developed in Europe in the sixteenth century, as central governments consolidated their power as against other groups and institutions in society, such as the Church and the aristocracy, and asserted their sole right to rule. As the sovereignty of governments within states became established, it simultaneously extended outwards, coming to refer also to the right of states to be free from external interference.

When the state fails in its obligations to its citizens, however, can other states intervene to protect them? As states have consolidated authority and control over national populations in the modern period, the international system has developed as a system of sovereign states, which claim the right to manage their own internal affairs without the interference or guidance of others. The principle of state sovereignty is enshrined in the United Nations Charter, which provides that states are allowed to use violence against others only in self-defence. But, as we see in Chapter 11, when governments turn on their own citizens, or fail to protect them, some argue that they are no longer entitled to the protections of sovereignty.

Theoretical paradigms and frameworks

As we have seen, theoretical frameworks and paradigms are constructed as philosophers, in order to explain and legitimize political action, link together particular interpretations and combinations of values. These include liberalism, conservatism, communitarianism, Marxism and feminism.

Some theoretical frameworks are not specifically political but, rather, explain human action on a private moral level as well. An example here is utilitarianism, which is a normative theory designed to guide private ethical, as well as public just, behaviour. Others focus on a specific issue, and are often combined with the frameworks or ideologies listed above; these include nationalism and cosmopolitanism. Although these theoretical frameworks do not line up neatly on all of the issues we deal with in this book, they can offer useful ways of grouping different theorists. What is more, they often figure in real-world political debates, so it is important that we are aware of their broad outlines. What follows is a brief sketch of the most important features of these frameworks. For more details, see Heywood, 2004.

Liberalism

Liberalism, the ideology that describes and legitimizes liberal democratic government, is hegemonic in the world today, and has been since the collapse of the Soviet Union and most socialist systems in the early 1990s. As a theoretical framework, liberalism emerged with modernity in Europe around the seventeenth century, associated with the transition from feudalism to capitalism, the emergence of Protestantism and the separation of religious from secular authority. Liberalism takes the moral value of each individual human being to be equal and irreducible, and its chief aim, in all of its varieties, is to protect individuals against threats to them from other people, from social groups and from the state. At its inception, liberalism was associated with a limited state and government by consent; concerns about state power are still powerful among liberals, as we see in several of the chapters in this book, especially Chapter 9. Classical liberalism – and its modern variant, libertarianism – is primarily concerned with defending the freedom of individuals against the reach of the law: or negative liberty (see p. 7).

But, since the nineteenth century, liberalism has also focused on positive liberty: enabling human beings to live free and autonomous lives, despite social and economic circumstances that might limit them. This has meant a greater role for the state, and explains why in popular political debate, particularly in the United States, 'liberal' refers to someone who defends state intervention and activism to ensure equality of opportunity. In some cases (see Chapters 4 and 8), liberals support state action to protect people from the powerful and damaging opinions of other people. Liberalism is usually seen as defending individuals against groups, but liberals do not always see groups in negative terms. Modern 'multiculturalist' liberals argue that because group membership has an important impact on individual identity and self-respect, minority groups should be given some protection – not because they have value in themselves, but because they have value, ultimately, to their members.

Liberalism has become the dominant theoretical framework for political philosophers writing in English, and has absorbed many of the arguments of its critics, such as socialists, feminists and communitarians. Many of the debates that we examine in this book take place within liberalism, as well as between it and its critics.

Communitarianism

Communitarianism developed as a theoretical framework in the 1980s, and posed a significant normative challenge to liberalism. Communitarians criticized liberalism's emphasis on individual rights, and what they saw as its 'atomistic' view of the individual – detached from any communal or social context. Because liberalism's ontology of the person – its view of what a person is – was mistaken, communitarians concluded, so was its view of how politics and government should be managed.

Communitarians see each individual as embedded in a social context, consisting of a network of social relations – including the institutions that make up society; such as the family, ethnic groups, religious communities – and shared norms and values. Some communitarians focus on the need to reinforce the associations and organizations of civil society, rather than the state. Others emphasize the importance of considering society's moral values when weighing up political issues, rather than merely analysing them in terms of individual rights. Many liberals have rejected the communitarian charge that they assume that individuals are disconnected and separated, pointing out that such ties are important to individual identity, but that they must separated from the public principles that guide cooperation and public debate.

Communitarians often assume that the relevant community is that of the nation-state, but this perspective has also influenced multiculturalist theorists, who emphasize the importance of cultural community for the individual, and the need to protect minority ethnic and national communities.

Marxism and socialism

Marxism is a theoretical framework based on the ideas of nineteenth-century theorists Karl Marx and Friedrich Engels. Marx analysed the development of societies in economic terms, and developed an argument that history progresses because of material factors: the way in which the economy is organized, the power structures that make it run, and the relations of social groups to each other on this power structure. (For more details, see Heywood, 2004.) Marx argues that history progresses forward as the internal contradictions within each system of production are revealed. Capitalism is the penultimate stage of economic development, and Marx thought that, as workers gained consciousness of themselves and their exploitation under capitalism, they would unite in revolution and capitalism would be replaced by socialism. Wealth would be earned by people using their abilities, and distributed to everyone on the basis of their need.

Since it is the economic system that drives society and determines its progress, Marx thought that factors such as ideas, moral and religious principles – which he described as ideology – are 'superstructural', which means that they reflect what is going on in economic relations, rather than causing it.

Marxism as a prescriptive theory of history, advocating and predicting a revolution of the workers, has very little relevance and support now, especially since the fall of the Soviet Union and communist states. (We should, however, also record that many leftist theorists argue that there was little correspondence between Marx's ideas and the state-run socialism that existed in the Soviet Union and its allies.) Even socialism, its more recent democratic heir, has become marginal in public political debate, as labour and social democratic parties in liberal democracies have abandoned the principle of state ownership. But other aspects of Marx's thoughts have been very influential, particularly his critique of ideology (meaning the ideas that legitimize a system of unequal economic power). Many feminists have adopted the Marxist critique of ideology but, rather than capitalism, they focus on patriarchy, the social system that assigns power and status to men, and subordinates women. (Socialist feminists believe that patriarchy is inherently related to capitalism.) Some theorists have combined the liberal focus on individual freedom and participation in self-government with a Marxist critique of ideology. However, when we look at debates about economic inequality (which we cover in Chapters 2 and 10 of this book) we see that most of the debate about redistribution is conducted not by Marxists or socialists but, rather, by liberals, who focus less on the elimination of capitalism and the full social ownership of the means of production, and much more on how the products of the system are distributed. In the Marxist model, distribution can be solved only after ownership of the means of production is changed.

Feminism

Feminism, now, includes such a diverse set of views that theorists often speak of 'feminisms' but, nevertheless, all feminism shares the fundamental commitment to achieving equality for women and to ending their subordination – legal, political, economic and social – to men. It requires no specific theory of how the economy should be organized, and there are liberal feminists and socialist feminists, as well as radical feminists who argue that patriarchy is trans-cultural and trans-historical, the primary form of human exploitation, and must be overcome before any other social change is possible. Feminism is a social movement as well as a system of ideas, and it has been particularly concerned with the relationship between theory and practice – feminists argue that theory should emerge out of women's critical reflections upon their own experiences of inequality.

Feminism, as a movement, arose first in the nineteenth century (in the 'first wave'), as groups of middle-class women became active in the suffrage movement, struggling to secure the right to vote. 'Second wave' feminism emerged in the 1950s and 1960s, and focused on equal rights – defined by liberals as legal and political, and by socialists and by radicals as social and economic. Feminism's concern with equal rights places it in the liberal tradition and, on many social issues that involve justice for women, feminists line up with liberals. But feminists have also been influenced by the Marxist critique of ideology, and many look more deeply at the way our social and cultural ideas and practices perpetuate inequality. We will see this in the debate over pornography in Chapter 5. One of the major contributions of feminism to normative theory is that it reminds us of how inequality is perpetuated in the 'private sphere' – in the family and domestic life. Previously, political theory had analysed status and power as it is exercised in the public sphere of politics, or in the economy and social life. Politics was assumed to exclude private life. Feminism reminds us to analyse as political any sphere of human life in which some people systematically exercise power over others.

Conservatism

Conservatism is more difficult to define and demarcate than many other theoretical frameworks. As is the case with liberalism, the way the term is used in everyday political debate is often distinct from its meaning as a theoretical framework. The positions often identified in politics as conservative are sometimes better seen as libertarian or liberal in a classical sense: respect for private property and support for a limited state with less government regulation in both the economy and people's private, moral and social conduct. Views that oppose regulation of the economy, but support state regulation of private behaviour and enforce moral views, are more likely to be influenced by conservatism. As a theoretical framework and a political movement, conservatism developed in response to radical and revolutionary movements and ideas that emerged in the eighteenth century and were embodied in the French Revolution. Conservatives, noting with alarm the wholesale change that radicals advocated, and the bloody course of the Revolution, rejected attempts to change social institutions and fundamental ideas and traditions based on abstract ideas. Conservatives argue that established social institutions deserve respect and protection because of the role they play in meeting human needs. They should not be abolished, changed or reformed in the light of abstract and utopian ideals. This view is behind much of the opposition to social change, such as same-sex marriage. Conservative views sometimes coincide with those of communitarians, as both schools of thought emphasize the need to protect common social institutions that shape and give meaning to people's lives.

This strand of conservative thinking is secular, although it incorporates respect for religious institutions. Christian conservatives, who take part in philosophical debates over social and moral issues, rely on the idea of natural law. They argue that traditional social and moral beliefs reflect God's law, as it is revealed in the 'natural order of things' and in each human conscience. This kind of social conservatism combines with economic liberalism to form the policies of the New Right.

Nationalism

Nationalism can also be described as a theoretical framework, an ideology and a social movement; unlike the other paradigms we have considered, however, it does not specify any particular organization of the national political or economic system. Nationalists might be liberals, socialists, conservatives or feminists, or a combination of these. We can distinguish here between ethnic nationalism, which views the nation as a community of people linked together in 'communities of fate' by ethnic, racial or kinship ties, and civic nationalism, which views the nation as a community made up of those who choose to commit to a common public life together, and to public institutions and principles. While these two forms of nationalism are based on different conceptions of the person, both justify normative commitments for citizens: nationalism assumes that we are at least to some degree fundamentally defined by membership in our nation, which binds us together with ties of sentiment and mutual obligation. It is similar here to communitarianism, with the important proviso that the communitarians do not necessarily see national communities as the only or most important ones in which people are embedded. It follows from nationalism that we have only limited duties to others outside national borders, whether to redistribute resources, and to go to war to protect them if their governments fail to do so (see Chapters 10 and 11).

Cosmopolitanism

In contrast with nationalism, cosmopolitanism is based on the principle that all human beings belong to a universal community, because of our common humanity. All people have equal moral status, which means that we must give full weight to the needs and interests of those outside our national or local communities. Cosmopolitanism is not a modern idea; it dates from ancient Greece and Rome, and was a key belief of the Stoic philosophers, in the third century BCE, and the early Christians. In its modern form, cosmopolitanism is associated with universal human rights, and with the challenge to nationalism. Cosmopolitans argue that those in wealthy countries have a duty to redistribute resources to meet the basic needs of the poor in other nations (Chapter 10), and that those who can prevent human rights abuses in other countries must intervene, if possible, to do so (Chapter 11). As with nationalism, cosmopolitanism does not imply any particular economic or political arrangements within states (classical liberalism and Marxism both have cosmopolitan elements) but, in modern thinking, it has been closely associated with liberalism, because of the liberal belief in the equal moral status of all individuals.

Utilitarianism

Utilitarianism is a philosophical tradition that argues that we should judge the worth of an action, a regulation, or a policy by how much it contributes to utility – defined variously as happiness, good, satisfaction or welfare. Actions, whether individual or governmental, are assessed in terms of their consequences, rather than by whether they conform to abstract moral principles or ideas. Unlike the other frameworks we have considered here, utilitarianism is primarily ethical: it covers all human action, and includes no specific provision for how political or economic life should be structured; it assumes that any political or economic system should be judged by how much it contributes to human happiness or welfare. Utilitarianism is not an ideology, neither is it the creed of a social movement, but it permeates our thinking on every political issue.

In this book, we will consider utilitarian thinking about the consequences of policy and legislation on both sides of all the questions we discuss. In contrast to the utilitarian approach, we will also consider deontological arguments. Deontological thinking evaluates policy and legislation according to whether they conform to moral and ethical principles, rather than on the basis of the consequences they produce. It is an approach to ethics, rather than an ideology, and does not prescribe particular moral or political principles.

The structure of this book

The chapters in this book address a range of political issues that are active and controversial in modern liberal democracies. While they have moral dimensions, all have been the subject of government regulation and policy, and we will examine them as distinctively political problems: those that concern our public lives together as individuals and members of social communities and nations, and as the subjects of state power. We begin in Chapter 2 by looking at the distribution of resources within states, and then turn to the status of minority groups in Chapters 3 and 4. Chapters 5, 6 and 7 continue the examination of controversial social issues with special implications for women, gays and lesbians, as well as the role of state in regulating the beginning and end of life. In Chapters 8 and 9 we look at the relationship between the state and civil liberties. Chapters 10 and 11 deal with global issues: the distribution of resources to those in poor countries, and whether or not to intervene to protect human rights abuses. Finally, Chapter 12 examines our obligations to save and protect resources for future generations.

Each chapter begins with a short survey of the issues and of the ways in which governments in liberal democracies have responded to them by legislation, regulation and policy. Then we turn to political theory to analyse the arguments relating to each issue. We examine the key concepts and values that underlie these arguments, where they come into conflict, and where they share common ground. It is not the purpose of this book to advocate one position or another on these issues; however, it does aim to help readers to understand what is really at stake in the arguments over such issues, and to become familiar with the concepts and values of normative political theory, so that they can go on to apply them to the full range of questions that we confront as citizens and students of politics.

Chapter 2

How Should Resources be Distributed? Taxation, Welfare and Redistribution

Debates over the ways in which governments should respond to poverty are some of the most controversial in modern democratic societies. In the past two decades, this controversy has focused on the welfare state: the range of institutionalized programmes through which governments aim to provide universal support to their citizens. The modern welfare state is a recent phenomenon, although its origins can be traced to the expansion of government assistance during the late nineteenth century in several European states – particularly in Germany, where Bismarck introduced social insurance programmes in the 1880s in order to counter emerging popular support for socialism. Some countries developed support programmes in response to the Great Depression of the 1930s, and American President Franklin Roosevelt declared that the ideal social security system would provide protection 'from the cradle to the grave'. It was only after World War II, however, that most western nations expanded their welfare policies to various degrees of comprehensive coverage of the population. The different ways in which welfare programmes have developed across nations reflect a range of political and cultural factors. In the United States, for example, welfare payments were channelled through one central programme – Aid to Families with Dependent Children. Australia and New Zealand have emphasized benefits and insurance for wage earners, while in many European countries, social and religious organizations have long-standing corporatist partnerships with the state for delivering support services.

None of these programmes, however, has been successful in eradicating poverty. By the 1980s, the growth in poverty rates and increasing numbers of beneficiaries on the welfare rolls in many countries, coupled with popular resistance to levels of taxation, had led to growing popular resentment and criticism of redistributive welfare policies. Critics of welfare argued that, rather than eliminating poverty, it had reinforced and perpetuated it by creating both individual attitudes and a social culture of passive dependency among beneficiaries. This, they claimed, benefited neither the recipients themselves, nor the tax-payers funding social support. Critics concluded that it was only when the receipt of welfare became explicitly linked to work and personal responsibility that it could succeed in lifting beneficiaries out of poverty.

With increasing government debt and the shift to neoliberal economic policies in the 1980s, welfare became a key electoral issue. Governments in most western countries responded by tightening and eliminating programmes. In the United States, President Clinton – who had been elected four years previously, promising 'to end welfare as we know it' – signed the Republican-initiated welfare reform legislation that marked the high point of a debate over welfare entitlement, personal responsibility and state obligation that had begun in earnest two decades earlier. The *Personal Responsibility and Work Opportunity Reconciliation Act* (1996) demonstrated in its title the shift in the way welfare was being discussed and defined. The new legislation, which transformed Aid to Families with Dependent Children into Temporary Assistance for Needy Families (TANF), shifted the focus of state redistribution away from the moral responsibility of the state to meet the needs of a defined group, and towards the duties of those receiving assistance to take steps to end their dependence. It imposed a time limit: no one could receive welfare benefits for more than five years, and funds for benefits were transferred from the federal government to the states under a 'block grant' system, which allowed states to impose their own rules and regulations regarding entitlements. States responded by directing funds into benefits that were directly linked to working, such as subsidies for childcare and transportation to work. Under the new system, the provision of assistance was linked less to the need of beneficiaries, and more to their work status.

The 1996 legislation came up for renewal in 2003 under President Bush, who claimed that it had successfully moved 4.7 million Americans out of welfare and into work, reducing the welfare rolls by 54 per cent. President Bush called for an increase in the number of hours of work required by welfare recipients. Critics countered that this requirement would result in more recipients working in low-paid and unproductive jobs, still requiring government support from other sources such as food stamps and Medicaid. The number of people officially recorded as being on welfare declined, but this masked continuing poverty. Nevertheless, the TANF scheme continued to operate during the term of the Bush administration.

Before these changes to welfare, other countries had criticized American policies as inadequate for dealing with poverty, because they were too punitive and restricted in scope. But, from the 1990s, key aspects of the American approach were adopted by European and other western countries – many of which had already begun to change their own approach to welfare as they adopted 'neo-liberal' policies of economic rationalism. The major reform strategies have focused on shifting funding from the unemployed towards low-income families and emphasizing 'welfare to work'. In many countries, benefits have increasingly been made conditional on the recipient's willingness to retrain, search for paid work and re-enter the labour force. In Britain, this trend began under the Conservative government of Margaret Thatcher in the 1980s. In 1997, the Labour government's New Deal programme introduced a raft of policies aimed at reducing the barriers to the unemployed entering the workforce, and offering tax credits and other financial incentives for low-income workers. In his first speech as Chancellor of the Exchequer in 1997, Gordon Brown announced that, under Labour, work would replace welfare. Britain adopted the working families tax credit, and similar tax relief for low-income work was introduced in France, the Netherlands and New Zealand. The conservative French government of Prime Minister Raffarin tightened the conditions under which people were able to obtain welfare, reduced the time period for which they could receive it, and required them to sign a contract stipulating that they were looking for work. In Australia, the welfare system, based on wage support, was transformed into a targeted needs-based programme. The Liberal party government elected in 1996 introduced a range of 'reforms' that implemented the same changes, making welfare payments dependent on active seeking of work. In New Zealand, the government shifted funds away from schemes directed towards the unemployed, and increased the tax credits available to low-income families with wage-earners. The National party government, which held office in the 1990s, introduced a 'work for the dole' scheme, later reintroduced by the Labour government. In Canada, cuts in federal funding led provinces to pass legislation designed to encourage welfare recipients into work, cutting eligibility for benefits, and providing supplements for low wages.

These changes in policy were accompanied by shifts in the arguments used to justify state support. Where benefits once were justified on the grounds of citizen rights, (Marshall and Bottomore, 1992) they have come to be seen now as temporary remedies designed to meet essential needs, while encouraging self-sufficiency. This has resulted in the introduction of means testing for child benefits that were formerly universal in Australia, Canada and New Zealand. But it has also meant that new requirements have been imposed on beneficiaries, as the justification for support has come to focus on fostering personal responsibility. The role of the state has been reduced to setting policy goals for welfare, and encouraging individual responsibility and a larger role for civil society in the provision of assistance. A further result of this is that many states have privatized the delivery of services and benefits – often to religious organizations. This has been particularly controversial in the United States, where the government is constitutionally prohibited from supporting religion.

Different explanations have been suggested for the decline, since the 1970s, in popular support for the welfare state. The German philosopher

Jürgen Habermas has argued that popular resentment towards it reflects the failure of the welfare state to avert the strains to the capitalist system that Marx had foreseen (strains that he predicted would lead to revolutionary crisis) (Habermas, 1975). What it did, instead, was to displace the crisis onto the social and cultural level, and threaten social integration – people's interests remained class-based, and they failed to develop a sense of shared commitment to a set of social values or norms. Communitarian philosophers also blame the decline in support for redistributing resources on a failure of commitment to a common good (Sandel, 1982, 1996). Some have suggested that the development of multiculturalist policies, or the ideology of multiculturalism is responsible (Barry, 2001; Miller, 2006).

Several different arguments can be advanced to support welfare, as we shall see, but perhaps the simplest is that the redistribution of resources to the needy increases the sum of human happiness. Utilitarians argue that the most just system is one that produces the greatest balance of satisfaction or

---

Box 2.1 Inheritance Tax

Taxing inheritance is a perennially controversial issue. As with gift tax, it raises a direct conflict between the wish of people to transfer their wealth to whomsoever they choose – here, in the form of their estate after their death – and the claim of the state to acquire and redistribute it. In the United Kingdom, Inheritance Tax is currently 40 per cent, but applies only to the portion of estates over £312,000. It affects about 6 per cent of estates, and accounts for less than 1 per cent of total government revenue. In the United States, federal estate tax (referred to as 'death duties', by its opponents) applies only to estates worth more than US$2 million, and is set at 45 per cent. It affects between 1–2 per cent of all estates. The tax is scheduled to be abolished for one year in 2010, and it is not clear what legislation Congress will pass on the matter after that. Some of the controversy about the tax focuses on the threshold value at which it should be applied to an estate. But broader issues of justice are also at stake:

- Supporters argue that it is less unfair than most taxes to the owner of the property, as it is not imposed during their lifetime. Moreover, it has wider social benefits. It helps to prevent the perpetuation and reinforcement of inequalities across generations, and it encourages productivity. Research has shown that older people who inherit more wealth are more likely to leave the labour force. Winston Churchill argued along these lines in 1924, that inheritance tax 'was a certain corrective against the development of a race of idle rich'.
- Opponents of inheritance tax contend that it interferes with people's fundamental right to transfer their property as they wish after their deaths. They also claim that it acts as a disincentive to entrepreneurship and saving.

happiness for all (Bentham, 1988 [1789]; Mill, (1969 [1861]). The welfare state provides a basic level of resources to the needy, thereby substantially increasing their happiness or satisfaction. At the same time, the reduction in happiness for higher income earners who pay to support the system is not very great, because of the diminishing marginal utility of income – the more money one makes, the less valuable is an increase in income. For the wealthy, the small loss of income is outweighed by the gain to those for whom the extra income makes a considerable difference (Goodin, 1995).

The critique of welfare has come from a wide range of political principles and perspectives. Much of it is neo-conservative, inspired by opposition to a large and interventionist state and to what critics see as 'social engineering' – the attempt by government to use legislation and policy to change people's ideas and behaviour. (These conservative principles were set out by Edmund Burke in the late eighteenth century to justify his opposition to the French Revolution (Burke, 1955 [1790])). Conservatives are inclined to hold an individual to be substantively responsible for his or her own choices, irrespective of the social factors that influence and limit choice. Neo-liberals also oppose an interventionist state. But there has also been criticism of welfare on the liberal grounds of individual freedom and autonomy. Liberals who give more weight to equality (egalitarian liberals) have argued for changing the system of welfare redistribution because they see it as minimizing individual choices and discouraging people from taking control of their own lives. Both liberals and conservatives have argued that welfare creates a 'dependency mentality' that effectively enslaves the poor. While egalitarian liberals have traditionally had more faith in the ability of the state to intervene constructively in people's lives, liberals and conservatives are critical of large bureaucratic institutions that are not responsive to the complex needs of beneficiaries. Liberals and social democrats who take the 'third way' perspective (dominant in left-of-centre governments in Britain, Canada, Australia and New Zealand) argue that the needy must be helped to become self-supporting, by taking an active role in decisions around the disbursement of welfare and in retraining themselves. The third way perspective tends to support the decentralization of welfare provision to social organizations in civil society.

Underlying these political perspectives and ideologies on welfare reform are some fundamental political questions:

• What is the purpose of government?
• How can we determine who should own wealth?
• How much income is the state entitled to take from those who earn it, and for what purposes?
• If income is to be taken, who is entitled to receive it through redistribution?
• Should the state or civil society organizations manage redistribution?

These questions, in turn, lead us to examine some basic political concepts: equality, property rights, the role of the state, liberty and autonomy (see Box 2.2, pp. 38–9). In the remainder of this chapter, we examine some key perspectives in political theory, and their interpretation of these values, to help us address the questions that underlie the welfare debate.

Redistribution and the right to private property

The most basic question that welfare raises is whether the state is justified in redistributing the income earned by its citizens. Given the right to private property of individuals – a basic value in all liberal democracies – how can governments justify appropriating, through tax, the income earned by some citizens, and redistributing it to others in need? The early social contract theorists of the seventeenth century, Thomas Hobbes and John Locke, argued that the primary purpose of the state is to ensure the security and safety of its citizens (Hobbes, 1962 [1651]; Locke, 1988 [1690]). Beyond this, however, there is considerable disagreement between political theorists. Some see the purpose of government as being to institute a particular, desired type of community – perhaps in line with particular moral principles, or religious beliefs. Those who support a more limited state argue that more extensive regulation by governments is an indefensible interference with individual freedom. Those modern liberals who take this view (libertarians) think that individual liberty is expressed in the fundamental right to private property, and that government should not interfere with property rights unless security is under threat. Rights to private property are essential to autonomy – to personal freedom and independence – and take precedence over any claims by citizens to support on the basis of need. Libertarian arguments can thus be made to oppose potentially all forms of welfare redistribution. An early case for this was made by F.A. Hayek in his attack on collectivism and central planning, *The Road to Serfdom*, written in 1944 (Hayek, 1962).

The most influential exponent of this view has been the American philosopher Robert Nozick (Nozick, 1974). His approach to distributing wealth is based on the rights of 'self-owning individuals' to their own property. Any argument for welfare redistribution must assume, Nozick argues, that there is a pattern of distribution that is just or fair, independent of how property is actually owned or distributed at the time. Such a pattern might be based on need or merit, or any criterion. The argument for welfare must also assume that the state can act justly, as a central redistributing authority, to correct the existing 'unjust' distributions of property. These assumptions are neither justified nor realistic, according to Nozick: all we have to go on in society are the unequal distributions that already exist, and that are the result of innumerable individual decisions. There is no reason to presume that original or desirable shares of goods were or should be equal; rather, our intuitions tell us that, in considering whether current unequal property holdings ought to be maintained or disturbed, we should consider the history of how those holdings came about, rather than whether they conform to a desirable pattern of distributions. Nozick argues that property owners are entitled to their holdings if they received them in accordance with principles of justice – either as the first acquirers of the property, in which case they acquired property through their ownership of themselves, or in transfer from someone who held them legitimately. We can thus assess the justice of property holdings by looking at the history of their acquisition.

If we can establish that people do have rights to their property, through self-ownership and historical entitlement, any redistribution on the grounds of, say, need or equality, will unjustly disturb their entitlement and compromise their autonomy. It diminishes the rights of individuals to transfer their property as they see fit – for example, to family members – and thus interferes with the relationships of love and care that exist within families. At a fundamental level, this view of property rights casts the legitimacy of all taxpayer-funded welfare programmes in doubt. Taxation is, after all, a system that requires people to surrender their property. Nozick comments that 'taxation of earnings from labor is on a par with forced labor' (Nozick, 1974: 169). It is justified to provide resources for state security, and the other functions of a minimal state. But requiring people to turn over the fruits of their labour to the state to redistribute to others forces them to work for the benefit of others. Welfare means that beneficiaries acquire a claim over property produced by others. In the same way that it would be illegitimate to force someone to spend their leisure time working for others, so it is, according to Nozick, illegitimate to force them to hand over the goods they earn from the labour they choose to perform, for others. If others have the ability to force us to perform work, or unrewarded work, Nozick argues, they become a part owner of us – they acquire a property right in us. So, any patterned view of distribution, Nozick argues, violates what he calls 'moral side constraints' concerning how people may be treated (Nozick, 1974: 172).

Nozick's conception of the self-owning individual assumes that we own our talents and abilities, and are entitled to what we earn by using them. While this is similar to the common claim that we *deserve* what we earn, Nozick makes no moral claim that we deserve our talents. Rather, we acquire rights in property as a result of our rights of ownership over our bodies. Private property in this view is entirely the product of individual action, rather than of the social structure and the context in which that action occurs. As we shall see below, other more egalitarian liberals argue that earnings are the product not only of individual labour, but also of shared social processes and institutions.

Of course, Nozick's argument against forced resource redistribution in the form of welfare holds only as long as the initial acquisition of property was just. If it was not, later transfers have not been legitimate, and redistributions might be required (to rectify the injustices that have occurred). Any argument that depends on a historical chain of transfer going back to original acquisition will be impossible to support empirically (in most cases). Nozick follows Locke regarding the question of original acquisition, in arguing that initial (unequal) appropriations of property are legitimate if, when the property was taken, there was 'enough and as good left in common for others' (Nozick, 1974: 175). Much depends on how we interpret this 'Lockean proviso', and Nozick takes it to mean '[a] process normally giving rise to a permanent bequeathable property right in a previously unowned thing will not do so if the position of others no longer at liberty to use the thing is thereby weakened' (Nozick, 1974: 178). If we follow the capitalist argument that the private ownership of property benefits all by increasing the social product, and allowing for production and wages, and the 'trickle down' of wealth to all, then most private acquisitions are justified, as they do not make the position of others worse. (The exceptions would be appropriations of all of a scarce resource essential to life.)

Nozick himself is ambivalent on the question of whether most previous acquisitions of property have worsened the situation of others – although he does think that the operation of the free market will not do so. Slavery and colonial dispossession raise obvious problems with the Lockean proviso, as they clearly involve illegitimate transactions along the historical chain of property transfer. In these cases, rectification might be required through a one-off redistribution of wealth. Nozick does not offer any detailed principle of rectification, but suggests that it would require trying to determine what would have occurred if the unjust transfer had not taken place. Only if it is impossible to determine what property holdings would have been had an injustice not occurred, would it be possible to look at considerations of distributive justice. We should note, however, that such redistributions made to rectify historical injustices are, for the most part, not tied to needs or aimed at equality, and so would not reflect the kinds of programmes usually delivered by welfare. They might, however, be used to justify affirmative action policies directed at particular social or ethnic groups.

One of the more radical redistributive proposals suggested by modern political philosophers is made by leftist libertarian philosophers, who argue that we should redistribute resource wealth through universal equal payments, in order to reinforce self-ownership and liberty. Left-libertarians concede that it is not legitimate to enact this equal division in an unequal world by redistributing the gains of labour through tax, because this violates self-ownership. Instead, there should be some distribution of capital – a monetary grant that represents each person's fair share of society's basic resources. This should be in the form of a 'universal basic income', which can be paid in one lump sum or through regular payments (Van Parijs, 1991, 1995). The income would not be means-tested, because all citizens, as 'stakeholders' in society, are entitled to equal shares of basic resources (Ackerman and Alstott, 1999). As the allowance is a right, recipients would not be accountable for how they spend their allowance – it would not be tied to looking for work. In 2005, the Blair government in Britain introduced a simple version of the stakeholder idea with the Child Trust Fund. Under this scheme, the government pays a sum of £250 (twice that for lower-income families) into a trust account for each child born in Britain. This payment is made at birth, and again at the age of seven years.

Advocates of the basic income argue that it should eventually be set high enough to replace other welfare benefits. In practice, it is likely to be set with reference not to needs, but to available resources. The basic income would, however, offer at least some support to those who perform unpaid labour in society, such as care giving, in a way that most benefit systems do not. Nevertheless, universal basic income proposals run counter to most of the ideas behind recent changes to welfare. They explicitly break the connection between work and personal choice, on the one hand, and income, on the other. Some critics have argued that they do not encourage a sense of social commitment or cooperation; others point out that the income will not necessarily satisfy basic needs. The basic income would have to be set at wage replacement levels in order for the scheme to ensure the individual freedom and autonomy it is meant to guarantee.

Nozick's approach, based on rights, self-ownership and historical entitlement, challenges all state-directed welfare redistributions – although it does not, of course, preclude private charity. Other right-wing libertarians have made even stronger arguments for the individual rights that flow from self-ownership (Narveson, 1988). While these have not been commonly expressed views in public debate about welfare, they are reflected in neo-conservative arguments for increased voluntary giving to take the place of tax-funded benefits. The Bush Administration in the United States was an enthusiastic supporter of this position, and promoted the delivery of social assistance by privately funded religious groups, rather than the state. Alternative approaches accord more weight to equality as a balance to liberty, or define liberty less in terms of the freedom to dispose of private property and more in terms of autonomy. Autonomous individuals exercise control over their own lives, and many egalitarian philosophers have argued that, in order for people to be autonomous, their basic needs must be met. Others have argued that the protection of liberty means aiming to achieve some rough equality at some level of resource distribution.

Equality and the case for redistribution

We now turn to arguments in favour of welfare redistribution, on the grounds of equality or autonomy. Egalitarian distributions are often associated with leftist political theory, although Marx himself argued that, under socialism, distribution should be on the basis of needs (Marx, 1978 [1875]: 531). Modern leftist theorists tend to endorse equal distributions of resources. Joseph Carens argues that every member of a society should make their most productive contribution possible towards it, and that distribution should be according to their needs (Carens, 2003). As, in practice, it is impossible fully to assess the needs of different people (this problem recurs with needs-based theories), it is best to focus on the basic needs shared by everyone – healthy water, food, air, housing, education and health care. Income should be distributed equally to everyone in order to satisfy these needs, and where people have special, or 'differentially incurred' basic needs – such as the disabled – these should be provided for separately by the state. We will look more closely at needs-based theories later in this chapter, but it is important to note here that Carens' system depends on everyone making a productive contribution to society through paid labour. We might see this as (ironically) compatible with the trend in welfare policy to require beneficiaries to work for their benefits.

Egalitarian thinkers take many different positions on the method and degree of redistribution, depending on how they interpret the requirements of liberty and autonomy, and how they balance liberty with equality. Debates over these issues reflect many of the controversies over changes in welfare policy described at the beginning of the chapter. As we will see, questions over people's responsibilities for their own choices, and the effect on our life chances of our ambitions, our natural abilities and luck are fundamental to liberal egalitarian theories as well as to the welfare debate.

We should note that while theorists who support the redistributions carried out by means of welfare are usually known as 'egalitarians', much controversy arises over what is being equalized. All democratic political theorists support the idea that all people should have equal political and legal rights. To egalitarian theorists, this usually means that there should be less disparity in ownership of material resources, although very few support the idea that there should be absolute equality, in large part because of differences in people's needs. One major point of disagreement among egalitarian theorists is over whether we should measure equality in terms of *resources* (how many resources we should have to use as we wish) or *outcomes* (how much wealth we should all ultimately have, irrespective of how we used our resources). Theorists often describe this distinction as one between equality of resources and equality of welfare.

Arguments in favour of state welfare rest on a fundamentally different way of seeing the relationship between the individual, his or her earnings and society, from that described by Nozick. As we have seen, the self-ownership principle means that everyone has the right to the fruits of their labour and to anything received in free exchange. Egalitarian thinkers assume, instead, that we are enabled to enjoy the fruits of our labour because we are working together in society, within a framework of shared institutions, laws and structures. As the influential political philosopher John Rawls puts it, society is a 'cooperative project for mutual advantage' (Rawls, 1971: 4). We have no automatic right to whatever we can earn ourselves, as we are only able to earn through our cooperation in a larger social project. It is because we are all members of such a project that we need principles of justice concerning the distribution of goods, to which we can all agree and which reflect our shared ideas.

If earned wealth is the result of the individual's participation in a shared social system, it follows that individuals should have no exclusive right to the property they earn. The egalitarian theories we examine here, beginning with that of Rawls, all apply different patterns of distribution, reflecting different interpretations of the relationship between liberty and equality, and corresponding to a range of welfare policies. In constructing his defence of redistribution, Rawls begins with the premise that the most basic assumption of society as a system of fair cooperation is the equality of citizens. We arrive at this premise by imagining the principles of justice that people would choose to regulate the 'basic structure' of society – its main political, social and economic institutions – if they were setting up a social contract and were not influenced by knowing anything about their talents and social position. Thus, they could not be biased in favour of their personal interests. In this 'original position', principles of justice and distribution would necessarily be chosen irrespective of factors such as class, race, sex and abilities. Rawls argues that, in these circumstances, people would insist on at least some degree of equality – as they would be unable to be sure that they would benefit from any inequalities. They would thus agree that all should be equal in terms of their legal, political and civil freedoms, and that this basic equality must be guaranteed. Rawls' first principle of justice is thus:

Principle 1:
Each person has an equal right to a full adequate scheme of equal basic liberties which is compatible with a similar scheme of liberties for all. (Rawls, 1993: 291)

This does not mean, however, that it is in the best interest of all to be economically equal. Rawls allows that incentives might increase the total wealth, in a way that benefits everyone – although the benefits might not be equal. He argues that, if people could choose fairly, they would decide to regulate institutions so that material inequalities could be justified only if they improved the situation of those who are the worst-off. Productive citizens might be allowed to make more, and to keep some of what they make, as long as the increased wealth improves the situation of the worst-off. This assumes that those at the bottom of the scale would be concerned more about their absolute economic well-being, than about how their status compared with that of others. Rawls' second principle thus reads:

Principle 2:
Social and economic inequalities are to satisfy two conditions. First, they must be attached to offices and positions open to all under conditions of fair equality of opportunity; and second, they must be to the greatest benefit of the least advantaged members of society. (Rawls, 1993: 291)

According to the second principle, economic inequalities may be justified if, first, there exists fair equality of opportunity for everyone to gain the positions that were best remunerated. This would prevent people from benefiting unfairly from the social and economic advantages that come from family, status and education. But, further, any inequalities in natural talents should also be harnessed to improve the position of the worst-off in society. That is to say, rather than insisting on a division of resources that would produce an equal amount for everyone, people in the original position would agree to goods distributed so that those who could put resources to the most productive use could have more, as long as the benefits would trickle down to improve the position of those who are least well-off. Rawls means us to follow these rules in order. Liberty (Principle 1) cannot be restricted in order to satisfy the reasons in Principle 2. And fair opportunity cannot be restricted in order to maximize the position of those who are worst-off.

Redistribution is thus justified to improve the position of the worst-off group in society, in accordance with the two parts of Principle 2. Both parts, it could be argued, justify substantial transfers of wealth. Under fair equality of opportunity, we might justify increased support for early childhood education, schools in low-income areas, subsidies for schooling of choice, or scholarships. It might be argued that most societies are a long way from ensuring fair equality of opportunity, as unequal social and economic positions in life have a substantial effect on the likely prospects of children. A major study of inequality in the United States in 1996 showed that the most reliable indicator of what children's socio-economic position would be was the socio-economic position of their parents (Fischer, 1996).

Rawls' second principle, part (a), the 'difference principle', is the most controversial part of his theory of justice, as it authorizes redistributing wealth to the worst-off even if those who earned it did so as a result of fair equality of opportunity. In practical terms, the principle means that high levels of earning are acceptable only to the extent at which taxing them improves the situation of the worst-off group. A balance must be struck: there is an assumed point for Rawls at which taxation is so high that the talented stop wanting to earn more. The task of policy-makers is to find the right rate of taxation – which will allow the wealthy to increase their wealth only while at the same time redistributing as much as possible to the poor. Many countries that have made the changes to welfare policy previously outlined (pp. 19–21) have also seen popular campaigns to reduce levels of taxation over the past two decades. Although those with the highest marginal tax rates (for example 52 per cent in the Netherlands, 45 per cent in Germany, compared with 35 per cent at the federal level in the USA) might be assumed to provide the highest level of welfare, this is not necessarily the case, as tax income must fund a wide range of government expenditures.

Rawls' difference principle and its defence of redistribution to the worst-off rely on several key claims. We have already discussed the idea that earnings and profits are the product of shared social systems and practices, and that, therefore, all in society have a possible claim to them. Further, as our intuitions tell us that social and economic advantages (such as family status and education) are unearned and undeserved, so also they tell us that our natural abilities and skills are unearned. We are born with them as a matter of luck, but we do not deserve them in a moral sense. It follows from this, and from viewing society as a shared project of cooperation, that our right to benefit from our talents should be limited by considerations of what is fair for everyone. Rawls argues: 'the more advantaged representative man cannot say that he deserves and therefore has a right to a scheme of cooperation in which he is permitted to acquire benefits in ways that do not contribute to the welfare of others' (Rawls, 1971: 104). This is a controversial claim: even if we do not actually deserve our talents and abilities, some might argue, as does Nozick, that they are so much a part of us that we are therefore entitled to what they bring us. And, of course, it can be very difficult to distinguish the success brought about by natural talents from the success earned by hard work in developing and applying one's talents.

Given that Rawls' scheme will limit the wealth that high achievers will earn, and redistribute it to the poor, why should high earners accept it? We have already considered Rawls' argument that his principles of justice are those that would be chosen if everyone were choosing under fair circumstances. Moreover, fair equality of opportunity is already accepted as a desirable social goal in all liberal democracies. Finally, and because of these reasons, Rawls argues that his scheme creates a sense of fraternity or solidarity. The fate of each member of the community is linked to that of others. As we have seen, some philosophers who have analysed the decline in support for welfare have ascribed it to insufficient communal loyalty and solidarity. Rawls suggests that that we might be able to build the same kind of mutuality and fellow feeling in society that exists, ideally, in the family, if we explicitly link the success of the wealthiest with the situation of the worst-off.

One possible disparity between Rawls' argument for redistribution and welfare systems as they exist is that he focuses on improving the position only of the economically worst-off group. Rawls defines this group mainly in terms of levels of income and wealth, although the contingencies of natural endowment and luck also play a role in identifying the 'least advantaged'. Physical and mental capabilities are explicitly excluded from the operation of the second principle. In some cases, they might be addressed, Rawls argues, by applying the fair equality of opportunity principle. In other cases, they should be the subject of separate state provision, designed to 'restore people by health care so that once again they are fully cooperating members of society' (Rawls, 1993: 184). Most welfare policies have identified the needs of the disabled and, as we have seen, in many countries changes to welfare policy have distinguished the needs of the disabled from other beneficiaries. Even if we put aside the question of compensating the disabled, Rawls' focus on the least-advantaged group means that the needs of those who fall elsewhere on the spectrum are not directly addressed. In fact, he assumes that there will be a 'chain-connectedness' between all groups on the scale of income, and that by improving the position of the worst-off, the situation of others between the two extremes will necessarily also be improved (Rawls, 1971: 80).

While needs-based welfare has focused on those at, or near, the bottom of the economic scale, the universal coverage of the postwar welfare state included provisions such as health care and pensions, which were accessible to all socio-economic groups. Contemporary welfare reforms are aimed not at improving the position of the worst-off in society but, rather, that of the working poor. As we have seen, welfare redistribution is now aimed at encouraging labour market participation. In Rawls' original discussion of his theory, the principles do not distinguish between those who work and those who do not – the position of the least-advantaged is targeted whether or not those in that position work or seek work. He has since suggested that 'leisure' might be included as a primary good and, thus, that someone who chose it would not be compensated under the difference principle (Rawls, 1993). The implications of this are, however, not worked out, and the objections we discuss below concerning the status of unpaid labour would apply here.

Bad luck or bad choices?

Much of the opposition to welfare is driven by the claim that the choices made by beneficiaries should matter – that there is a meaningful difference between being poor as a result of bad luck, and being poor as a result of bad choices. This is particularly the case with welfare assistance for able-bodied adults. In the case of children and the disabled, where it is clear that recipients are, by definition, prevented from choosing to become self-supporting, the debate has continued to focus on meeting need. Most European reforms to welfare provision have excluded the disabled from new restrictions. Those programmes that restrict benefits to those actively in search of work, or working in low-wage positions, however, are designed to reward those who make 'good' choices – to work – and penalize those who choose not to.

Several liberal egalitarian philosophers have addressed the question of whether those in need due to circumstances beyond their control should be treated in the same way as those who might be seen as contributing to their hardship by irresponsibility or negligence. In doing so, they argue for a more limited view of equality – focusing on equalizing luck, rather than equalizing material circumstances. One way to address this is to draw a distinction between the qualities with which we are naturally endowed and our ambitions to make use of those qualities. This also has the effect of emphasizing liberty, by holding that individuals should be bound to the consequences of the free choices they make concerning the use of their talents and resources. Ronald Dworkin has developed a scheme that aims to correct for disadvantages in terms of natural talents, but not to adjust for ambition and hard work when justifying redistributions. Theories such as this are sometimes referred to as 'luck egalitarianism' (Anderson, 1999) because they aim to equalize luck: to support those in need due to bad luck, but not those whose circumstances are caused by bad choices. Dworkin describes this distinction as being between two different types of bad luck: 'brute' bad luck (circumstances to which we did not contribute in any way) and 'option' bad luck (which occurs when we experience unfortunate circumstances as a result of our poor choices).

Dworkin agrees with Rawls that the benefits we derive from our choices and our luck are the product of our shared membership and cooperation in society: 'For the distribution of wealth is the product of a legal order: a citizen's wealth massively depends on which laws his community has enacted – not only its laws concerning ownership, theft, contract and tort, but its welfare law, tax law, labor law, civil rights law, environmental regulation law, and laws of practically everything else' (Dworkin, 2000: 1). Within this context, he outlines two basic principles of 'ethical individualism':

Principle 1:
That human lives should be successful, rather than wasted.

Principle 2:
That the ultimate responsibility for the success of each life lies with the person living it. (Dworkin, 2000, 5)

The first principle justifies the state redistributing resources by means of welfare policies, in order to provide the conditions for autonomy. However, the second principle emphasizes the importance of individual responsibility. This resonates with the concerns of conservatives about welfare, but we could also see in it a more liberal concern with the importance of people being actively involved in their lives, rather than the passive beneficiaries of assistance.

This focus on free and autonomous human choice helps to distinguish between two different approaches that might be taken by theories of distributional equality: either to equalize welfare, or to equalize resources. (Welfare here refers to outcomes that are good for citizens.) As Dworkin points out, equalizing welfare as outcomes has an immediate appeal. It focuses on ends rather than means, and recognizes that people have different needs, and will need different amounts and kinds of resources to achieve equal welfare. Needs-based welfare programmes can be understood as an effort to bring about greater equality of welfare in terms of outcomes. There are, however, some problems with this approach, which arise from the rather nebulous way in which welfare as outcomes can be defined. It is difficult to measure and compare people's level of personal happiness, or overall success in life. (This problem of 'interpersonal comparisons' also besets utilitarianism.) Certainly, a large and intrusive state bureaucracy would be required to make these comparisons. Some people's welfare might depend on preferences that we consider illegitimate, perhaps because they are uninformed, or irrational, or because they involve the denigration of others. Others might have preferences that they regard as essential to their welfare, but which the state cannot ensure are satisfied, for example an end to global warming, world peace, no more deaths from cancer.

Given these problems, Dworkin argues that the better egalitarian strategy is to aim at equality of resources, rather than welfare. If everyone has an equal amount of resources, some will choose to do more with these than others, or be less or more happy – but these are personal matters in which the state need not be involved. Focusing on equality of resources re-emphasizes the principle of individual responsibility and accords with many of the practical critiques made of the effects of welfare. Naturally, people will want different resources and different combinations of them, based on their own abilities and desires. Dworkin proposes a thought experiment to show how this would work. Imagine a group of castaways on a desert island who had to work out a scheme for sharing resources. In order to ensure a just distribution, an auction is held at which everyone has equal purchasing power. Each castaway then bids for bundles of resources. These bundles are re-divided after each successful bid, until all resources are accounted for. Eventually, everyone will be happy with their bundle of resources – because if they were not, they would have bid differently. Individuals are free to choose what collection of resources they would most like, and a fair and open market allocates resources.

However, Dworkin, as does Rawls, believes that people should not be penalized for lacking abilities. Neither should they receive unregulated rewards because they have socially valued talents. Once the castaways have their initial distribution, the degree to which they will amass more resources and be successful depends on a range of different factors. Some people will choose more remunerative occupations than others and, in this case, they should be entitled to the profits they make. In some cases, luck will be a factor. Where castaways make more wealth as a result of luck that depended on them choosing to take risks – Dworkin calls this 'option luck' – they should be entitled to any gains they make – and they should also have to bear any losses. Choice entails risk. But what people can make out of their initial bundle of resources can also be affected by the bad luck that befalls them. As this is not a result of their free choice, they should not have to bear the brunt of it. Resource redistribution should thus compensate for what Dworkin calls 'brute luck'. The best way of assessing compensation would be to look at what the castaways would have agreed to pay in insurance, against such bad luck happening. Then, because not all would choose to take out insurance, a compulsory insurance scheme would be instituted, financed by progressive taxation, which would compensate people for brute bad luck – including natural or physical handicaps.

Unlike Rawls' theory, Dworkin's scheme addresses the central concern of those who support changes to welfare: it distinguishes economic hardship caused by choice from that caused by bad luck. It also targets a wider range of those in need: Rawls focuses only on the worst-off group in society, defined in terms of income and wealth. Dworkin's compulsory insurance scheme recognizes a range of hardships that might be produced by bad luck, notably including physical and mental disabilities. However, Dworkin also wants, as does Rawls, to prevent people benefiting from the possession of unearned talents. This, he argues, can be achieved by the periodic redistribution of resources through taxation. These redistributions would be based on the same principle as the insurance scheme; individuals would make a compulsory contribution to redistribution, through tax, contributing to insure themselves against having no or few marketable talents. This is, of course, an ideal scheme, and the challenge is to implement policies of 'defensible egalitarian redistributions' that most closely approximate its underlying rationale.

Dworkin's defence of equalizing resources assumes that a clear distinction can be drawn between the demands on us that result from our choices, and those that result from circumstances that we did not choose. If we have desires or tastes that are expensive to satisfy, we should not be compensated for them by the state, because it can be assumed that they are freely chosen. Gerald Cohen has pointed out, however, that we do not necessarily choose our expensive tastes, although we might be impelled to satisfy them (Cohen, 1989). It follows that, when we are considering redistribution, we cannot avoid looking closely at what was chosen and what was not. Rather than equalizing resources, Cohen concludes, we should equalize access to advantage, which recognizes the legitimacy of redistributing so that those with unchosen expensive preferences are not disadvantaged. This accords with Marx's call for resources to be distributed 'to each, according to his need' (Cohen, 2004). We might note here the difficulty in implementing a policy of redistribution that requires the circumstances of individual choices to be assessed. In order to carry this out, the state would require an unimaginably large and intrusive bureaucracy. This objection is, as Cohen points out, practical rather than theoretical; it does not affect the egalitarian case that he makes against equalizing resources (Cohen, 1989). It does, however, point to the difficulty in applying 'ideal' theory to real world problems.

Ensuring human capabilities

Dworkin's is a more complex scheme for redistribution than Rawls', but has the possible advantage of aiming to separate clearly between the chosen and unchosen determinants of our own fortunes. This is clearly in accord with some recent changes to welfare that tighten requirements for eligibility for benefits. But is it possible to make such clear distinctions? Some egalitarian thinkers have criticized the idea that people should or should not receive financial assistance on the basis of whether or not they made good choices. Elizabeth Anderson argues that whether luck egalitarians focus on equality of welfare or equality of resources, their mistake is to think that luck is what should be equalized. In fact, people's abilities to utilize resources depend not on luck, but rather on the social, economic and cultural structures within which they make choices, and which constrain those choices. As Marx put it, people make their own history, but not under the circumstances of their own choosing (Marx, 1978 [1852]: 595). Instead of equalizing luck, justice should aim to end the oppression that constrains human choice (Anderson, 1999).

The real problem with luck egalitarianism is its assumption of free choice.

Focusing on luck ignores the way in which systems affect choices and prospects, and, instead, sets up the state as a moral arbiter, tasked with judging individual decisions. It forces people to live with the consequences of 'bad choices', no matter how that choice was constrained. Consider, for example, a young woman with a poor education, a family history of abuse, and no social support, who becomes pregnant with a second child (a common group of potential beneficiaries targeted by recent welfare changes). Her 'decision' to become pregnant might have been due to lack of education about contraception, an uncooperative partner, or her lack of direction in life. Or consider a young man who 'chooses' to work at a local automobile plant, because that is overwhelmingly the main employer in town, and his school and family have not prepared him for other options. When the plant closes because production has moved offshore, and the worker finds himself unemployed and, without retraining, unemployable, is his situation the result of option or brute luck? These examples are importantly different from the case of someone from a wealthy background who chooses to drop out of university and go surfing. Even setting aside the structural constraints of choice, those who 'choose' to care for dependants – work necessary for society to continue – will find themselves penalized under a system that cannot distinguish between the various reasons why people do not engage in remunerative labour.

What these and other similar critiques suggest is that, rather than assuming freedom of choice, and assessing choices made, an egalitarian system should focus on redistributing resources to ensure that people can actually make free and autonomous choices in the first place. Some theorists have suggested that the aim of redistribution should be to ensure that everyone had enough resources to exercise their human capabilities, in order to make autonomous choices about the important things in life. Anderson calls this a system of 'democratic equality' – and adds that, once enough resources are redistributed to ensure essential human capabilities, there should not be limits on additional gains by the wealthy. Amartya Sen argues, similarly, that the goal of justice should be to ensure that all people are equally capable of functioning as free human beings (Sen, 1992). Martha Nussbaum lists a range of 'core capabilities' that she sees as essential to being human, and argues that a just society must distribute resources in such a way as to provide for these. Her list of basic capabilities ranges from physical survival and bodily health to the capability to exercise practical reason, and the capability to exert some control over one's environment, including political control (Nussbaum, 1999).

As we have seen, before the current wave of reforms, the welfare state was aimed at satisfying the basic needs of citizens, on the grounds that everyone must have the resources required to satisfy these needs in order to function as citizens. The capabilities-based theories I have outlined argue that the satisfaction of essential needs is necessary to living free and autonomous lives. We should note here that this conception of autonomy is quite different from that of self-ownership libertarians such as Nozick. However, a more complex concept of autonomy presents its own problems:

- Can we clearly identify the capabilities essential to autonomy?
- Is it possible to fix a point at which we could be sure that enough redistribution had occurred in order to ensure that these capabilities were fully provided for?
- How, given scarce resources, are we to deal with the problem of expensive needs?
- Should all redistribution, for example, be targeted towards improving the condition of the severely disabled, with very high needs?
- Should support be limited on the basis of the likely degree of improvement in human capabilities that it can sustain?

Notwithstanding these difficult questions, the separation between needs and choices becomes particularly attractive when we concede more weight to the structural and institutional factors that constrain and limit choice. Feminist theorists argue that economic, cultural and ideological factors combine to limit women's free and autonomous choices to carry out their plans and projects in life (Okin, 1989: 4). Women in most modern societies are still assumed to be the primary care-givers for children and other dependants, and their average income is uniformly lower than that of men. At the same time, women have tended to be the focus of anti-welfare campaigns, particularly in the United States, in the figure of the 'welfare queen' – the young, low-income, single mother. As we have seen, a needs-based approach avoids penalizing women and children in this situation for the results of their constrained choices. The left libertarian basic income scheme also provides at least some resources for this group. Stricter luck-egalitarian arguments might attempt to satisfy the child as an innocent victim from its mother, but it is not possible to achieve complete separation of the interests of dependent children from their care-givers.

The fact that even liberal egalitarian arguments do not take into account women's socialization into care-giving roles in the family might be due to the fact that liberal political philosophy historically has relegated the family to the 'private sphere', exempt from regulation by political principles of justice (Okin, 1989; Elshtain, 1981). Susan Okin comments that a central source of injustice for women is that the law 'treats more or less as equals those whom custom, workplace discrimination, and the still conventional division of labor within the family have made very unequal' (Okin, 1989: 4). The feminist critique suggests that more is required for justice than merely redistribution. Rather, institutions (such as marriage and the family), and the ideas and ideologies that underlie them, must change in order to make society more fair, and to provide for those in need. But, in the meantime, in the non-ideal world, redistribution on the basis of choice must recognize how constrained choices actually are.

Sustaining communities through redistribution

Some feminists argue that redistribution in the form of welfare is important, not because it reflects the claims of individuals to justice, but because it embodies an 'ethics of care' (Tronto, 1993). Feminists who work in this tradition argue that we should think of justice not as the balancing of individual rights but, rather, in terms of recognizing and maintaining the

---

Box 2.2 Taxation and redistribution: competing norms and values

The philosophical debate over taxation and redistribution centres on different interpretations of some key concepts:

• Private property

Supporters of redistribution – liberal, communitarian and feminist – argue that private property is not an absolute good, but is legitimate as long as it supports principles of justice or the good of the community.

Opponents of redistribution see private property rights as fundamental, and independent of questions about the fair distribution of resources. Individuals who acquired property justly may do with it what they wish, and there are no grounds for the state to take it forcibly and redistribute it to others.

Marxists think that property is produced through social cooperation, and should be owned in common.

• Equality

Supporters, across the spectrum from liberal to Marxist, hold that justice requires equality, whether of overall welfare, resources, or access to opportunity.

Some libertarian opponents of redistribution argue that equalizing resources or overall welfare is incompatible with liberty. Left-libertarians, however, claim that everyone is entitled to an equal share in the world's resources, and that the benefits and proceeds of resources should be equally distributed to everyone – not merely to the needy.

→

network of social relations that sustains the community. The concept of the individual underlying this perspective is different to that which shapes most of the liberal theories we have discussed: individuals here are not unconnected, 'atomistic' selves driven by self-interest but, rather, interdependent members of communities that make them who they are. Theorists of the ethics of care base this view on the experience women have gained through their social roles as care-givers, particularly in families. This experience (rather than what male philosophers have historically often seen as women's 'essential nature') endows them with what moral psychologist Carol Gilligan has called a 'different voice' (Gilligan, 1982), less attuned to regulating competing claims under justice, and better suited to social reproduction. When it comes to redistribution, theorists of the ethics of care tend to support a needs-based approach, which reflects a common

• **Liberty**

Supporters of redistribution think that freedom is expressed through the abilities of individuals to make independent and autonomous decisions, or to exercise their human capabilities. The right to private property must be subordinate to personal freedom and autonomy, and redistribution is thus justified if it enables people to achieve these.

Communitarian thinkers argue that personal liberty is defined and limited by communal ties. Redistribution must reflect a sense of shared social commitment and obligation, and must be accompanied by the strengthening of social institutions.

Libertarians emphasize people's liberty to do what they wish with their own property. For Nozick, this means preventing the state from forcibly acquiring and redistributing the resources of some to others. For left-libertarians, it means granting everyone their rightful equal share of resources, and allowing them to spend it as they wish.

• **The role of the state**

Libertarians argue for a minimal state that will protect the security of citizens and enforce contracts, but not forcibly redistribute resources from some citizens to others.

Communitarians share this sceptical view of state welfare, but emphasize the role of civil society organizations and institutions in managing redistribution.

Other liberals think that the state should play a more activist role in creating the opportunities people need to enjoy their liberties. Redistribution that is tied to choice and responsibility requires close regulation by the state. But a strong state is also necessary for leftist schemes to redistribute on the basis of need.

responsibility to care for our fellow community members. We might note here that Rawls' liberal theory also reflects the idea that all members of a society share their fates – that is why the wealth of the richest is tied to that of the poorest.

Communitarian thinkers more generally support at least some redistribution on the grounds that large-scale material inequalities are corrosive to social cohesion. The flip side of this is their argument that communal responsibility should be re-emphasized as the justification for welfare redistribution. Some communitarians, as we saw at the beginning of this chapter, think that an excessive focus on individualist rights-based arguments is responsible for the decline in commitment to the welfare state (Sandel, 1982, 1996). Redistribution through welfare can only be justified insofar as all citizens are committed to a common good. The remedy for this involves not only changes in the way we think and talk about politics, but also changes in the institutions we expect to achieve social change. Rather than the state and its bureaucracies, we should reinforce the role played by the social institutions of civil society (Bellah *et al.*, 1985; Elshtain, 1995). Right-wing communitarians have argued from this that social – particularly religious – organizations should be charged with the responsibility for social support. To some extent this involves voluntary aid through charity – of the same kind envisaged by libertarians, although for different reasons. The latter emphasize the private right to give charity, while communitarians stress the ways in which charitable institutions contribute to the common good. These ideas have been influential in justifying the state provision of funding to social groups – as we have seen, a common change to welfare policies in many countries has been the privatization of service provision and delivery.

Conclusion

All of the theorists we have discussed in this chapter are concerned with the balance between private ownership and fairness or justice. For Nozick, justice is defined in terms of private ownership: as long as people acquired their property as a result of free transfer from the previous owner, they are under no obligation to transfer it to others in need. For egalitarian thinkers, private ownership is an institution that only has meaning in the context of society and its regulating principles of justice. Ownership and entitlement must thus be balanced with fairness, reciprocity, the common good, the intrinsic importance of developing human capabilities, and other principles such as the value of taking personal responsibility for our choices. How they strike this balance determines where theorists line up in their support of redistribution.

We might also see the debate over welfare as turning on the relationship between distribution and resources, on the one hand, and human autonomy, or free and self-directed action, on the other. Some political theorists who support welfare redistribution against the current trend to restrict benefits argue that redistribution is not enough to achieve justice. Fairer redistribution of resources might provide people with the resources they need to develop themselves freely, but structural changes to our institutions and values might be required to allow people to think about themselves in such a way as to enable them to use their resources. Iris Young, one of these more 'critical theorists' argues that people need to be able to exercise two capacities: self-determination and self-development. Self-development requires (at least) adequate material resources, while self-determination means that people must be free to make their own decisions, and choose the conditions of their actions. Domination prevents this, and that is exercised through constraining institutions and social relations (Young, 2000). So, while welfare will redistribute resources, broader social change is required in order to treat beneficiaries truly justly and equally. At the same time, as we saw at the beginning of this chapter, opponents of welfare see the system itself as a source of domination, preventing recipients from becoming autonomous, in the sense of taking responsibility for their own lives. As with many of the issues we encounter in this book, the debate over redistribution is, at least in part, over what is required in order for people to be autonomous.

Chapter 3

Are Minority Cultures Entitled to Recognition and Rights?

One of the most important new political developments in western democracies towards the end of the last century has been the emergence of minority cultural groups claiming official recognition and rights. As immigration has made democratic societies increasingly pluralist and multicultural, minority ethnic and cultural groups have argued not only that their individual members must be granted equal rights and protections, but also that groups themselves are entitled to recognized status and collective rights. The groups making these claims are diverse: they include ethnic immigrant and refugee communities, indigenous peoples, religious communities that draw members from different ethnic backgrounds, national minorities that have existed with some degree of separateness for the entire history of a nation, and the descendants of those brought to their country against their will. Their claims also cover a wide spectrum: some groups demand that their language, cultural customs, religious beliefs or history be included in public ceremonies or school curricula. They might go so far as to claim that cultural practices and beliefs should be taken into account as a defence or mitigation in criminal trials. Some groups request that they be exempted from usual regulations covering dress or Sunday trading. Indigenous groups or national minorities might demand limited self-determination and self-government, perhaps over territory or resources, or over policy issues that specifically affect the minority.

Despite their differences, these groups share in common the view that the identities of individual members are importantly shaped or influenced by their unchosen or ascribed membership. It is the 'deep' and unchosen nature of group membership that differentiates cultural groups from other kinds of association, based on shared interests or opinions. As Paul Hirst puts it, cultural groups constitute 'communities of fate' rather than 'communities of choice' (Hirst, 1994), and deserve to be treated differently from the voluntary groups and associations to which people belong. Because of the link between political claims and collective identity, these arguments are sometimes referred to as 'identity politics'.

While cultural diversity is a fact of life in most modern democracies, relatively few have official policies recognizing minority cultures. In Australia and Canada, multiculturalism was officially adopted at the federal level in the 1970s, and the policy was entrenched in the Canadian Constitution in

1982. In both countries, governments formally committed themselves to recognizing the diverse cultural backgrounds of their citizens, and to supporting projects aimed at maintaining and publicly celebrating minority cultures. Some European countries – including Sweden, the Netherlands and Denmark – followed suit. Recent years, however, have seen a widespread popular backlash against multiculturalism. In Australia, the right-wing One Nation Party emerged in the 1990s, and elected representatives to parliament on the platform of attacking immigration, multiculturalism and Aboriginal rights. In many culturally diverse nations, anti-immigration parties increased their support in the same period, as pressure has grown for minorities to assimilate and to drop claims for recognition or rights.

Some of the most controversial of these claims recently have involved the rights of members of cultural minorities to substitute ethnic or religious dress for uniforms, either in school or at work in public institutions such as schools, hospitals and the police force. These claims are not new: in the 1960s, Sikhs in Britain employed by bus companies demanded and won the right to wear turbans to work, and the Canadian government ruled that Sikhs could serve as members of the Royal Canadian Mounted Police without removing their turbans and beards. Most recent cases have involved Muslim immigrants and, while the most publicized has been that of the headscarf in France (see Box 3.1), similar cases have arisen in many other European countries, as well as Britain, the United States and Canada. These cases raise issues of the freedom of religious expression, but also the status of minority cultural communities.

Concerns about the assimilation of Asian immigrants had been publicly debated in Britain throughout the 1990s in response to the Salman Rushdie affair of 1989 (in which Muslims protested against blasphemy against the Prophet Mohammed in one of Rushdie's novels, *The Satanic Verses*). Cases in which young girls were forced into marriages in accordance with alleged traditional cultural practices provoked further public debate about the status of minority cultures. In fact, many disputes concerning minority cultural customs centre around the dress and treatment of girls and women, as feminist theorists, whose work we consider later in this chapter, point out. The official policy in Britain has been that integration does not mean assimilation, and that ethnic and cultural differences can be maintained unless they are contrary to the public interest. This has increasingly come to be extended – not without controversy – to minority religious groups. The government provides funding for schools reflecting minority religious cultures and has recently extended this to Muslim schools. Nevertheless, the recognition of acceptable differences has run up against limits. The *hijab* is largely uncontroversial – female Muslim police officers have been permitted to wear it – but forms of dress that cover the whole body or face have been much more controversial. In 2002, Shabina Begum, a pupil at Denbigh high school, was

Box 3.1 The headscarf controversy in France

In France, where the secular character of public life has historically been fiercely defended, small numbers of Muslim girls began to wear the *hijab* (or headscarf) to school during the 1980s. Teachers complained, but the state left the decision about whether to ban this dress to individual schools. After the terrorist attacks of 2001, however, the issue attracted increased public anxiety about radical Islam and the apparent failure of Muslim immigrants to assimilate into French society. In 2002, right-wing presidential candidate Jean-Marie Le Pen attracted substantial support when he campaigned on an anti-immigration agenda that included such policies as a ban on the building of mosques in France. In September 2004, France enacted a national ban on the wearing of all conspicuous religious symbols in state schools, including Muslim headscarves, Jewish skullcaps, large Christian crosses and Sikh turbans. While this controversy also raised issues of religious freedom, much of the dispute focused on questions of cultural rights:

- Supporters of the ban argue that religious coverings impede free movement and imply that women's bodies are shameful, and that girls and women – if freely allowed to make their own decisions, uninfluenced by religious and patriarchal authority – would not choose to wear them. Girls who do claim to choose to wear the veil cannot really be free to consult their own wishes. Moreover, allowing Muslim citizens to wear religious dress means treating them differently, and exempting them from general uniform rules. The effect of such a policy would be to encourage separatism among Muslim immigrants to France.
- Opponents of the ban counter that many girls and women who choose to wear religious dress insist that they are acting freely. To assume that a decision not to appear in a sexualized manner in public must be coerced is to assume that western values are universal. To prevent Muslim women from following what they see as their religious duty is to discriminate against them. Moreover, it will force them to be educated privately, and thus, paradoxically, will increase their alienation from French institutions and political values.

expelled for insisting on wearing the *jilbab*, a long gown, in contravention of the school uniform policy. After a lengthy appeals process, the House of Lords in 2006 upheld the school's right to expel the girl, given that it had determined its uniform policy in full consultation with local minority community group leaders. In 2007, the courts ruled that schools could ban pupils from wearing the full-face veil on the grounds of security, safety or learning. Also in 2006, a young Muslim woman who was a teaching assistant in a Yorkshire school was dismissed for insisting on wearing her *niqab*, a veil worn by some Muslim women that covers all of the face except the eyes. The debate this sparked about minority cultural and religious practices was further fuelled when Cabinet Minister Jack Straw remarked that he asked Muslim women attending his office in his Blackburn constituency, where some 30 per cent of residents were Muslim, to remove their veils. Straw argued that covering the face undermined community relationships. Prime Minister Tony Blair asserted that all immigrants had a duty to embrace the values of 'democracy, the rule of law, tolerance, equal treatment for all, respect for this country and its shared heritage', stating that immigrants should 'conform to it, or don't come here' (Associated Press, 2006).

In the United States, the issue of religious dress has been viewed primarily as one of freedom of expression, and the government has maintained that banning religious dress would violate a basic right that should be protected. The US Justice Department, for example, intervened when an 11-year-old Muslim girl was banned from wearing her headscarf as part of a wider ban on head coverings, and the school eventually changed its policy. However, courts refused the request of a Muslim woman in Florida to be photographed for her driver's licence wearing a face-covering *burqa*, on the grounds that facial identification was an essential aspect of the licence. The question of minority communities' rights in the United States to exemption from legal provisions was addressed in 1972 in the Yoder Supreme Court case. Here, the Amish community were granted the right to exempt their children from education in a state curriculum that contravened their values.

Where ethnic minority groups and separatist communities such as the Amish have requested exemption from legal requirements, indigenous communities and long-standing national minorities argue for formal constitutional or legal recognition of their status, and varying degrees of self-management. In the United States, Native American tribes have powers of self-government similar to those of states in the federal system. They manage natural resources and law enforcement: most Native American communities have local court systems that deal with matters that relate to local ordinances. In Canada, the indigenous First Nations, Inuit and Metis peoples are officially recognized in the Constitution, and claim varying degrees of self-determination and sovereignty. Nunavut, the new self-governing territory formed in 1999, has a population which is 85 per cent Inuit, and its own territorial legislature and institutions. Indigenous First Nations are not, of course, the only national minorities in Canada: the province of Quebec has demanded autonomy and self-determination, and two referenda have been held on whether or not Quebec should secede from Canada. Although these failed, federal legislation recognizes Quebec as a distinct nation within Canada. French is its sole official language, and English speakers are a recognized linguistic minority within the province.

Indigenous peoples in Australia do not enjoy the same degree of self-determination, although, since the landmark Mabo High Court case in 1992, their rights as native title-holders over their land have been legally recognized. Activists have demanded that Indigenous Australians be recognized as a culturally and historically distinct group, with original rights to their land, but they have achieved limited success in mainstream politics. The situation for indigenous peoples is very different in New Zealand, where the Maori people are a strong and active force in mainstream politics, and Maori cultural practices and language are, to some degree at least, incorporated into public life under policies of 'biculturalism'. Since the 1980s, New Zealand has recognized the Treaty of Waitangi, signed by representatives of the Crown and Maori chiefs in 1840, as a foundational legal and political document that apportions sovereignty and grants limited rights to self-determination and self-management to Maori. Separate seats have been allocated for Maori representatives to New Zealand's parliament since the 1860s, and currently number seven.

The myriad of policy responses that nations have taken to the claims of minority communities must be viewed in an international political and legal context. The rights and status of cultural minorities are protected by the United Nations' International Covenant on Civil and Political Rights. Article 27 prescribes:

> In those states in which ethnic, religious or linguistic minorities exist, persons belonging to such minorities shall not be denied the right, in community with the other members of their group, to enjoy their own culture, to profess and practice their own religion, or to use their own language.

A UN Special Rapporteur confirmed the view that this article does not mean only that members of minority cultures should not be discriminated against. It concluded that special measures granting rights to minority cultures might be required (Capotorti, 1979). A UN Declaration on the Rights of Indigenous Peoples eventually passed in the General Assembly in 2007, with negative votes from the United States, Australia, Canada and New Zealand. These four countries opposed self-determination for indigenous peoples on the grounds that it was contrary to international law, and would result in the creation of two separate classes of citizens.

Many of the underlying political and philosophical questions that arise in these cases concern the relationship between group and individual rights, for example:

- To what extent should we see individuals' identity and status as dependent on the groups to which they belong?
- Is individual freedom or autonomy affected by the way cultural groups are treated?

• Does granting rights to groups threaten individual freedom – particularly in cases where individuals disagree with or reject their groups' cultural values and practices?

These debates also raise questions about the relationship between the state and cultures: Should – or can – the state be 'benignly neutral', not supporting any cultural group, or maintaining even-handedness between all groups? Related to this are issues around social cohesion: Do recognition and rights for cultural minorities threaten the cohesion and commonality of the nation? The answers to these questions might be seen to depend on the cultural minority in question. Critics have asked, for example, whether indigenous cultural groups, or historical national minorities should be treated differently, and have more collective rights than other minorities – for example, those of ethnic immigrant communities (Kymlicka, 1995). And, in all cases, we might ask:

• What should be the extent of these rights?
• Is simply official recognition of minority cultures required, or should they be granted some degree of self-government or self-management, so that they can make their own rules respecting their members?

We might also look critically at the relationship between cultural recognition or rights and the broader issues of justice we considered in Chapter 2: Should we focus instead on ensuring that the members of minorities – and all in need – receive fairer distributions of material goods? Some critics, as we will see, view the claims of multiculturalism as a distraction from the real causes of injustice and inequality.

We can group together the arguments in favour of cultural recognition and rights into three basic categories:

1 Liberal concern for the relationship between cultural membership and individual freedom.
2 The empirical grounds that people belong to a range of cultural groups that are of value to them.
3 History-based arguments that indigenous peoples have been dispossessed and subordinated by colonization.

Arguments opposed to cultural recognition and rights can also be divided into three groups:

1 Liberal concerns for individual freedom (including the freedom of groups and individuals within minorities).
2 Arguments based on national unity and the common good.

3 Leftist concerns with the relationship between multiculturalism and
  distributive justice.

We examine first the liberal individualist case against minority cultural
rights, because the centrality of individual rights in modern liberal democratic societies means that the presumption tends to be against recognizing
collectivities. We then turn to liberal and non-liberal theories in support of
cultural rights, before considering a range of critical perspectives in greater
detail.

Cultural rights versus individual freedom

Our contemporary ideas about multiculturalism and the rights of cultural
minorities are deeply rooted in the history of modern politics. In the wake
of the Protestant Reformation, the emerging plurality of religious beliefs
formed the major social context for the development of liberal thought in
the seventeenth century; John Locke's *A Letter Concerning Toleration*
(Locke, 1983 [1689]) is an early expression of the liberal view that the
business of politics and government should be distinguished from the
range of different religious convictions that exist in private life. As we shall
see, Locke's separation of public from private concerns still forms the basis
of much contemporary liberal criticism of cultural rights.

Most modern liberals have not argued that cultural membership and
identity is unimportant but, rather, that it is a matter for private and social
life, not to be regulated by the state. 'Political liberals' such as John Rawls
argue that the public business of politics must be regulated by principles of
fairness that can be agreed on by people who have a range of different
moral views – and, by implication, cultural identities – in private life
(Rawls, 1993). Throughout the history of western political theory,
philosophers have divided human activity into separate spheres of action,
each of which is concerned with different aspects of life, and has different
goals. Since the seventeenth century and the development of liberal
thought, these spheres have included the private (the sphere of individual
action, which often includes the family), the social (human activity that
involves others, but not formal political activity), and the political or
public. The private sphere is where individuals are socialized and accultur-
ated, and where we derive our sense of what is good, important and
morally valuable in life. Liberals maintain that there is a distinction,
however, between the 'deep' or 'thick' identities of private life, and the
'thin' selves who debate and make political decisions in public.

Some of the strongest opposition to policies of multiculturalism is associated with a libertarian liberalism, which emphasizes individual freedom

and a limited state. Philosophers who take this perspective insist that giving groups rights will endanger important individual rights. This does not mean, however, that they assume that individuals are necessarily 'atomistic' and unconnected individuals, for whom culture is unimportant. They argue, rather, that cultural identities should be freely chosen, and that cultural communities should be seen as voluntary associations or communities of choice, composed of members with shared interests, and thus be no more deserving of protections and rights than other voluntary groups (Kukathas, 1992: 239). Chandran Kukathas claims that the job of the state is to offer security to individuals, and to provide a safe and secure environment in which they can pursue their private interests and goods (Kukathas, 1992). The state should not intervene to protect and preserve cultural groups, which exist only as the product of free individual action and allegiance – such groups will thrive if they are successful in attracting individual followers and adherents; if they are not successful, Kukathas concludes, they are not worth preserving. Moreover, state intervention to recognize minority cultures will inevitably favour some over others, thus dragging the states into conflicts between groups. An example in point is the tension that sometimes exists in countries such as Australia and New Zealand between immigrant ethnic groups and those indigenous peoples who argue that their cultures merit special recognition and rights (Walker, 1993/4).

Opponents of cultural rights argue that the right to join and leave groups is essential to human freedom. Political philosophers have particularly emphasized the 'right of exit', as it is clear that most of us are born and raised within cultural communities, rather than actively choosing to join them. Individualist liberals argue that we must be free to review our membership, that we must be aware of options, and that we must be free to leave our communities if we choose to do so. As Martha Nussbaum puts it when discussing women members of cultural groups: cultural membership and the norms, practices and beliefs that flow from it should only be assumed to apply to a member of that group if 'on due consideration, with all the capabilities at her disposal', she has consciously adopted that identity (Nussbaum, 1999: 46). We discuss this in greater detail below, but it raises some basic problems:

- Can we really exit from cultural communities based on race or ethnicity?
- What is meant by a meaningful review of our membership?

The Yoder case in the United States is a good example of the difficulties here: If the children of cultural minorities are excluded from the mainstream system of education, or curriculum, and are educated only according to the mores and values of their culture, can they meaningfully assess and review their allegiance to their culture? If adults have not been exposed to alternative cultures and lifestyles, it is hard to see how they could be said to have sufficient knowledge with which to exercise their right of exit. The same applies to all cultural practices and customs that might make it diffi- cult for people to leave their communities, or which might restrict their options. In practice, this might cover a wide range of customs that, for example, restrict the education and opportunities of some group members, such as women. The individualist position that cultural communities should be treated as voluntary associations potentially justifies significant governmental intervention into groups that do not allow a real right of existence. On the other hand, it does mean that cultural groups should not be discriminated against if they advocate restrictive or illiberal practices, as long as these do not limit the freedom of members to exit.

Some philosophers have suggested that it is the voluntary associations that emerge out of identity groups that have real moral value. The rights of these groups to regulate their members should not be interfered with, as long as there exists an effective right to exit from them. Nancy Rosenblum argues that voluntary organizations that have formalized representative structures and decision-making procedures allow true representative voices to express group interests – thus avoiding the charge that majority and powerful groups tend to be allowed to define the identity of the minor- ity (Rosenblum, 1998). Identity groups, she argues, can too easily be attributed unity and coherence, with self-appointed spokespersons claim- ing to speak for the 'latent voice' of the group. They do not encourage an active group life, and might not be happy to see themselves as a part of a 'pluralist mosaic' including other cultural communities (Rosenblum, 1998: 323).

Critics concerned about individual liberty have also pointed out that granting cultural rights can result in pigeon-holing, or forcing into fixed categories, individuals who are members of many groups. Jeremy Waldron, for example, argues for a 'cosmopolitan' view of the self, which recognizes 'the chaotic co-existence of projects, pursuits, ideas, images and snatches of culture within an individual' (Waldron, 1992, 2000). The autonomous individual does not have a single, unitary life-plan, but has a complex identity, with many different forms of expression and identifica- tion. Waldron warns us against assuming that, in order to be a real or authentic individual, one must be unitary and singly focused. Anthony Appiah argues similarly that ethno-racial identities tend to become an obsessive focus of people's lives, leading them to forget that their individ- ual identities are complex and multifarious (Appiah, 1996: 103). As Rosenblum reminds us, individual identities might be formed just as much in reaction against the communities to which they belong as they are shaped by them (Rosenblum, 1998).

Group rights and cultural change

Recognizing cultural rights has an impact not only on individual freedom, but also on the nature of groups themselves. Opponents of rights point out that groups are not fixed and unchanging but, rather, are always changing and evolving. There will always be a plurality of group interests and identities, but the groups that comprise that plurality will change, and state policies that attempt to identify and fix groups will inevitably lag behind social realities. Yael Tamir argues that official recognition 'freezes' groups in the historical moment, treating as timeless cultural practices that are in a constant state of change, and might themselves be shaped by experiences such as colonialism, or recent oppression, or the adoption of Christianity (Tamir, 1999). In addition, granting rights to groups assumes that they are fixed not only across time, but that they have single and unified identities themselves. In reality, individualists argue, groups are not homogeneous; they are frequently riven by serious conflicts of interest. We are, in fact, no more justified in assuming minority cultural groups to be united and homogeneous than the larger pluralist societies of which they form parts.

Allowing collective rights to minority communities runs the risk of legitimizing and privileging group elites that are better educated and integrated into mainstream political processes, and that consequently are better able to make claims. Apart from reinforcing power differentials within groups, it would make it more difficult for those trying to change cultures from the inside to do so. This argument is sometimes made by feminists, who argue that granting cultural rights makes it more difficult for women within minority cultures to change discriminatory customs and practices. We discuss this in greater detail later in this chapter. In the case of Muslim dress for women, the claim is frequently made that male leaders of the community are demanding that women wear the forms of dress in question, and that Muslim women are denied free choice in the matter.

Defending cultural rights: autonomy and the role of culture in personal identity

Waldron's cosmopolitan view of the individual leads us to one of the more common arguments in favour of the protection of minority cultures: the utilitarian argument that it generally improves the lives of everyone, including members of majority cultures, to have more cultural choice available. Many pro-multiculturalist arguments defend cultural diversity as a good thing for everyone. There are two reasons why this argument does not make a strong case for the protection of minority cultures:

1 It does not matter, for cultural diversity, which cultures exist. All existing cultures could disappear provided they were replaced by others; so there is no particular reason to protect and preserve any existing culture.
2 We could fall back on the individualist liberal rejoinder here: if people from the majority culture want to preserve the benefits they derive from the existence of the minority, they will support it themselves, without requiring intervention from the state. (Although in order to take into account the good produced by cultural diversity over time, state intervention to protect cultures in the short term might be justified.)

The stronger argument in favour of cultural protection and rights relies on the good of individual members of minorities. While some political philosophers oppose granting rights and recognition to minority cultures, on the grounds that doing so will threaten individual liberty, others argue that the preservation and maintenance of cultural communities is essential to liberty and to individual autonomy. These philosophers tend to be influenced by the Enlightenment and Romantic belief that cultural membership deeply shapes who we are and our destinies. This idea was developed by the French philosopher Montesquieu in the seventeenth century, and later by the German Johann Gottfried Herder in the eighteenth century. In this early Romantic view, national cultures are deeply rooted and natural – they shape individual identity and demand political expression. These ideas have influenced modern nationalism, as well as arguments for the protection and recognition of minority cultures.

The connection between individual autonomy and culture might be described in several ways. Charles Taylor argues that individual self-respect is bound up with cultural membership (Taylor, 1994). People derive an important sense of who they are from their cultures and, if the culture is not recognized and respected generally, their individual self-respect and dignity will suffer. There must therefore be, Taylor argues, a presumption of equal recognition for all cultures – at least those that 'have animated whole societies over some considerable stretch of time' (Taylor, 1994: 66). Taylor explicitly excludes 'partial cultural milieux' within a society. But this is, he warns, only a presumption. An actual judgement of value can only come with real knowledge and understanding, when there has developed a 'fused horizon of standards' – an attempt to understand other cultures in their own terms, rather than simply applying the standards of our own (Taylor, 1994: 70). Avishai Margalit and Joseph Raz similarly claim that the culture in which we are born and raised forms the primary focus of our personal identification, because it is based on belonging rather than accomplishment. If a culture is not generally respected, the self-respect and dignity of its members suffers also (Margalit and Raz, 1990). Other philosophers have followed suit in applying this argument about cultural identification to nationality and national self-determination, arguing that national identification is a key factor in building solidarity and shared commitment to the common good (Miller, 1997; Tamir 1993). We should note, however, that national identification is not necessarily compatible with recognizing minority cultural groups. We discuss nationalist-based objections to multiculturalism later in this chapter.

Perhaps the most influential argument linking the individual to cultural membership is made by Will Kymlicka. His approach is based on the fundamental liberal assumption that 'a liberal democracy's most basic commitment is to the freedom and equality of its individual citizens' (Kymlicka, 1995). There is a deep connection, Kymlicka argues, between the freedom and autonomy of individuals, and the 'societal cultures' to which they belong. It is important to look carefully at his definition of societal culture, as key distinctions in his argument, and the strong case he makes for particular minority group rights, depend on this. A societal culture is 'a culture which provides its members with meaningful ways of life across the full range of human activities, including social, educational, religious, recreational, and economic life, encompassing both public and private spheres. These cultures tend to be territorially concentrated, and based on a shared language' (Kymlicka, 1995: 76). Societal cultures provide a focus for members to feel solidarity, as Margalit and Raz argue, and to make sacrifices for one another (such as giving up income to be redistributed by the welfare state). Immigrants are encouraged to integrate into this dominant societal culture, rather than to re-establish their own societal cultures in their new countries.

All this might be uncontroversial if every nation had only one societal culture, or if there were several and the state was neutral between them and did not favour any over the others. However, nations that were formed as a result of colonialism and the subordination of indigenous inhabitants have both dominant and subordinated societal cultures. Indigenous peoples, unlike immigrants, did not choose to give up their societal cultures; neither did national groups who came together and agreed to form a new state. These cultural communities have resisted integration into the dominant societal culture. Individualist liberals often defend this view of the neutral state, taking a position of 'benign neglect' towards private and cultural matters. As Kymlicka points out, however, governments do not take a neutral position towards cultures but, generally, support – both tacitly and expressly – the dominant societal culture (Kymlicka, 1995). These cultures enjoy a range of advantages: their language is used, their history is taught, and their cultural and religious practices are observed in public life. As a result, minority social cultures that are not recognized and supported in the same ways are doomed to increasing marginalization, and eventual disappearance. We can see evidence of this in the way that indigenous cultures have been marginalized, and their languages have declined since European settlement in the United States, Canada and Australia. By 1990, of the original 60 indigenous languages spoken in Canada at European settlement, 13 per cent were extinct, 21 per cent were near extinction and 38 per cent were endangered (with no children learning them). In Australia, by 1990, 64 per cent of indigenous languages present at European settlement were extinct, while 28 per cent were seriously threatened, and the process of decline has continued (McConvell and Thieberger, 2001).

From the liberal individualist, anti-collectivist position, as we have seen, this does not matter; if minority cultures cannot attract the support necessary for their survival, there is no reason to maintain them. If, however, there is a deep connection between the individual and their societal culture – as Kymlicka and other 'culturalist' liberals argue – then the loss of cultures will mean an injury to the individual. Kymlicka describes the nature of that connection in terms of individual autonomy: in order to be free, each individual must be able to make choices about how to live their lives, and what kind of person they will be. Our societal cultures provide us with the options we need to make those choices, and they also make those options meaningful to us: in order to choose between different paths in life and different role models to follow, we must be able to attach value to our options, and we derive these values, at least in the first instance, from our cultures. Thus, some cultures will strongly value solidarity, sacrifice and commitment to the community over the acquisition of material wealth. Others will value an individualist drive to succeed. The traditions, norms and narratives of our cultures – the myths, legends and stories we tell our children – provide us with ways of seeing our world and our place in it, and ways of valuing certain courses of life more than others. If we are deprived of these traditions, norms and narratives because our cultures have become marginalized by a dominant societal culture – especially one with a sophisticated technology, media, advertising industry and consumer ethic – we cannot make the kinds of choices we need to in order to live autonomous lives.

Even if Kymlicka is correct in arguing that societal cultures provide us with the tools we need in order to live autonomous lives, does it matter whether these are the cultures we are born into, or others that come to take their place? We might argue that, if a dominant culture marginalizes a minority culture, then that dominant culture will take over the role of providing the norms, roles and narratives that we need in order to shape our lives and identities. Or perhaps individuals will grow up in a cultural context that is transitional between a traditional and a western societal culture, or draws elements from both of these (Tomasi, 1995). Nevertheless, there does seem to be an important distinction between cultures into which one is born, and those to which one has to adapt later in life. Margalit and Halbertal have argued that the culture in which a person is born and grows up has a particular role because it is unchosen, and so shapes his or her identity (Margalit and Halbertal, 1994). We might also agree with Kymlicka that it is very difficult to shift from one societal culture to another, and that people whose societal cultures have been eroded are more likely to feel stranded between cultures, or be prey to a shallow, consumer-oriented popular culture, and to drugs and alcohol. The literature of Native American writers such as N. Scott Momaday, Leslie Marmon Silko and Louise Erdrich explores the alienation of indigenous people caught between their own marginalized culture and a hostile majority society. Their situation is quite different from, for example, the young, white, British woman who enjoys eating Chinese and Indian food, and listening to Caribbean music. This kind of lifestyle is possible within a varied societal culture, but does not involve shifting from one to another. On the basis of this argument, we could defend special rights and status, and even self-determination for indigenous cultural communities and national minorities. These are essentially nationalist claims, made by 'nations within'.

Some of these rights are already exercised by indigenous communities; for example, the right to be educated in their own language, to manage their own resources and to adjudicate local disputes. Quebec limits the use of written English in public, and Native American and Canadian First Nations communities place restrictions on land use, particularly on the alienation of land, or on people's entitlement to remain in communities (if, for example, they marry non-members). Indigenous peoples in Canada are entitled to have cultural considerations taken into account if they are convicted of crimes, and might be offered restorative justice processes instead of jail sentences. Specific statutory provisions of Australian criminal law exempt Aboriginal people following customary law from criminal responsibility in certain defined situations. Kymlicka describes these measures as 'external protections' that are justified to protect the minority societal culture (Kymlicka, 1995).

Societal cultures and ethnic groups

This is a strong argument for indigenous rights, but it is important to remember that it applies only to societal cultures. Kymlicka suggests several reasons why immigrant groups do not constitute such cultures: they tend not to be territorially concentrated, and they develop as the result of conscious decisions to leave an original culture. Immigrants are already in the process of joining the societal culture to which they have come. This does not, however, mean that they must give up all their cultural practices and marks of difference, and assimilate into the majority. We can usefully distinguish, as Kymlicka does, between assimilation and integration: we might argue that immigrant – or polyethnic communities – should aim to integrate into the mainstream society, while still retaining aspects of their ethnic heritage. Assimilation, by contrast, entails incorporating oneself into the majority culture. Integration allows ethnic minorities to continue to express their cultural practices and customs, while also making new commitments to the political processes, institutions and ideals of their adopted society, and to the language in which these are carried out and expressed (Kymlicka, 2001, ch. 8). Immigrants can demonstrate their commitment to these without adopting all the cultural practices and customs of the former, and while retaining their ability to speak their native tongue. We could defend policies of bilingual education along these lines. In the case of dress, for example, we might conclude, as Kymlicka does, that the desire to wear religious dress to school or work in public occupations indicates a desire to participate and integrate in public schooling and life, rather than a desire to remain separate. This argument has been invoked to support the right of girls to wear religious dress, from the headscarf to the *burqa*: if they are prevented from doing so, they will be forced out of the public school system and into private schooling, with their sense of cultural separation, and perhaps alienation will only increase. Similarly, laws and regulations that grant students from non-Christian religious communities exemptions from attending classes and sitting exams on their religious holidays are aimed at making it fairer and easier for them to participate in education.

Groups in most countries can be categorized as either societal cultures or polyethnic groups, but there are some exceptions (Kymlicka, 2001). Isolationist religious groups are one: in the Yoder case in the United States, some of the arguments made by the Amish were similar to those claimed by national minorities or indigenous groups. Although they are not national minorities, the exceptional historical isolation and voluntary marginalization of these groups have meant that their demands for exemption from civic duty have been tolerated. Refugees are another difficult group to categorize: unlike immigrants, they do not come voluntarily to their new homelands; once they have arrived, however, their aims to integrate might be similar to those of migrants. African Americans are a more complex case. Historically, they have followed both the integrationist and the national separatist approaches, demanding both equal rights as Americans, and recognition as a 'nation'. Many of the demands African-Americans make are concerned with rectifying historical injustices, and seeking fair equality of opportunity. We address these in the next chapter.

Intrinsic rights for minority cultures

So far, we have examined arguments for cultural rights on the liberal grounds of self-respect, freedom and autonomy. As we have seen, these have been used to defend quite extensive rights to self-management and protection for some kinds of cultural minorities. But the fact that these defences are based on liberal values inevitably means that, when cultural minorities threaten those liberal values, or treat their members illiberally, they abrogate their rights. External protections for cultures are defensible for liberals, but not internal restrictions that allow minority groups to limit the freedom of members (Kymlicka, 1995: 35).

Some political philosophers have criticized this approach on the grounds that it assumes that western liberal standards should be applied to other cultures, to determine whether or not they are worthy of support and protection. As Bhikhu Parekh argues, this is incompatible with the view that culture plays a fundamental role in human life, not necessarily because it allows us to be autonomous, but because it is through culture that we make sense of our lives and world (Parekh, 2006). Ideas about what is reasonable and moral are not universal, as liberals claim, but are embedded in and mediated by culture. It follows that minority cultures must be recognized and granted rights because these cultures form a deep basis for human beings' sense of self. The basic respect we owe one another implies a basic respect for each other's culture. We have already considered Taylor's argument that self-respect and cultural membership are deeply intertwined (Taylor, 1994). However, Parekh specifically rejects liberal arguments for recognition of culture on the grounds that it is essential to individual autonomy. He counters that there is no reason to assume that autonomy is crucial to all people – many people want to value the beliefs and decisions that they inherit or derive from communities, rather than consider and evaluate them. Members of non-liberal cultures often relate to their cultures differently, and do not attempt critical judgement of them or their allegiance.

If we do not tie cultural membership to individual autonomy or the exercise of liberty, we are not restricted to defending cultures that promote, or even allow for, autonomy as understood by western liberalism. Parekh rejects the 'crude' dichotomy drawn by liberals between liberal and non-liberal cultures, arguing instead that cultural communities should be respected and allowed to transmit their culture, as long as they do not contravene any basic universal values, such as respect for human life (Parekh, 2006: 110). A culture has a right to exist, and to be recognized if it is important to members and would not survive without protection. The specific form that recognition should take will vary. In some cases, communities require non-interference (as in the case of the Amish); in some cases, exemptions from general laws and requirements (in the case of religious communities exempted from holiday closings and dress laws), and, in some cases, positive support from the state (as in the case of indigenous groups to maintain language and culture.) Notwithstanding his critique of the 'false universalism' of western liberal ideas such as autonomy, Parekh maintains that – as individual rights remain as or more important than the rights of the group to survive – members of the group should have a say in its decision-making, they should have collectively acceptable modes of redress, and they should be able to exit the group without undue loss (Parekh, 2006).

Neither Parekh's nor Taylor's arguments depend on a specific distinction between the rights claimed by indigenous or national minorities, and those claimed by polyethnic or religious groups. A special case might be made for indigenous groups, however, without the liberal link Kymlicka makes between such groups and individual autonomy. James Tully argues that indigenous communities are distinctive political communities that have been subjected to 'internal colonization' by the majority societal culture (Tully, 1995, 2000). We can defend the rights of indigenous peoples to sovereignty on the same grounds that we would any independent state now threatened with imperial control. Indigenous sovereignty should be recognized over territory that is reserved by such peoples for themselves, and territories that are shared by the dominant cultural community and the indigenous people should have shared jurisdiction. Both the indigenous and the majority culture should recognize each other as 'equal, self-governing and co-existing entities', constantly negotiating the terms of shared sovereignty (Tully, 2000: 53). Claims similar to this are made by the Maori in New Zealand, who have increasingly come to argue for shared sovereignty on the basis of the Treaty of Waitangi. Some argue that this amounts to defending the rights of indigenous peoples to secede from their state, but, in the case of New Zealand, no such right is claimed. The Maori insist, rather, that sovereignty should be shared within the confines of a single territorial state.

Group interests versus the common good

As we have seen, one argument made against minority cultural rights is that these interfere with individual freedom. Such rights might also be opposed, however, on the grounds that they threaten a shared commitment to the common good. The nineteenth-century utilitarian philosopher Jeremy Bentham warned of 'sinister interests': the agendas of minority groups that threatened to take over individuals and blind them to the interests they shared in common with all citizens (Bentham, 1824). The 'civic republican' tradition of political thinking has been very suspicious of organized internal diversity within societies. The eighteenth-century French philosopher Jean-

Jacques Rousseau thought that factions or 'partial associations' interposed their own partial viewpoint between the individual and the social good – the goal towards which they would otherwise strive (Rousseau, 1973 [1762]). This republican line of thinking has been particularly influential in France, and much of the opposition to French schoolgirls wearing the headscarf has been on the grounds not that it compromises their individual rights but, rather, that it encourages identification with a sub-national group, rather than commitment to a common French identity.

A similarly strong strand of thinking along these lines continues in the United States, where commitment, particularly to racial or ethnic groups, has often been viewed as contrary to a common American identity. Jean Elshtain argues that it is only in the context of incorporation within a single body that diversity becomes meaningful (Elshtain, 1995). Too much focus on group identity, which she terms 'the politics of displacement', becomes group triumphalism, in which no recognition of commonality is possible. Elshtain claims that our commitment to democratic values – including equality, justice, freedom and fairness – turns on our acknowledgement that we share a common identity with our fellow citizens. David Miller argues similarly in his defence of civic nationalism that 'radical multiculturalism' – strong identification with ethnic and cultural groups – detracts from identification with the nation. It is that shared national identity that forms the basis of trust that makes democratic debate about common problems possible (Miller, 1997). Approaches such as these are not opposed to the observance of separate cultural practices in private, but insist that cultural difference should not be emphasized or officially recognized in the public sphere. Schools are particularly important institutions here, because of the role they play in inculcating a national culture, and bringing people together from different communities and backgrounds. Without this experience of commonality, civic republican theorists fear that society will become 'balkanized' – fragmented into small groups.

Cultural rights versus egalitarian distribution

Egalitarian philosophers – both liberal and, more explicitly, socialist – have also questioned state support for minority cultures, on the grounds that it undermines effort to achieve distributional equality. Brian Barry defends an egalitarian liberalism based on equity and fairness, and the assumption that all human beings share common interests or 'conditions of self-development' that are deduced from 'universal human nature' (Barry, 2001). Barry argues that everyone has the same basic needs and wants, and that the state should treat all its citizens equally and uniformly, granting them an equal basket of legal, political and social rights. Equality of opportunity means making these identical rights available to everyone – and, in practice, is more likely to mean encouraging cultural assimilation rather than separateness.

Socialist critics have agreed that multiculturalism's focus on recognition distracts attention from the true source of injustice: economic inequalities. Marx himself was suspicious of cultural identity and inheritance, and their constraining effects on human freedom, writing that 'the tradition of all the dead generations weighs like a nightmare on the brain of the living' (Marx, 1978 [1852]). Marx and Engels believed that the international proletariat would unite irrespective of local cultural and national differences, all of which only served the interests of the ruling class. Marxists, historically, have regarded cultural identification as a form of 'false consciousness' that prevented workers from realizing their real class interests. Modern leftists have pointed out that economic inequalities have become greater while minority groups were agitating for cultural recognition. They argue that cultural claims distracted attention from growing inequalities in wealth, and made it more difficult for alliances to be forged across groups (Gitlin, 1995). Sociologist Todd Gitlin argues that multiculturalism emphasizes the differences between people, rather than their common humanity, and detracts from the solidarity required to agitate for and support programmes of equitable redistribution. In a more nuanced approach to the issue, critical theorist Nancy Fraser argues that justice requires redistribution and recognition – that cultural recognition cannot be a goal in itself without the fairer redistribution of material resources (Fraser, 1995). Iris Young agrees that the cultural recognition necessary for individual self-determination must be combined with structural changes in the distribution of resources in order to allow for self-development (Young, 2000).

Cultural rights versus gender equality

The final critique of rights and recognition for minority cultures that we consider develops from the first – from liberal individualist arguments that cultural rights are incompatible with individual freedom. It deals with the difficult case of minority cultural groups that do not either recognize liberal rights or endorse liberal practices that respect individual freedom and autonomy. Feminists have raised this issue in the case of groups that are, in western liberal democratic terms, discriminatory against women. Susan Okin argues that a tension exists between the rights of women and increasing multiculturalist concern for cultural diversity (Okin, 1999). This is particularly clear when cultures openly discriminate against women, and attempt to deny them rights to which they have legal or constitutional guarantees in the wider society – the right, say, to be educated, or to marry freely, or to be allowed to move around or vote or express themselves freely. We should note that, in many of these cases, most theorists that we have discussed who defend minority cultural rights, including Kymlicka and Parekh, would argue that such rights should not be invoked over the wishes of members.

But there are also many cases, Okin argues, in which cultural groups are apparently liberal but actually discriminate against women. As with other critics we have considered, she points out that cultures are not homogeneous, and groups within minorities are often engaged in struggles to define what the minority culture itself means and requires. It is easy to overlook the way men impose cultural definitions and regulation on women, because most such discrimination occurs in the private sphere, out of public view. It is here that people's identities are importantly shaped by cultural communities in the ways described by liberals; here, that norms, roles and narratives are passed on to the young. In the private sphere, however, women are often treated as second-class members of their culture. Okin points out that the sphere of personal, sexual and reproductive life is crucially important in many cultures and an area subject to considerable regulation in terms of cultural expectations and normalized practices. Issues of marriage, child custody, the division of labour and inheritance are at the centre of many cultural differences, and because of women's central role in these issues, regulation of them will impact particularly strongly on women.

According to this argument, we might see many of the demands of cultural minorities for group rights as, in effect, claims to be able to exert control over women members. Cases in which people accused of crimes cite their cultural customs as a defence, or to mitigate their sentence, are a good example here (Phillips, 2003; Renteln, 2004). Feminist philosophers such as Okin and Anne Phillips point out that such cases often involve the status and treatment of women and children. The 'cultural defence' has been invoked by many ethnic groups in the United States, often to reduce the crime (and sentence) for defendants accused of beating or murdering women in cases of sexual infidelity, but also in a case (*People* v. *Kimura*) where a Japanese mother killed her children and attempted suicide after learning that her husband was being unfaithful. The cultural belief invoked here was that her husband's rejection of her rendered the lives of herself and their children worthless. A Laotian Hmong man in the United States invoked the cultural defence in *People* v. *Kong Pheng Moua* to justify the practice of 'bride capture' after he was charged with kidnapping and rape. He was found guilty of the lesser crime of false imprisonment and was sentenced to 120 days in prison and a fine of US$1000. A Chinese immigrant to New York invoked it after he battered his wife to death with a hammer after discovering that she had been unfaithful to him (*People* v. *Kong Pheng Moua*). Here, the judge accepted that the man was 'driven to violence', convicted him of second degree manslaughter (a lesser homicide charge) and sentenced him to five years' probation.

In Britain, legislation has now been passed preventing the arranged marriage of underage girls. However, the defence is still sometimes raised to mitigate the seriousness of an offence on the basis of how it would be seen in the defendant's home culture. One such case involved a British man born in Pakistan who murdered his sister-in-law because she defaulted on a marriage arranged for her when she was a child, and began an affair with a married man. At retrial, after an appeal, the defendant pleaded manslaughter on the grounds of provocation, because the victim's behaviour was particularly shocking to his cultural beliefs. The judge reduced his original sentence from life to six-and-a-half years (Phillips, 2003).

We might argue, as does Okin, against decisions such as these on the grounds that they compromise the individual rights and equality of the women involved. But we might also focus on the view of culture they imply. Critics of the cultural defence often allege that cultural customs in the home country do not justify the violence that is the subject of the charge. There may be considerable internal debate about cultural practices, and the 'defence' might rely on a dominant interpretation. Moreover, as Phillips points out, there are particular dangers in allowing a cultural defence when those involved are children, and cannot give an alternative view of what their culture might require and entail.

Okin has been strongly criticized for attempting to judge other cultures and the ways in which they treat women. Critics allege that she mistakenly applies western standards of what is acceptable, in what is often referred to as 'cultural imperialism'. Thus, she misses the particular ways in which western culture subordinates and manipulates women, and fails to notice the meaning that non-western cultural rituals have for women in those minority communities. She assumes that western values of liberty and autonomy, interpreted in western ways, must apply universally to everyone. This is, ironically, similar to the criticism made of Kymlicka, although his defence of minority cultures is one of her targets. The extent to which they scrutinize minority cultures for illiberal practices differs, with Okin focusing on the private sphere; but both agree that cultures should only be recognized if they promote liberty and autonomy.

Conclusion

The claims of minority cultures are likely to be a continuing feature of the political landscape in western democracies, given the increasing ethnic pluralism of their populations. In Australia, for example, the 2001 Census recorded that 16 per cent of the population spoke a language other than English at home – an increase of 8 per cent since 1996. The 2001 Census in Canada found that 13.4 per cent of the population identified themselves as

Box 3.2 Recognizing minority cultures: competing norms and values

The debate over recognizing minority cultures centres on some key norms: autonomy, liberty, equality and the common good, but the ways in which these are interpreted lead to very different conclusions:

• **Autonomy and liberty**

Multicultural liberal philosophers who support the recognition of minority cultures argue that membership in cultural groups has a profound effect on individual identity. Autonomy requires making choices, and liberty allows us to act on them. Supporters claim that our cultures are essential in providing us with the options from which we choose. Given that the majority culture is recognized and supported, if implicitly, by the state, minority cultures must also be supported so that their members can act autonomously and freely.

Libertarian opponents of cultural rights see individuals as more distinct from their cultural communities. People must be free to exit from their communities or change them from the inside. Both of these actions are potentially more difficult if the state officially recognizes cultural groups. This is particularly important for feminist critics who argue that women are oppressed in patriarchal cultures.

• **Equality**

Supporters of cultural rights argue that treating people equally does not mean treating them as if they were the same. Because the state, either officially or unofficially, supports the majority and dominant culture, to refuse recognition to minority groups means that their members are being treated unequally. Recognizing minorities allows everyone more equal access to culture. For liberals, this means equal opportunity for autonomy.

Opponents claim that recognizing cultural minorities, and allowing specific cultural practices, means treating their members differently, and creating two classes of citizens. They maintain that, in order for the state to treat all citizens equally, they must be treated the same.

• **The common good**

Supporters of cultural rights argue that, paradoxically, recognizing people's cultural differences will encourage social cohesion. If members or minority cultures can express their cultural difference in public, they will be more likely to participate in and support common political principles, processes and institutions.

Civic republican and communitarian opponents counter that encouraging the public expression of cultural difference encourages a sense of difference and separatism inimical to common citizenship.

'visible minorities' (excluding Aboriginal peoples) – as compared to 4.7 per cent in 1981. In New Zealand, the 2006 Census found that the population of Maori had increased by 7.4 per cent since 2001, and the proportion of Europeans in the population had declined from 83 per cent to 80 per cent. Asian ethnic groups increased by a total of almost 50 per cent. In Britain, where there is more homogeneity, the 2001 Census nevertheless found that the white or non-minority population had dropped from 94.3 per cent in 1991 to 92.1 per cent.

As we have seen, rights and recognition for minority cultures can be defended on quite different grounds. The differences between the liberal arguments based on freedom and autonomy, and the more general cultural rights based on belonging or identification might only emerge when illiberal cultural practices are considered. Even explicitly non-liberal arguments, however, such as Parekh's, are based on the assumption that cultural membership is a good for the individual. Similarly, opposition to cultural rights has most commonly been based on liberal concerns about the ways in which individual freedom might be limited by recognizing and protecting collectivities. There are signs, however, that this might be changing in the post-September 11 context, where national security and public safety have come to be seen as balancing individual rights. As public anxiety about the threat of terrorism from fundamentalist religious groups within society increases, along with ethnic and cultural plurality, concerns about social fragmentation and the importance of committing to a common good are likely to become stronger.

Chapter 4

Is Affirmative Action Fair?

Affirmative action covers a wide and controversial range of programmes designed to benefit disadvantaged groups: from advertising jobs to women or minorities who tend not to apply for them, to special training schemes for minorities, to the consideration of race as a factor in university admission or employment, to establishing quotas for hiring or appointing under-represented groups. Unlike the redistribution of wealth, and cultural rights, which we considered in previous chapters, affirmative action refers to specific policies, designed to serve goals that are particular to each national case. Some countries do not refer to these policies specifically as affirmative action, and the term has been particularly controversial in the United States, which is where it first entered common currency. In 1961, with the aim of eliminating discrimination in employment by the US federal government, President John F. Kennedy established the Committee on Equal Employment Opportunity, and issued an Executive Order directing state employers to take 'affirmative action to ensure that applicants are employed, and that employees are treated during employment, without regard to their race, creed, colour or national origin'. Since then, many other countries have developed policies designed to offer special assistance to disadvantaged minority groups and women.

Affirmative action emerged in the United States as a response to the Civil Rights movement and is fundamentally intertwined with America's history of slavery and segregation. It became part of federal government policy with the 1964 Civil Rights Act, which banned discrimination on the grounds of sex, race, colour, ethnicity and religion. President Johnson's statement is worth quoting in full, as it explains the rationale of applying affirmative action – which formally takes race into account – to achieve equality:

> You do not wipe away the scars of centuries by saying: 'now, you are free to go where you want, do as you desire and choose the leaders you please.' You do not take a man who for years has been hobbled by chains, liberate him, bring him to the starting line of a race, saying 'you are free to compete with all the others,' and still justly believe you have been completely fair. Thus it is not enough just to open the gates of opportunity. All our citizens must have the ability to walk through those gates. This is the next and more profound stage of the battle for civil rights. We seek not just freedom but opportunity – not just legal equity but human

ability – not just equality as a right and theory, but equality as a fact and result. (Johnson, 1965)

The Civil Rights Act and subsequent presidential Executive Orders prescribed affirmative action to eliminate discrimination, to ensure equality of opportunity and provide remedial relief to those who had been injured by discrimination. This was interpreted to cover a wide range of measures and, in the early 1970s, the Nixon Administration began to push employers to develop goals and targets with respect to minority hiring. Since then, critics have complained that affirmative action was being applied not only to ensure equal opportunity in employment and education, but also to justify race-based preferential treatment contrary to the provisions of the Civil Rights Act. They have singled out preferences in hiring for less qualified minorities and race-based quotas in employment and universities. In 1978, in *Regents of the University of California* v. *Bakke*, the Supreme Court held that, given the under-representation of minorities in the professions, racial preferences could be used by universities in admissions decisions as a remedial measure. However, the Court rejected strict quotas for minorities and stipulated that the process had to be subject to 'strict scrutiny'. In the case of affirmative action, this meant that such measures could only be justified if they were closely designed to achieve racial equality and were, in addition, the least restrictive means of achieving racial equality in the case in question.

Much of the academic discussion of affirmative action in the United States turns on interpretation of the American Constitution – particularly the Fourteenth Amendment, adopted after the American Civil War, which guarantees equal protection for all citizens under the law. We will not consider the constitutionality of affirmative action in the United States in this chapter but, instead, the broader philosophical issues that these policies raise. Many of these emerge in some key Supreme Court decisions (see Box 4.1.)

United Kingdom law permits measures designed to increase the likelihood that members of ethnic and racial minority groups and women will be hired and promoted, but not preference in hiring on the grounds of race or gender. The 1976 Race Relations Act prohibits discrimination on the grounds of race, except in special circumstances where it is required to provide members of particular racial groups access to services and facilities to meet their special needs. The Act specifically allows for the direct targeting of training, education and benefits to the needs of particular minorities. The Race Relations (Amendment) Act of 2000 requires public authorities, including universities, to have regard to the need to promote equality of opportunity and good race relations. The Sex Discrimination Act of 1975 similarly outlines discrimination on the grounds of gender. It prohibits 'positive discrimination' to advantage women, with 'limited exceptions' allowing discrimination in training and recruitment to favour either men or women in

Box 4.1 The University of Michigan cases

In 2003, the US Supreme Court ruled on two cases concerning the use of race in admissions at the University of Michigan – one for undergraduate entry to the University, and one for the Law School (*Gratz* v. *Bollinger* and *Grutter* v. *Bollinger*). The court held that the Law School was justified in using race preferences in admissions with the purpose of ensuring that a 'critical mass' of minority students was enrolled. This was crucial in order to gain the benefits of diversity for the Law School student body, and to promote integration by ensuring that minorities were represented in the next generation of Michigan's professionals and leaders. However, the Court struck down the University's use of race in undergraduate admissions because it gave automatic preference to race, rather than considering each student's case individually.

- Supporters of the University's policies argued that members of racial minorities still suffer because they belong to groups that have experienced discrimination in the past. This affects both their self-esteem and their access to resources and opportunities. While minor injustice is done to applicants who lose places due to race, those applicants still benefit from their membership in the majority group.
- Supporters maintained that no applicant could be said to have a right to a place at university. Decisions about the appropriate criteria for admitting students should be made by society as a whole, with a view to broad moral goals such as diversity.
- Finally – and not least – the increased presence of minorities on campus would lead to better understanding between racial groups, and stronger social solidarity.
- Critics argued that universities have, in the past, used race to exclude some groups of applicants, and preferences now amount to continuing unequal treatment. Those minorities who benefit now are not those harmed by past race discrimination. And those who lose places to less-qualified minority applicants are not guilty themselves of wrongful discrimination, so should not have to bear the burden of restitution.
- Moreover, the best-qualified students are entitled to assume they have a right to a position, because of their qualifications.
- Finally, critics argued that, if race is counted towards admission, under-qualified students would be admitted who would be unable to succeed at university – thereby further damaging their self-esteem. Moreover, racism would increase as a result of resentment on the part of better-qualified white students who missed out on places, and a sense of superiority among white students towards struggling minority classmates.

professions where their gender is under-represented. The Act refers to these exceptions as 'positive action' rather than positive or reverse discrimination; the difference being that positive discrimination involves discriminating against men in favour of women, while positive action means introducing measures to ensure that women can compete more equally with men. We discuss these differences in greater detail in the next section. The Blair Labour government responded to increased racial unrest in Britain by encouraging positive action in recruitment in a number of areas, including the police force. This has, however, proved difficult to achieve.

European countries have taken a cautious approach to affirmative action, for some time restricting it to programmes designed to promote equal opportunity for women, particularly in the provision of childcare services and provisions designed to allow women to balance family and work. In the 1997 *Marschall* case, the European Court of Justice upheld public sector programmes targeting women. It is only recently that the increasing ethnic plurality of many European nations, the rise of racial tensions and the perceived failures of integration have led some, such as the United Kingdom, to consider extending affirmative action programmes to ethnic minorities. The Treaty of Amsterdam was amended in 1999 to allow positive action in the area of gender equality and, more recently, the EU has issued directives allowing member states to consider positive action against all forms of discrimination. France, for example, has traditionally taken a strongly assimilationist and 'colour-blind' approach to ethnic diversity as discussed in Chapter 3. In 2004, however, several French companies signed a 'Diversity Charter', committing them to take action against ethnic discrimination in the workplace. After the 2005 riots, the Interior Minister, (and now President) Nicholas Sarkozy, admitted that Muslims were not treated equally in France, and called for the introduction of affirmative action policies.

In Canada and New Zealand, human rights legislation has allowed affirmative action to extend beyond gender. In Canada, the Charter of Rights and Freedoms (1982) provides constitutional protection against discrimination, but specifically exempts laws and programmes that are designed to overcome disadvantage experienced by people because of race, ethnicity, sex, religion, colour, age or disability. The federal Employment Equity Act of 1986 aims to ensure that these groups are represented in the workplace. Canadian courts have interpreted federal legislation as being designed to ensure not only formal, but also substantive equality, and to consider the effects of systemic discrimination.

In New Zealand, the 1993 Human Rights Act prohibits discrimination on the grounds of race, ethnicity and sex (among other factors). However, it specifically exempts provisions designed to ensure the equality of disadvantaged groups, such as training schemes or employment assistance measures. The politicized relationship between the New Zealand government and the country's indigenous Maori people has led to considerable public controversy over the legitimacy of special measures designed to ensure the equality of Maori. The conservative National Party has called recently for an end to affirmative action programmes targeted at Maori on the grounds that these programmes are patronizing and socially divisive. Some programmes have been refocused so that they target economic need, rather than race. As we shall see later in this chapter, the charge that affirmative action should address economic need rather than group membership can be supported on both empirical and philosophical grounds.

Quotas, preferential hiring programmes and other positive discrimination measures have been adopted in countries with large minority populations, and histories of racial exploitation and conflict. Instituted after race riots in 1969, Malaysia's New Economic Policy has given preference in jobs, business and universities to ethnic Malays, at the expense of the Chinese and Indian populations. In India, 'protective discrimination' for scheduled castes and tribes is set out in the Constitution. Quotas in government positions, employment and education are reserved for members of scheduled castes and tribes.

The wide variety of affirmative action policies that has developed in different countries, and the controversy they have provoked, raise some fundamental questions. The most important of these centre around the meaning of equality:

- Does treating people equally mean treating them in the same way?
- Should different needs justify different treatment, in order to achieve an egalitarian result?

Other questions at stake include:

- Do we deserve our talents and what they make possible for us in society?
- What counts as the kind of disadvantage that should be remedied by government?
- Is damage to self-respect and confidence as important as having fewer material resources?
- Is diversity essential to a good society?
- Should our elites and institutions mirror demographic patterns in society?

In order to consider these, we will first identify some basic categories of affirmative action policies and then consider the philosophical arguments, both for and against. Much of the philosophical debate about affirmative action has taken place in the United States, and most of the philosophers whose work we discuss here are American – the principles they discuss, however, apply to these policies more broadly.

Weak and strong affirmative action

We can identify two main types of affirmative action (Pojman, 1992). The first, 'weak' affirmative action policies, are mainly designed to remove unfair barriers to equality of opportunity. This typically includes the removal of all prejudicial selection criteria, advertising jobs aggressively to minorities and the gender that does not usually apply for them, and, in the case of tertiary education, special scholarships for disadvantaged groups who would not otherwise be able to attend university. These policies fall into the category of 'positive action'. 'Strong' affirmative action (or 'positive discrimination') involves more active steps to eliminate the effects of past injustice, and might include preferential treatment in employment or education to minority candidates with lesser qualifications, requiring representation in a job or institution proportionate to the ethnic composition of the wider population, and quotas (Beckwith, 1999). It is important to note that, while strong affirmative action might involve selecting minority or female candidates with comparable (although not equal) qualifications, no affirmative action programmes in Europe, the United States, and most other countries permit the hiring of unqualified employees, irrespective of their race, ethnicity or gender. Some measures are difficult to categorize: treating membership in a group previously subject to discrimination or under-representation as a tie-breaker when candidates have approximately equal qualifications for a job or place is sometimes also considered to be weak affirmative action. Some critics, however, are sceptical of the way in which such a policy is applied, and argue that other factors, such as class or degree of hardship experienced by the applicants, might also be used to make the final decision. This, in turn, suggests that it operates as strong affirmative action. (This was the decision of the US Court of Appeals in the 1997 *Piscataway* case, which considered the use of race as a tie-breaker (1996).)

Both types of affirmative action aim to eliminate wrongful discrimination and to reduce the inequalities suffered by minorities and women. The fundamental distinction between them, however, lies in *what* is meant to be equalized. Weak affirmative action focuses on equality of opportunity and process, while the strong version aims, in addition, at achieving outcomes that are more equal for disadvantaged groups. Advocates of strong affirmative action argue that it involves looking at the deeper causes of inequality, and at the social consequences of inequalities that might continue, even if formal equality of opportunity has been achieved. There are other important differences: weak affirmative action assumes that all obstacles, both direct and indirect, should be removed so that people can freely exercise their natural talents (Goldman, 1976). This would mean, for example, prohibiting regulations that prevented women from applying for and being hired into positions, but it would also mean ensuring that bathroom facilities are available for women, and possibly even that childcare is provided. It could also encompass special advertising targeted at women if they tend not to apply for jobs in this area. Of course, as individuals have different abilities and preferences, these policies are not aimed at ensuring that all groups are equally represented in jobs or universities (although this could happen).

Advocates of strong affirmative action, by contrast, do not believe that people necessarily deserve their talents and abilities, neither that they are necessarily entitled to gain any position or place because of them. They argue that the need to break down discrimination and its effects are more important than an individual's claim to a particular job on the basis of their abilities or skills. In practice, this might mean companies or institutions giving preference to women applicants for a job, even if they are less qualified than men, until a substantial proportion – if not half – of employees are women.

Most of the contemporary political thinkers discussed here share the general consensus in liberal democracies that weak affirmative action programmes designed to promote and foster equality of opportunity are generally justifiable. There are, as we shall see, differences of opinion on the degree to which the state is justified in intervening in order to bring this about. It is strong affirmative action – also referred to here as 'preferential treatment' – that attracts the greatest controversy. Its critics argue that it defeats the very egalitarian purposes it is designed to achieve. According to its supporters, however, weak affirmative action policies are only effective in dealing with cases where any discrimination is obvious on the surface. Where discrimination and inequality are deeply entrenched in social and economic structures, and social and cultural attitudes, more radical measures will be required.

The case in favour: justice and fairness

Arguments in favour of affirmative action can be divided into deontological and consequentialist categories. According to deontological arguments, affirmative action is fair and just as a remedy for past injustice. Advocates argue that group preferences are not the same as group discrimination, and that we must take into account the broader context in which racial and gender preferences are applied. In addition, group preferences do not compromise fairness, because individuals do not have an automatic entitlement to any particular benefits as a result of their natural talents and abilities. It is the task of society to distribute benefits according to reasonable and publicly justified criteria, and in pursuance of broader social goals. According to consequentialist or utilitarian defences, affirmative action has a range of positive effects – which either reinforce the justice of the policy, or outweigh any injustices it might involve.

The fundamental argument in favour of affirmative action is that set out by US President Johnson in 1965: merely removing legal barriers to advancement will not, by itself, enable historically disadvantaged people to compete equally. In order to achieve true equality of opportunity, extra help, encouragement and support is needed, as well as addressing inequalities built into the popular attitudes, and the social and economic system. Both weak and strong affirmative action programmes are justified, their supporters contend, because they aim to change structures, rather than being just in every individual case.

In response to what is perhaps the most common critique of affirmative action, advocates maintain that the preferential treatment of minorities is not morally equivalent to discrimination against them, and does not seriously compromise individual rights. We must look at these programmes in their broader social context. Ronald Dworkin argues that 'malign forms of discrimination' violate a fundamental individual right that most preferential treatment programmes do not: the right of each citizen to be treated as equally worthy of concern and respect (Dworkin, 2000: 405). Affirmative action does not reflect prejudice against white people or men, and does not entrench their inequality, as discrimination does. Richard Wasserstrom suggests a similar defence of preferential treatment programmes such as quotas: discrimination against people of colour was 'part of a larger social universe which systematically maintained a network of institutions which unjustifiably concentrated power, authority and goods in the hands of white male individuals, and which systematically consigned blacks and women to subordinate positions in the society' (Wasserstrom, 1997). On this account, quotas that favour minority groups do not entrench their positions, or add to their already disproportionate share of resources.

A major hurdle for defenders of affirmative action is the claim that those who are best qualified are entitled to their job or position. Supporters of affirmative action make a complex argument about desert (deservingness) and the ownership of goods and resources. First, they point out that we do not morally deserve our natural talents and abilities. John Rawls points out: 'It seems to be one of the fixed points of our considered judgments that no one deserves his place in the distribution of native endowments, any more than one deserves one's initial starting place in society. The assertion that a man deserves the superior character that enables him to make the effort to cultivate his abilities is equally problematic; for his character depends in large part upon fortunate family and social circumstances for which he can claim no credit' (Rawls, 1971). Thus, it cannot be said that we deserve anything except what has been agreed to by all in a just system of distribution. Rawls and other egalitarian liberals take the view that all have a claim on primary goods, resources and the benefits they produce, because it is only in society, as a voluntary scheme for fair cooperation, that these benefits can be generated, produced and made valuable. The relationship between natural talents and incomes, jobs or places at universities is not a natural one – it is, rather, the product of social agreement, and can be altered or modified to achieve other social goals. In Rawls' scheme, this allows contracting parties to agree to his principles of justice (see Chapter 2) and to goals such as the equal representation of minorities.

Some critics have also pointed out that the assessment of qualifications is not a simple matter. Dworkin argues that, in the case of university admissions, qualification is a matter of forward-looking promise (Dworkin, 2000). The aim of universities is, in part, the advancement of knowledge, for which high academic achievement at school might be a good indicator of future success. (Although we might add here that a range of qualities is required to make a good doctor, for example, some of which have more to do with personality or character than academic ability.) But Dworkin adds that universities also aim to improve the collective life of their communities and the nation – to make it more just, more secure. When they are assessing the forward-looking promise of candidates with this goal in mind, race and other markers of diversity might be considered as relevant indicators. We will consider this in greater detail when we turn to the consequentialist arguments in favour of affirmative action, later in this section.

There are difficulties involved in defending affirmative action from an individual rights perspective. Dworkin (as other liberals) relies on a rights-based liberal theory to defend his claim that no individual deserves, or is entitled, to be admitted to university. This theoretical perspective assumes individuals to be discrete, distinct bearers or owners of rights. In the communitarian view, by contrast, individuals are embedded in their communities and networks of social relations – relations that constitute them and make them who they are. Communitarian philosopher Michael Sandel points out that Dworkin abandons the claims of the meritocratic individual, who is 'entitled' to benefits, in favour of the community, which is to establish its own goals and the criteria for benefits and positions (Sandel, 1982). A rights-based argument provides no grounds, however, as Sandel argues, for showing how the goals of the community are developed, or for assessing them. Supporters of the rights-based argument are forced to fall back on the utilitarian arguments they reject – as we discuss later in this chapter. Sandel argues that a stronger case can be made for policies such as affirmative action, which require individuals to sacrifice some of their prospects for a common endeavour, if we accept that people are 'participants in a common identity' (Sandel, 1982).

Once they have established that those with natural talents and abilities do not necessarily deserve jobs and positions, supporters of affirmative action must show that the policy is a legitimate response to injustice. Judith Jarvis Thomson argues that, even though the beneficiaries of affirmative action might not have directly suffered discrimination themselves, the damage of past discrimination is sufficiently recent to continue to affect young African Americans and women (Thomson, 1973). Young African Americans and women 'have not merely not been given that very equal chance at the benefits generated by what the community owns which is so firmly insisted on for white males, they have not until lately even been felt to have a right to it' (Thomson, 1973: 381). Even if they are not downgraded themselves, they experience a lack of self-confidence and self-respect as a result of the way other African Americans and women are treated. This affects their sense of what they can achieve, and the way in which they choose to develop their skills and abilities.

Ideally, Thomson argues – and other supporters of affirmative action concede – the wrong that minorities suffer as a result of their membership in unjustly treated groups should be redressed without causing harm to any individual – so that the burden of making good past mistreatment is shared by the community as a whole. Some opponents of preferential treatment agree with this, and argue for weak affirmative action programmes such as training schemes and scholarships to ensure equality of opportunity. Leftists, as we have seen, favour fairer redistribution of wealth to those who are worse off. Thomson suggests, however, that professional jobs are an excellent way of redressing past damage. What the recipient has missed and wants is equal membership in the community and self-respect, and a job confers this better than a welfare payment. Preference in employment and education does mean that the burden of making good falls harder on the shoulders of the white male candidate who misses out on a job or place at university due to preferences. Supporters of affirmative action contend, however, that while these candidates may never have discriminated against others themselves, they have benefited from a system of historical discrimination because of their race and sex.

Before we turn to consequentialist arguments in favour of affirmative action, we will consider a libertarian defence. As we have seen, the libertarian position, emphasizing individual liberty and a minimal state, is most often opposed to affirmative action because it involves state interference with commercial and contractual decisions. As we saw in Chapter 2, however, Nozick argues that ownership and transfers of property are only legitimate if they are based on an unbroken string of legitimate transfers, starting with first acquisition. If property has been unjustly transferred at any point in the historical process, the state might be justified in intervening to rectify the injustice. We might view affirmative action as a form of rectification, as Andrew Valls argues in the case of African Americans (Valls, 1999). As rectification is designed to improve the situation of those who would have been better off if the injustice had not taken place, it may legitimately focus not only on those who were most directly discriminated against, but also on any who have suffered as a result of the unjust transfer. But rectification is notoriously difficult to apply: How are we to work out what would have happened if an unjust transfer had not taken place? Many intervening circumstances between the historical injustice and the present complicate this matter. Further, rectification simply assumes that a past wrongdoing can be corrected. We might conclude that affirmative action incorporates a stronger claim, not only for rectifying past wrongs, but also for compensating as a group those who suffer as a result of them. Finally, we should note that the libertarian view rejects any assumption that rectification would necessarily lead to an egalitarian result today.

The case in favour: positive consequences

Consequentialist or utilitarian arguments in favour of affirmative action depend on claims about the effects of the policies that must be assessed by looking at the facts of particular cases. They reflect a utilitarian approach to politics, according to which policies and principles are assessed solely in terms of the social welfare they produce. They are particularly important, as several political philosophers concede that such programmes might involve some small burden on those denied jobs or places, but that such injustice is outweighed by the overwhelming social good that affirmative action brings about (Nagel, 1973; Thomson, 1973). All supporters of affirmative action, whether strong or weak, make their case, at least in part, on the basis of the positive consequences of the policy, both for beneficiaries and for the wider society. Consequentialist arguments are particularly relevant in cases where the targeted groups have not necessarily been subject to long historical injustice, but nevertheless experience social and economic inequalities – for example, recent Asian and Muslim immigrants in the United Kingdom and Europe.

The advantages of affirmative action to beneficiaries are not only tangible; Peter Singer, who relies on a utilitarian position, argues that inequalities between members of different groups are likely to produce feelings of superiority and inferiority. This leads to feelings of hopelessness on the part of the minority, as they feel they cannot do anything about their race or gender (Singer, 1993). Feminists from nineteenth-century British philosopher John Stuart Mill to the present have pointed to the ways in which women have been socialized to think that, because of their biological and social roles in the family, they are incapable of and unsuited for professional employment (Mill, 1989b [1869]; Okin, 1989). Affirmative action is required to overcome this self-perpetuating cycle of low self-esteem, low achievement and reinforced inequality (Singer, 1993). It is important to remember here, in balancing these positive effects against efficiency, that preferential treatment policies do not award jobs or places to unqualified candidates. Proponents of affirmative action concede that a minimal level of qualification is required in order to perform the basic requirements a job, or to participate meaningfully in an institution such as a university. A recent study, by former presidents of Harvard and Princeton universities, of the effects of thirty years of affirmative action in American universities found that African American graduates accepted into prestigious institutions under affirmative action applauded the policy, and were more likely to go on to successful professional careers, with higher incomes, than their counterparts who had not taken advantage of affirmative action (Bowen and Bok, 1998).

We might also claim that affirmative action has positive consequences for non-beneficiaries because it fosters diversity, and it is better for people at work and university to come into contact with others who are different from themselves. It introduces new perspectives, experiences and views, and encourages learning and new ideas. This argument depends on the liberal view that diversity of opinion is socially valuable irrespective of how true various opinions might be – a principle set out by Mill in the nineteenth century (Mill, 1989a [1859]). As critics have pointed out, however, the groups that affirmative action targets – minorities and women, who have historically been discriminated against – are not the only sources or varieties of diversity. We might argue that it is diversity of ideology or opinion that should be represented; critics of affirmative action sometimes argue (facetiously) that it would better be applied to political conservatives, who tend to be under-represented in university faculties. Even if we took a more identity-based approach to diversity, we might think that different geographical areas should be represented, or perhaps different age groups. Nevertheless, Bowen and Bok found that, by 1989, a majority of white and black respondents reported that they valued the ability to get along with people of other races, and that their university experience had helped to prepare them for this (Bowen and Bok, 1998).

Other utilitarian arguments are also advanced in support of affirmative action: it will result in more minorities and women in universities and positions of social prestige, to act as aspirational role models for young people with similar identities. In addition, minority professionals might be more likely to want to work amongst and for people of their own race group, and have a better understanding of the problems facing fellow group members.

One of the more ambitious consequentialist arguments in favour of affirmative action is that advanced by Elizabeth Anderson, who defends the policy on the grounds that it promotes democratic civil society (Anderson, 2002). Analysing the American case, Anderson argues that de facto racial segregation is the chief barrier to equal opportunity for racial minorities. Segregation is not only the result of past race discrimination, but also the cause of racial inequality, and a threat to the legitimacy and stability of democratic government. The empirical evidence in the United States shows that African Americans are likely to attend school predominantly comprising students of colour, and to work mainly with other people of colour. The effect of this self-reproducing pattern is entrenched economic inequality: African Americans tend to be concentrated in low-wage jobs, and find it difficult to build up wealth over generations. Because of de facto segregation, the effects of discrimination tend to last longer, become entrenched, and spread across families and social groups. But, in addition, de facto segregation means that there are few opportunities for social interaction, political cooperation and the sharing of public goods across lines of race. A robust civil society requires the participation of people from all walks of life, and the legitimacy of political outcomes depends on our knowing that everyone affected by them participated in deciding the policies that led to them. If minorities are not effective participants in the political process, society cannot function, in Rawls' terms, as a scheme of fair cooperation. The purpose of affirmative action is to end de facto segregation and to reshape democratic politics. This perspective builds on a deliberative and participatory approach to democratic government (Young, 2000) and, while Anderson applies it to the American case, the de facto segregation of immigrant groups in major cities in Britain and Europe suggests its broader relevance.

This argument assumes that the (roughly) proportional representation of race, ethnic and gender groups in the economy and in government will increase the likelihood that people's viewpoints and experience will be represented. As we have already seen, however, it might be claimed that ideological diversity is at least as valuable as a range of group identities. We might also point out, with leftist critics of affirmative action, that economic or class diversity is also crucial. The emphasis on identity groups based on race, gender and ethnicity raises some of the same concerns about internal ideological and economic diversity within these groups that we discussed in Chapter 3. One of the most common criticisms made of affirmative action is that it tends to benefit the middle-class members of the target groups only – we could extend that argument to suggest that affirmative action only draws into democratic debate the perspective of middle-class minorities and women. Affirmative action might well be only one part of a wider strategy required to increase democratic participation and legitimacy.

One final challenge confronting consequentialist arguments for affirmative action is to show why the policy continues to be required, many years after it was first introduced. (We might apply this to race in the case of the United States, and gender in the case of European countries.) Critics point out that, if preferential treatment was successful at raising the self-esteem, and social and economic status of its beneficiaries, creating role models, and teaching the wider society the benefits of diversity, why do members of minorities continue to suffer the ill effects of past discrimination? The ultimate aim of affirmative action must be to eliminate these ill effects, so that individuals can compete equally for jobs and places. However, as many supporters of preferential treatment have argued, the ill effects of wrongful discrimination are deeply embedded in the social and cultural views of majorities and minorities, and in social and economic structures. This is particularly clear in the case of women, who continue to suffer economically as a result of their role in the family. Change is slow in these areas. Moreover, as Anderson has shown, the economic inequality and segregation that discrimination produced cannot be eliminated over a single generation.

The case against: justice and fairness

Arguments against affirmative action fall into four basic categories:

1 The policy is self-defeating, as preferences on the grounds of race and sex are incompatible with the goal of ending wrongful discrimination. According to this view, any discrimination on the grounds of group membership or identity is unfair, whether it is positive or negative.
2 It interferes with individual freedom of contract, by regulating employment decisions.
3 It fails to rectify past injustices, as it does not assist those who were actually victimized by direct discrimination.
4 It produces negative consequences both for minorities themselves and for society more broadly.

The first three of these arguments are deontological; that is, they argue that affirmative action is contrary to justice, irrespective of its consequences. They are based on the liberal principles of individual freedom and the equality of persons. Of course, these principles can be used both to support and oppose preferential treatment: all liberals, whether opponents or supporters of affirmative action, agree that direct discrimination interferes with the freedom and autonomy of individuals by preventing them from carrying out their life plans and projects. Discrimination on grounds such as race or gender fails to recognize people as individuals, with their own particular characteristics, talents and abilities, and, instead, treats them as identical members of a group. While supporters of preferential treatment believe that it is required to combat the effects of such discrimination, opponents of the policy see it as simply another form of wrongful discrimination: establishing preferential treatment to counter past injustice, critics argue, continues to disregard the needs and rights of individuals in order to benefit a group. This runs counter to the fundamental liberal maxim set out by Immanuel Kant, that individuals must never be used as the means to others' ends and purposes, but must always be treated as ends in themselves (Kant, 1993 [1785]). Accordingly, whether the benefited group is a majority or a minority, discrimination on the grounds of group identity is simply wrong. In strictly individualist terms, the state should treat people in all cases as individuals, their membership in groups a matter of free and private association, with no relevance in the public sphere. This position is similar to that used to oppose collective multicultural rights, as we discussed in Chapter 3.

The strict individualist position might appear to be incompatible with support for weak affirmative action, which focuses on disadvantaged and under-represented groups. But, as such policies are aimed only at fostering and encouraging members of minorities to succeed, and at removing legal, economic and cultural barriers that might stand in their way, we might also make individualist arguments in favour of weak affirmative action. Affirmative action policies in Britain, for example, which encourage positive action, are based on the grounds of equality of opportunity and individual rights. However, the argument from individual liberty suggests a stronger critique of affirmative action in both its forms.

Both strong and weak affirmative action can impose state requirements on private employers, regulating, at least, the support and training services they offer, and, at most, their decisions to enter into employment contracts. From the libertarian perspective, commercial activity and the contractual employment relationship are domains of free action (Nozick, 1974). Private property, freedom of association and freedom of contract are fundamental values, and any interference with these is regarded as problematic. This freedom extends to the right of corporations to discriminate against minority groups. Such rights and liberties, libertarians argue, cannot be overridden by considerations of social welfare. As Nozick concludes, considerations of fairness cannot overcome the requirement that people voluntarily consent to any limitation or regulation of their activities. Nozick does not admit even weak affirmative action to ensure equality of opportunity, although other libertarians have conceded that the state's duty is to ensure formal equality of opportunity (Hayek, 1962). Of course, this argument defines freedom in terms of property and contractual rights. If we take a broader view, and interpret freedom as including the ability to formulate and carry out life plans and projects, then the damage to self-respect and the unequal social and economic status caused by discrimination might be interpreted as an impediment to freedom.

Opponents of affirmative action also argue that it fails as a form of rectification for past injustice, largely because it does not address the problem of discrimination where it actually occurs. As Alan Goldman (who supports some affirmative action programmes) points out, reduced numbers of people of colour in University departments do not necessarily indicate discrimination against people of colour with PhDs – rather, they probably indicate discrimination at the level of primary and secondary education, which led to fewer minorities achieving PhDs in the first place (Goldman, 1976). Similarly, lower numbers of women in professional positions might well reflect not discrimination in professional recruitment, but less support available to women to enable them to combine families with career. Weak affirmative action policies increasing equality of opportunity are more likely to address these problems – and this is the rationale behind the positive action/equal opportunity approach adopted in several countries.

Moreover, those who benefit from preferential treatment in hiring are usually not those who were directly harmed by institutionalized discrimination – such as slavery, segregation, colonialism, or the denial of civil rights to women (Sher, 1975). If we accept that even those who were not directly harmed by legally sanctioned discrimination still suffer because they are members of a group against which prejudice exists, it is difficult, as Thomas Nagel points out, to identify the contribution that such injustice makes to inequality (Nagel, 1973). It is also not clear that strong affirmative action is the best way to redress such harm; many arguing along these lines advocate ensuring equality of opportunity instead. Moreover, not all women or members of minorities will have experienced harm from prejudice to the same degree. In fact, we might question the assumption behind affirmative action that membership in minority groups and gender are important determinants of individual identity. Critics often point out that affirmative action programmes have the effect of encouraging people to identify with minority groups that might not otherwise have played an important role in their sense of who they are. Even in cases where people do identify strongly with historically disadvantaged groups, strong affirmative action policies do not favour those who are suffering the worst harms as a result of discrimination; some critics argue that, as they benefit middle class minorities and women, they are likely to advantage those amongst their group who have suffered the least (Goldman, 1979).

This last argument is consistent with two quite different philosophical perspectives: liberal individualists reject the view that collective factors such as race or gender define personal identity. The same arguments as those discussed in Chapter 3 against ascribing a group identity to people who share a common sex, race or ethnicity might be made here. To assume that women or people of colour must have diminished self-respect and abilities because of their sex or race, and thereby be the victims of prejudice, is to ignore their individual experience and identities. But, in addition, leftist philosophers concerned about economic equality will oppose measures that maintain inequalities. Goldman suggests, for example, that affirmative action might be justified if the economic status of the minority is also taken into account (Goldman, 1979). The point of affirmative action is to produce fair equality of opportunity for all, and it is the chronically poor, he argues, who are least likely to be able to do this. This argument is similar to the critique of multiculturalism by leftists, who see economic status as far more important a source of injustice than membership in a less-respected social or cultural group.

From this perspective, all forms of affirmative action are inadequate to bring about real equality. While affirmative action policies aim to produce more equal results in terms of gender and race, they do nothing to change the underlying unequal distribution of wealth based on educational and employment opportunities. Inequalities are not abolished, they are just rearranged. At the most, these measures could only be a step towards a more fundamental change to the economic system that would produce more egalitarian outcomes. At the least, they reinforce an inegalitarian system, by co-opting economic elites amongst women and minority groups. It is important to note a significant difference between these leftists and libertarians, although both believe that strong affirmative action is misguided. The latter argue that people are entitled to whatever values and benefits they can gain on the free market from the use of their talents. (We should note that this does not mean that people morally deserve their natural talents.) Leftists contend that it is society's task to distribute goods and benefits. This basic position is shared by many liberal egalitarians, as we saw in Chapter 2: they reject the argument that anyone deserves or is entitled to a job or position. The difference lies in whether the ultimate goal of society's distribution of benefits is to share them out unevenly, but without regard to race or sex, or to share them out more evenly to all.

Thomas Nagel defends affirmative action in the limited circumstances where injustice has caused specific disadvantage (Nagel, 1973). In other cases, he argues, justice is better served by separating the criterion of efficiency – by which performance and skills criteria best select people for jobs – from the question of whether people deserve the benefits that come from jobs. The most fundamental cause of injustice is differential reward. Fair equality of opportunity – as might be achieved through weak affirmative action policies – cannot produce just outcomes when some natural talents and abilities earn more income than others. The real injustice, Nagel argues, is that those with higher intelligence are disproportionately rewarded by society. Justice requires that we reduce the connections between material advantages, cultural opportunity and institutional authority. But we can only do this by large alterations in the social system, including major changes to taxes and salaries. We cannot do this by changing the hiring policies of corporations or the admissions policies of universities (Nagel, 1973).

The case against: negative consequences

We have already considered utilitarian arguments in favour of affirmative action; critics emphasize other more negative consequences of the policy. They contend that preferential treatment for minorities and women is wrong because it damages the very groups it sets out to assist, as well as producing more general negative social consequences. Carl Cohen argues, for example, that strong affirmative action hinders the quest for an integrated society, and damages and corrupts institutions (Cohen and Sterba, 2003). This critique has both individualist and communitarian dimensions. From a liberal individualist position, affirmative action affects those who lose positions and places simply because of their race and gender. But it also damages its beneficiaries, by refusing to treat them as individuals. On a psychological level, critics allege that this reinforces their sense of inferiority and victim-hood, and their fear that their fates are determined by their race, ethnicity or sex (Pojman, 1992). It leaves them vulnerable to charges of tokenism, and places them in jobs and universities where they do not have the skills to cope and achieve, thereby setting them up for failure.

The central problem with claims such as this is that the evidence supporting them is anecdotal and difficult to assess. Richard Rodriguez, for example, describes the helpless failure of unprepared minorities admitted under affirmative action to study at the elite University of California Berkeley (Rodriguez, 1982). However, the Bowen and Bok study of affirmative action in a range of American universities tells a different story (Bowen and Bok, 1998). A study of employees conducted in 1994 found that there was no evidence that affirmative action 'blighted the psychological functioning' of beneficiaries (Taylor, 1994).

Similarly, communitarian concerns might suggest that affirmative action creates division and resentment, and reduces the legitimacy of social institutions and the commitment of citizens to them. Pojman argues that hiring less qualified people will not break stereotypes against them but, rather, will only reinforce them – presumably because such people will perform in a less than satisfactory way (Pojman, 1992). Even if they do not, affirmative action might reinforce the perception that members of minority groups are inferior, and unable to achieve their positions on their own merits. Again, the evidence is mixed and often anecdotal, although the US study discussed in the previous section suggests that affirmative action – by increasing racial diversity in the workplace, the professions and public life – builds, rather than diminishes, social solidarity.

Finally, critics of strong affirmative action allege that allocating jobs to candidates who are less qualified is contrary to efficiency. The most efficient and productive way to organize an economy is to allocate jobs and responsibilities to those best qualified for them. The economic evidence for this claim

Box 4.2 Affirmative action: competing norms and values

The debate over affirmative action centres on different interpretations of equality, justice, liberty and the common good.

• **Equality**

Supporters of affirmative action argue that, in order to treat people equally, differences between them must be taken into account. Minority group membership and gender are relevant differences, because of the way minorities and women have been treated historically, and also because of the consequences of this for their present position.

Opponents respond that, in order to treat people equally, the state must treat them the same. Recognizing differences in a 'positive' way is just as unfair as recognizing them negatively.

• **Justice**

Supporters of affirmative action argue that justice requires compensating for historical injustices, and recognizing the effects of these injustices upon members of minority communities and upon the distribution of wealth and power in society more broadly.

Opponents counter that justice requires considering people as individuals rather than group members, and rewarding or advancing them based on merit and performance.

• **Liberty**

Supporters argue that freedom of contract means that the state must not intervene in hiring decisions to mandate affirmative action.

Opponents counter that freedom of contract must be balanced against other considerations of justice.

• **Social cohesion**

Supporters argue that affirmative action will lead to greater representation of minorities and women at university, in the professions and in public life. This will improve communication and relations between the majority and minorities, and ultimately foster social cohesion.

Opponents contend that the resentment that majorities will feel towards positive discrimination will undermine community cohesion.

is not conclusive (Holzer and Neumark, 2000). Moreover, as Nagel has argued, we cannot assume that economic efficiency should trump moral considerations (Nagel, 1973). If, as Rawls does, we take a contractarian approach to politics, according to which the basic structures of society must be subject to reasonable agreement by all, society might reasonably decide that economic efficiency is only one of the important goals of social policy.

What, then, if anything, do the opponents of affirmative action suggest should be done by the state to bring about greater racial and gender equality? After all, if minority groups and women were represented in institutions and professions in proportion to their share of the population, and this pattern seemed likely to continue into the future, there would be no need for the policy. Some libertarians, as we have seen, insist that it is not the business of the state to pursue such a goal. Other critics argue that equality of opportunity will go a long way towards ensuring more equal representation, and that any final differences in outcomes will be because of individual differences in talent and performance. Still others – controversially – ascribe these differences in outcome to biological or cultural differences between races and sexes. According to the biological 'essentialist' position, different races and sexes have different levels of intelligence and different kinds of ability (Herrnstein and Murray, 1994). The former President of Harvard University, Dr Lawrence Summers, made a similar suggestion in 2005, when he commented that the small proportion of women at higher levels in maths and sciences might be due to their lack of innate abilities in these areas – a deficiency that might be genetic in origin. Many have criticized these essentialist assertions (Fischer, 1996); taking a critical position, however, does not necessarily entail support for strong, over weak, affirmative action. Other critics argue, without making a link to innate intelligence, that the cultural practices of groups lead them to take fewer opportunities to educate and develop their children (Pojman, 1992). Thus it is not discrimination that limits the success of minority group members but, rather, their own identities and decisions. Those who hold this position are likely to support equality of opportunity but not strong affirmative action, as they believe that state regulation cannot achieve equality without change from members of minority groups themselves.

Conclusion

While much of the discussion of affirmative action has focused on the American experience, recent increases in ethnic diversity and race-based conflict are likely to mean that these preferential treatment policies will be considered more closely in Britain and Europe. As we have seen, while there is fairly wide support for measures that promote equality of opportunity, both deontological and consequentialist arguments can be offered on both sides of the issue of preferential treatment. Despite the claims of opponents, however, recent evidence does seem to suggest that the consequences of years of affirmative action in the United States are generally positive. Utilitarian arguments are the most powerful offered in support of preferential treatment – even philosophers such as Dworkin who offer a deontological defence of the policy also rely heavily on consequentialist claims.

This might appear to be less than satisfactory to supporters of affirmative action for two reasons. First, consequentialist claims will always be subject to dispute – empirical evidence is frequently cited both for the positive and negative consequences of the policy. Second, claims about beneficial effects do not address the most powerful argument made by critics of preferential treatment: that it is unfair to those individuals who are passed over for jobs or education by apparently less-qualified minorities. The stronger case for affirmative action depends on principles of justice, and on the view that justice cannot be considered ahistorically. The benefits and goods of society should be distributed in a way that takes into account membership in groups that were the subject of historical injustice and that aims to compensate for, and ultimately overcome, those injustices.

Chapter 5

Should Prostitution and Pornography be Legal?

Every year, billions of dollars are generated by the global sex industry – a term covering a wide range of activities, from prostitution in its various forms, trafficking and sex tourism, to pornography, adult entertainment and advertising. The exact worth of the industry is impossible to gauge, in part because much of it is, at least in some countries, illegal. A vast network of law and regulation to regulate the sex industry has developed at every level of government, from local ordinances to international treaties. Some of this – particularly those aspects dealing with children, human trafficking and sex slavery – is uncontroversial; it deals with activities that are widely agreed across cultures to be wrong. The United Nations Convention on the Suppression of the Traffic in Persons and the Exploitation of the Prostitution of Others, signed in 1949, declared that forced prostitution was incompatible with human dignity. The controversy over commercial sex focuses on two issues:

• Should prostitution be legal when it involves women who appear to consent to working as prostitutes?
• Should the voluntary distribution and consumption of pornography by adults be legal?

Pornography and prostitution are regulated separately, but both have been substantially liberalized in developed countries over the past three decades. Both activities raise issues of consent and the status of women: the great majority of prostitutes are women, and the great majority of consumers of pornography are men – although there are also male prostitutes, and women who use pornography. (Women comprise the fastest growing group of consumers of Internet pornography.) In both cases, the arguments against legalization were traditionally made on the grounds of community morality, although, as we shall see, the debate is increasingly driven by feminist arguments that prostitution and pornography are inherently exploitative of women. As we explore these debates, it will be clear that liberty, equality, consent and power are not merely academic issues: some of the most central questions of political theory are invoked by policy-makers, activists and sex workers themselves in arguing their cases.

The legal regulation of prostitution is complex: in countries in which it is legal, it is often closely regulated, with special licences required for brothels. Where it is illegal, national laws differ on whether they target those who sell or buy sex. 'Pimping' (living off the prostitution of others) – also targeted in the 1949 UN Convention – is illegal in most countries, as is soliciting on the street. Some countries impose stringent penalties: in Iran women convicted of prostitution face the death penalty, while Chinese law imposes the death penalty for those who organize prostitution rings in which women are abused. Among western countries, the United States has some of the strictest legislation. Prostitution is regulated by the state, and both the buying and selling of sexual services is illegal in almost all states, while street prostitution is illegal throughout the country. Nevertheless, prostitution is common (as it is in most countries where it is illegal), and there are periodic public calls for legalization. Critics point out that, following the 1988 California Supreme Court decision *People* v. *Freeman*, actors can be paid for sex if they are being videotaped for commercial pornography, while the same activities are criminalized in the case of prostitution.

Prostitution is legal in almost all European countries, although most impose restrictions on where it can be carried out. The most liberal regime is that of the Netherlands, where prostitution (including streetwalking) was legalized in 1988, and brothels in 2000, with the express aim of protecting the rights of sex workers (see Box 5.1). Some other developed countries have followed the Dutch model: prostitution is legal in Germany, for example, although local authorities are permitted to regulate it, and several restrict streetwalking, and impose a tax on brothels. New Zealand fully legalized prostitution, including streetwalking and living off earnings, in 2003.

While policy in these countries is directed at normalizing prostitution, others aim to eventually eliminate it on the grounds that it exploits women. This was the position taken by the UN Women's Conference in Beijing in 1995, which declared that prostitution and pornography – as well as sexual harassment, gender-based violence, sexual slavery and exploitation – 'are incompatible with the dignity and worth of the human person and must be eliminated'. The strongest approach along these lines is taken by Sweden, which, in 1999, became the first country in the world to criminalize all activities around prostitution, including the buying of sex, but not its sale (see Box 5.1).

Several countries take a regulatory and restrictive approach, which criminalizes not the actual sellers and buyers of sex but, rather, third parties who benefit from prostitution. This commonly involves prohibiting all of the commercial activities around prostitution, although not the transaction itself. In France, for example, the actual buying and selling of sex is not illegal, but owning or operating a brothel, advertising for prostitution and soliciting customers in public places are all banned. The United Kingdom also

Box 5.1   The Dutch and Swedish approaches to prostitution

The Dutch and Swedish approaches to prostitution both aim to empower women, but go about doing so in very different ways. Neither country criminalizes prostitutes themselves. In the Netherlands, prostitution (of adults) is recognized as work, and is fully legal. No health checks are required of prostitutes, who have full rights to join unions and are treated by law no differently from other self-employed workers. Pimping and trafficking in people are prohibited. In Sweden, by contrast, buying sex and third-party involvement in prostitution are criminalized, although prostitutes themselves are not.

- The Netherlands' liberal legislation has widespread popular support. A 1999 opinion poll found that 78 per cent of Dutch regarded prostitution as a job, in the same way as any other.
- Opponents of decriminalization claim that, by recognizing prostitution as work, the state makes it acceptable to see it as a legitimate avenue of employment for the poor and immigrants. The number of prostitutes in the Netherlands has increased since legalization, as also has the proportion of them who are foreign. The government has only recently attempted to crack down on the trafficking of women. Opponents claim that the legalization of prostitution has increased the demand for it in all its forms – including child prostitution.
- In Sweden, the ban is supported by 80 per cent of the population, and supporters point out that it has drastically reduced the number of prostitutes, including the numbers of foreign women illegally trafficked in the sex industry.
- However, some Swedish sex workers have complained that the ban forces them to work in unsafe conditions, and increases their risk of violence and abuse. The government has had to invest in drug treatment services and social support for prostitutes forced to leave the industry.

permits the buying and selling of sex, but bans pimping, soliciting and the operating of brothels. Prostitution is regulated under the Sexual Offences Act of 1956, which reflected the findings of the Wolfenden Committee on homosexual offences and prostitution. The Committee concluded that street prostitution, unlike homosexuality (see Chapter 6) caused community instability and the weakening of the family, and could be regulated as a moral issue. Similar restrictive legislation is in force in most Australian states, and in Canada, where prostitution is not illegal but many of the business activities associated with it are. The Canadian Criminal Code prohibits brothels, soliciting and living on the profits of prostitution. Sex workers in Ontario launched a constitutional challenge in the courts in 2007, claiming that these provisions violate the Canadian Charter of Rights and Freedoms, by denying sex workers their rights to liberty and security.

As with prostitution, pornography has been increasingly legalized in developed countries. Most restrictions focus on the age of users and performers, and the extremity of the material permitted. Pornography covers a wide variety of material – from soft to hardcore, to violent pornography, material depicting sexual fetishes, bestiality and child pornography. Child pornography is illegal in almost all countries (although there are some differences with respect to the cut-off age for children, and some states criminalize distribution but not possession) and all pornography is illegal in some states, including Iran, Pakistan, Malaysia and Indonesia. But pornography is notoriously difficult to regulate – in the past because much of it has been delivered by mail, and more recently because much of it is accessed over the Internet. Few countries have been able to control access to Internet pornography, although China has tightly regulated service providers, with the aim of blocking pornography as well as political dissidence. Many countries have attempted to impose filters to block material that is illegal in their own jurisdiction.

Most developed countries have adopted policies of legalizing pornography, often with exceptions for violence and some fetishist practices, and focusing efforts at control on child pornography. Much of the international political and academic debate on the issue has taken place in the United States, where regulation is a matter for states, and where defenders of legalization base their arguments on the constitutionally protected right to freedom of speech. First Amendment protection of freedom of speech was held by the US Supreme Court in the case of *Miller* v. *California* (1973) to apply to material that is not 'obscene'. The Court acknowledged the possibility of a threat to freedom of speech, and set up three requirements classifying material as obscene. In order for regulation to be permitted, the average person, applying contemporary community standards, must find that:

1 The material appeals to the prurient interest.
2 The work must define, in a patently offensive way, sexual conduct or excretory functions.
3 The work must lack 'serious literary, artistic, political or scientific value'.

It is important to note that, in the United States, the standards to be applied in determining whether material is obscene or not are those of local communities, rather than the nation as a whole. Since the Miller decision, local communities have banned sex shows, pornographic materials and, sometimes, art exhibitions on the basis of these community standards.

Legislation in the United Kingdom permits 'obscene' material to be published and sold, as long as it does not 'tend to deprave and corrupt' those who read, see or hear it (there are no restrictions on possession of such material). In practice, the courts have increasingly limited their assessment of what is held to deprave and corrupt – endorsing, instead, protective measures such as age limits and restrictions on places of sale. The UK Criminal Justice and Immigration Act of 2008 prohibits 'extreme pornography', which includes, for example, threats to the lives of those involved, bestiality and necrophilia. During the debate over these provisions, opponents claimed that they would prohibit non-abusive behaviour freely engaged in by consenting adults. In New Zealand, government censors are charged with banning 'objectionable' material that is 'injurious to the public good'. Objectionable material is defined as promoting the sexual exploitation of children, sexual violence and other extreme sexual acts. A similar approach prohibiting child sex, violence and extreme acts is followed in Australia.

Denmark, the Netherlands and Sweden take the most permissive approach to pornography, allowing any material except child pornography to be distributed to adults. In Canada, by contrast, the Supreme Court decision in 1992 in *R. v. Butler* defined as obscene – and subject to ban – material that promotes gender inequality. Gay and lesbian bookstores allege that Canada's border officials apply the definition of objectionable material in a discriminatory way to target gay and lesbian pornography.

This chapter addresses prostitution and pornography together, as case studies in the commercialization of sex. While they raise important separate issues, as we shall see, those who defend legalization in each case base their arguments on liberty: in the case of pornography, freedom of expression and, in the case of prostitution, freedom of contract. The case against both can be divided into two basic categories:

1 Conservative or communitarian arguments, which emphasize the damage that commercialized sex does to the moral character of society.
2 Feminist arguments, which focus not on the alleged immorality of prostitution and pornography but, rather, on the damage that they cause to women and gender equality.

Conservative and communitarian arguments apply to prostitution and pornography involving men as well as women, while the feminist case naturally focuses on women, but sees male prostitution, which mainly involves gay men, as repeating gendered power relations between men. Liberals arguing for the legalization of sex work rely on principles that apply whether the workers are male or female – but, in practice, because they are responding to feminist claims, focus more on women.

Both prostitution and pornography raise questions about how to balance different freedoms, and what it means to act freely:

- Does liberty mean being permitted to act or to make any kind of contract one wishes, even actions or contracts of which the majority disapproves, and believes to be damaging?
- Should individual freedom to engage in activities that deeply offend others be limited?
- Can there be contractual freedom in a society in which groups, such as women, do not have equal social and economic power?
- What is the relationship between sex and women's equality?

Some of these issues concerning liberty will also arise in Chapter 7, in which we consider censorship and freedom of speech more broadly. We begin here by outlining conservative, communitarian and feminist arguments against prostitution and pornography, and then turn to the liberal case for legalization. As we shall see, both sides in these debates employ both deontological arguments, based on their respective views of what is right and just, and consequentialist arguments, based on the implications for individuals and society of regulating the sex industry.

The conservative case against prostitution and pornography

The case against both prostitution and pornography has traditionally been made on conservative or moralist lines, and depends on particular views of sex, the family and the obligations of the individual to the common good. Liberals, as we shall see, are committed to the idea that adults should be able to make their own sexual choices, and oppose government regulation of people's sexual activities and transactions. This is consistent with the broader liberal belief that individuals should be free to behave in private in ways not approved of by others. Conservatives, however, want to preserve traditional morality's restriction of sex to marriage. Christian (and Jewish and Muslim) conservatives cite injunctions against prostitution in their holy scriptures. However, Christian conservatives also base their opposition to all forms of commercialized sex on natural law, which they believe to be established by God (Finnis, 1980).

The idea of natural law dates back to ancient philosophy, but became central to the Christian view of politics and ethics with the work of the medieval Roman Catholic philosopher Thomas Aquinas (Aquinas, 1952, written 1265–74). Natural law theorists believe that God's laws for the universe and for human society are revealed in nature and human nature, and are made known to human beings through their reason. Christians believe that if people reason properly and follow their natural moral instincts, they will know what is right and good. In terms of sex, this means restricting sexual activity to heterosexual married couples, where sex enables men and women to unite together – the physical procreative act expressing a deeper religious or spiritual union. (We discuss some related implications of this in Chapter 6, on same-sex marriage.) The problem with pornography and prostitution, according to this perspective, is that they treat sex as a commercial commodity, rather than part of an intimate and married relationship, and they assume that its purpose is pleasure and enjoyment, rather than procreation and commitment.

Conservatives (both religious and otherwise) also focus on what they believe to be the consequences of commercialized sex – both for the individuals involved in it, and for the broader community. They argue that sexual behaviour shapes and influences public life, and that to allow people unlimited liberty from regulation of their sexual choices will degrade public life and the good of families and the community. The state must therefore take a 'paternalist' approach, protecting people from their own worst impulses. Both prostitution and pornography are viewed as being corrupting – as destructive to people's willingness both to commit to a permanent sexual relationship, and to maintain their commitments. (Again, a similar argument is made about homosexuality, as we shall see in Chapter 6.) Critics argue that the legalization of prostitution and pornography will damage the family, by encouraging men to abandon marital fidelity. Prostitution obviously provides a ready alternative to sexual fidelity, and publicly available pornography, critics claim, destroys the sense of shame that restrains people's sexual impulses (Kristol, 2004). The American neoconservative Irving Kristol insists that the ready availability of pornography coarsens society, and basically changes its moral character. More specifically, religious conservatives blame pornography and prostitution for rape and sexual violence, adultery, family breakdown, premarital sex and the sexual abuse of children. In 1986, American conservatives persuaded President Reagan to commission Attorney General Edwin Meese to investigate pornography. The Meese Commission, which numbered several religious conservatives among its members, focused on the alleged harmful social effects of pornography. It concluded that pornography represented a clear danger, and recommended stricter and more extensive controls on sexually explicit matter. The Commission was widely criticized by liberals for its biased and unscientific approach to evidence; as we shall see, liberal critics contend that there is no evidence of a causal relationship between either pornography or prostitution and social dysfunction.

Arguments about the negative consequences of sex work for women, both individually and as a group, are also made by feminists, and this is why the work of the Meese Commission, for example, was supported by both anti-pornography feminists and pro-family conservatives. But some conservative arguments, such as Kristol's, also reflect a communitarian view that communities should be able to maintain and enforce their collective moral views and commitments, against the claims of individuals.

Community values and sex work

The claim that pornography and prostitution should be regulated by the state to reflect and reinforce community morality is also based on harmful consequences – but the harm invoked is the destruction of the character of a community generally, rather than specific effects on the family or children. In 1957, the Wolfenden Committee's Report into prostitution and homosexuality in the United Kingdom recommended that homosexuality should be decriminalized, but that street prostitution was destructive to the family, and should continue to be banned. The British High Court Justice Lord Devlin, commenting on the report, made the public case that the state was justified in banning an act or practice if it were regarded as morally unacceptable by popular opinion, in order to protect and preserve the moral fabric of society (Devlin, 1959). (For a fuller discussion, see pp. 120–1 in Chapter 6.)

This communitarian defence of prohibitions against pornography and prostitution does not imply that all communities necessarily would, or should, prohibit either. If public debate and discussion revealed no strong feeling in a particular community against the commercial availability of sex or images of it, and no feeling that the community would be damaged by it, then there would be no reason for a prohibition. Michael Sandel has argued that communities should be able to choose, and protect in law, their own moral standards. Debates about what a community finds acceptable and unacceptable are an essential part of the political process (Sandel, 1984). As we have seen, this local community standard approach is used to define what counts as obscenity in the United States.

Sex as a commodity

Religious opposition to pornography and prostitution, as we have seen, depends not only on concern about social consequences, but also on the belief that sex should express a spiritual union between a husband and wife. The view that sex and sexual bodies should not be treated as commodities to be bought and sold underlies not only conservative thought, but also leftist and feminist opposition to pornography and prostitution. These critics see sexual activity and expression not as divine gifts, but as fundamental to what makes us human – aspects of the person that must not be exchanged for money, any more than human beings themselves should be bought or sold.

Marxists have termed the process by which human relationships are transformed into commercial relationships 'commodification'. Under capitalism, the worker's labour power, an integral part of him, becomes a commodity to be sold and, as it is, part of the worker is sold away, and he becomes alienated from himself (Marx and Engels, 1978 [1848]). Marx and Engels thought that that the process by which human relations become commercialized, and governed by market forces and market power, was an essential aspect of capitalism. The ascendancy of the bourgeoisie – the capital-owning class – destroyed all earlier forms of human relationships: 'The bourgeoisie has torn away from the family its sentimental veil, and has reduced the family relation to a mere money relation' (Marx and Engels, 1978 [1848]). We see this process particularly clearly in slavery, the selling of human organs, or surrogate motherhood contracts, where intimate bodily services – and body parts themselves – are transformed into commodities.

In the cases of pornography and prostitution, sex itself, images of it – and, critics argue, bodies themselves – are turned into commodities. As the prostitute and sex worker sells her (or his – the argument applies irrespective of gender) sexual labour, she becomes alienated from herself, and exploited, in the same way as other workers, by the agents of capitalism – pimps and others who live off the profits of her or his labour. Marxists see commodification and exploitation as the real problems with prostitution and pornography (as they are with all labour under capitalism). But it is not only Marxists who see similarities between prostitution and other forms of labour. The liberal philosopher Martha Nussbaum, for example, argues that there is no more reason to prohibit prostitution than there is to proscribe other forms of low-paid labour requiring bodily exertion, often performed under conditions of exploitation (Nussbaum, 2008). By the same token, there is a strong argument for improving the conditions of people who work in the sex industry.

This analysis of commodification has been very influential on a range of leftist critics, who share a broad concern about applying the norms of the market to other human relationships. Michael Walzer suggests that human beings exist and act in the world in a range of different spheres of action, each of which has its particular social good – for example, education, political power, or love and affection. In each sphere, the principles by which goods are distributed are based on principles agreed to by and meanings shared among the community. Each good must be distributed according to its appropriate principles, and money, particularly, must not be used as a universal criterion of distribution. Wealth should not mean automatic success in other spheres of action, because some things should not be sold: such as human beings, political power, basic freedoms, public honour, marriage, love and friendship. Sex can be sold only when it is not understood exclusively in terms of love and commitment (Walzer, 1983). Elizabeth Anderson argues similarly that personal relations should be governed by the norms of intimacy and commitment, rather than market norms. Both prostitution and pornography have commodified women's bodies, making it more difficult for women to be fully recognized as sexual beings (Anderson, 1993).

Marriage and prostitution

Modern feminists have sometimes argued that (heterosexual) prostitution was not very different from traditional marriage, which required a woman to guarantee her sexual availability to her husband, in exchange for income and support (Jeffreys, 1997). This argument was first made at length by Marx's collaborator Friedrich Engels in *The Origins of the Family, Private Property and the State*. He traces the relationship between prostitution and marriage, which he describes as 'inseparable opposites, poles of the same social conditions' (Engels, 1948 [1884]). Engels argued that the ideal of monogamous marriage developed so that men could ensure that they could pass on their private property to their heirs. As sexual fidelity was only required of women as mothers, prostitution allowed men to continue to enjoy sexual freedom – a freedom denied to their wives. It has continued to be tolerated, despite remaining illegal, because it is necessary as an outlet to keep men stable in otherwise monogamous marriages. Efforts to ban prostitution in the name of morality or community standards are merely hypocritical moralism, as the institution is essential to bourgeois marriage. It is, thus, not surprising that the situation of the prostitute is not all that different to that of the wife under bourgeois marriage. Unlike the prostitute, the wife does not 'hire out her body like a wage-worker, on piecework, but sells it into slavery once and for all' (Engels, 1948 [1884]).

Engels concludes (rather romantically) that when the economic foundations of monogamy disappear, so will prostitution. Once private property and class power are abolished, men will no longer have to marry to ensure they can pass on their private wealth, and men and women will be able to enter into sexual relationships purely out of choice. As we shall see, the argument for individual freedom of choice is also made by liberals in defence of the legality of prostitution and pornography. Unlike liberals, however, Marxists do not believe that such freedom can be established while property remains concentrated in the hands of a capitalist class.

False consciousness

One further Marxist concept helpful to understanding radical feminist opposition to pornography and prostitution is that of 'false consciousness'. In Marx and Engels' terms, the role of ideology in capitalism is to persuade workers to believe that they are rational economic agents making free choices, and that they can improve their class position through labour. This false consciousness (as later Marxists referred to it) of who they are and what their interests are maintains the very system that dominates them. Leftist critics sometimes use this idea to describe what happens when people identify in ways, or claim interests, that critics believe to be contrary to their 'true' identities and interests (Eagleton, 1991). For feminists, this helps to explain why women often reject feminism, and claim to subordinate themselves to men freely. Women who insist on their rights and liberties to participate in prostitution and pornography might be seen as identifying with their patriarchal oppressors, rather than with their true interests. Most feminist opponents of legalizing prostitution and pornography do not make the false consciousness argument by name but, rather, rely on a version of it to answer the objection that some women claim to choose freely to participate in and enjoy both institutions.

The feminist case against pornography and prostitution

Feminists opposed to pornography and prostitution believe that these institutions do not merely represent the private career choices of individuals, or the expression of women's sexual freedom. Neither is the issue with sex work its immorality or the danger it poses to the community good. The real problems of prostitution, pornography and all forms of sex work are, according to this argument, both deontological and consequential. Sex work is unjust and wrong in itself, because it subordinates women to men, and it causes damage both to those engaged in it and to all women. Feminists see the sex industry as being linked to broader systems and relationships of power. Where, for Marxists, class economic power shapes all social institutions and practices, feminists believe that the underlying cause is patriarchy – the system of gender relations by which men are able to subordinate, exploit and exercise control over women. While the industry might involve men as workers – particularly gay men – its terms of operation are set by patriarchy, so that when men are subordinated in gay male pornography, or work as prostitutes, they are treated in the same way as women. Banning or ending pornography or prostitution is not an end in itself for the feminists who support these policies. Rather, it is part of a broader reform of socio-economic and cultural structures that will ensure women's freedom and equality. This, broadly, is the approach behind the Swedish ban on prostitution – although it is notable that Sweden takes a very different and much more liberal attitude to pornography.

The most influential feminist case that pornography is inherently unjust and damages women directly and indirectly has been made by the American feminist legal theorist and activist, Catharine MacKinnon (MacKinnon,

1985, 1995). MacKinnon argues that pornography is a violation of women's civil rights: it causes (rather than simply reflects) their inequality, and diminishes their liberty. MacKinnon's work – together with that of Andrea Dworkin (Dworkin, 1981, 1985) – has been a powerful support to international women's groups arguing for more restrictive laws against pornography in many countries. In the 1980s, MacKinnon and Dworkin drafted city regulations in the American cities of Minneapolis and Indianapolis, allowing women to sue the makers and distributors of pornography. The Ordinances were based on the claim that pornography was unjust because it subordinates women, but as the basis for legal action was damage actually caused to victims, the hearings on them were dominated by women's (often shocking) accounts of the harm that had been done to them by male consumers of pornography.

The direct harm experienced by many (although not all) workers in the sex industry is well documented; many studies of the lives and experience of sex workers have found evidence of systematic violence and abuse (Renzetti *et al.*, 2001). The indirect harm done to all women – particularly by pornography, because its nature is to be circulated beyond those involved in making it – takes two forms:

1 Critics allege that men who consume pornography use it to abuse and coerce other women sexually, both intimates and strangers (Itzin and Sweet, 1993; Russell, 1993; Weaver, 1993).
2 Pornography justifies and reinforces the continued social, cultural and economic exploitation of women, because it perpetuates the sexist stereotype that women are servile beings who exist for male sexual pleasure.

While no defender of legal pornography would wish to deny the reality of women's experience of sexual abuse, the difficulty of arguments based on harm lies in drawing a causal connection between pornography and abuse. Some empirical studies have shown a relationship between consuming pornography and sexual abuse or rape, but have not shown that pornography causes abuse: it would be ethically impossible to undertake the kind of controlled study that would prove this. Critics point out that sexualized imagery and messages are common in popular culture, and that ordinary advertising and entertainment might also inspire men to abuse women. In fact, by concentrating on pornography, we run the risk of ignoring the way the mainstream media and advertising sexualizes women and girls (Dworkin, 1991; Strossen, 1995). In addition, there is considerable variety in women's responses to pornography – some of it is made by women, either for profit or for amateur websites, and, as we have seen, women are a fast-growing proportion of the market for Internet pornography.

From a philosophical point of view, it is the argument that pornography is inherently unjust and subordinating that is most controversial. MacKinnon rejects the traditional definition of pornography as material that is sexually explicit or obscene. She restricts it to material that is not only sexually explicit, but that also shows women – or, indeed, anyone – being dominated, subdued, coerced or humiliated, or in servile positions, in such a way that endorses what they depict. From this feminist perspective, images and text that are sexually explicit but do not subordinate women are categorized as legitimate erotica. Pornography, prostitution and other forms of commercialized sex must, MacKinnon argues, be seen in the context of women's subordination to men. Pornography is not, as liberals claim, a form of speech, and prostitution is not an expression of contractual freedom – rather, both are actual political practices that reflect and reinforce the power of men and the powerlessness of women. Pornography makes abuse, domination and harassment erotic. It defines sex as being about domination and submission. Its practical effect is to reinforce patriarchy and the subordination of women.

One of the most controversial aspects of MacKinnon's argument is the way in which she categorizes so much sexually explicit material as pornographic and objectionable. She condemns not only violent or obviously degrading materials, but also anything that depicts women in a way that could be construed as servile. Images that many liberals see as neutral performances of sexual acts can be interpreted according to this feminist perspective as objectifying women – as treating them as objects that are acted on by men, rather than autonomous individuals who direct their own lives. As we shall see, other feminists have been strongly critical of this approach, arguing that pornographic images can be interpreted as empowering to women.

In order to understand MacKinnon's perspective, we have to bear in mind that she sees patriarchy as a powerful system of meaning that shapes the way we interpret, and the way in which we are affected by, images of sex. Pornography exists in a context of social ideas and relations of power – as with ideology for Marxists, it reflects and reinforces social structures. For this reason also, MacKinnon argues that women cannot be said to choose to participate in pornography. The inequality of gender relations makes it virtually impossible for women to consent freely. As for the claim of some women to enjoy pornography, this is in fact a sign of the overwhelming power of patriarchy to define sex for women as well as men. As a result, women accept their servile status as normal, and even pleasurable. This observation was first made by the nineteenth-century liberal feminist philosopher John Stuart Mill, who wrote in his critical analysis of marriage that men want not only women's obedience, but also their sentiments (Mill, 1989b [1869]). MacKinnon is describing something close to the concept of false consciousness here – although she rejects the term itself, arguing that women's consciousness of themselves as objectified cannot be said to be false, when it is the reality of the world in which they live.

The main target of anti-pornography feminists is the liberal defence of pornography on the grounds of freedom of speech (which we examine later in this chapter). The debate between them addresses one of the fundamental problems in modern political philosophy: How to balance liberty with equality. MacKinnon does not deny that consuming pornography is an exercise of individual liberty, but argues that other factors outweigh the value of that liberty. Her argument has several strands here

- First, she maintains that the freedom of men to consume pornography should not outweigh the damage to women's equality that it causes (MacKinnon, 1985). This argument on the basis of women's equality was substantially accepted by the Canadian Supreme Court in the Butler case (see p. 90).
- Second, the liberty of men to consume is incompatible with women's freedom – because while women are structurally unequal in society, they cannot really be free.
- Third, on the specific question of freedom of speech, pornography silences women, and prevents their free speech. It does so by creating an environment in which women are unwilling to complain of sexual abuse and unlikely to be believed. Moreover, by creating the illusion that women are always happily available for men's sexual pleasure, it causes their speech to be misunderstood – suggesting, most obviously, that 'no' to sexual invitations actually means 'yes'.

Ronald Dworkin points out that MacKinnon's argument turns on the distinction between negative and positive liberty (see Chapter 1). Negative liberty refers to freedom from restraints – whether imposed by the state or by others, while positive liberty means being able to direct and manage one's own life, and to participate in public decision-making about matters of common concern. MacKinnon argues that men's negative liberty from censorship damages the positive liberty of women to act as equals in public life (Dworkin, 1991).

As in the case of pornography, feminists are divided on the issue of prostitution. The case against legalization is based on a rejection of the claim that prostitutes are exercising contractual freedom, and on the evidence of harm caused to them (Jeffreys, 1997). Critics who take this position argue that economic and social inequalities, and lack of opportunities for women, drive some into prostitution. Because they believe prostitutes to be the victims of wider social and economic injustices, they advocate criminalizing men who employ prostitutes and all those who make a living as third parties from the industry, rather than prostitutes themselves. The Swedish legislation reflects this perspective. MacKinnon, for example, argues that women cannot be said to be free to enter into contracts to sell sex when their place in society is structurally unequal. To pretend that they are equally free to contract is to deny them both equality and freedom. The vast majority of prostitutes, she claims, are forced into the work by lack of other choices, histories of sexual abuse and drug dependency. Criminalizing the practice, however, would punish women for being victims (MacKinnon, 2005).

Similarly, the feminist political philosopher Carole Pateman argues that prostitution is based in gender inequality and the subordination of women (Pateman, 1988). The fact that the overwhelming majority of prostitutes are women, while clients are men, is not an accidental or contingent fact – rather, it reflects gendered power structures. What women are selling are not sexual services but, instead, the right of someone to impose their will over the body of a woman. Prostitution is the public recognition of men as sexual masters.

Feminist opposition to pornography and prostitution on the grounds that private choices are not free under current social and economic conditions is always vulnerable to counter-arguments by women who claim to work in the sex industry of their own free will and choice. Some feminists deny that consent to prostitution can ever be meaningful. Kathleen Barry maintains that, with or without consent, prostitution is the 'institutional, economic and sexual model for women's oppression' (Barry, 1996). As we have seen, feminist opponents respond that patriarchal culture and ideology persuades women to enjoy their subordination, and to identify with the perspective – what Laura Mulvey calls the 'gaze' – of their male oppressors (Mulvey, 1975) – rather than with their own true interests. Some go further, to argue that the norms of the market, such as the right to contract, can never liberate women – that the rules of free market behaviour were formulated assuming the exclusion of women and, unless they are fundamentally restructured, can never be extended to include women. Against this, liberal feminists counter that equal access to the market, and freedoms of contract and expression will liberate women, freeing them from their gendered status. This reconciliation of equality with liberty, by defining equality in terms of equal access to and rights in the market, forms the basis of the feminist anti-censorship position. Before we examine it, however, we turn to the mainstream liberal argument in favour of legalized prostitution and pornography.

Liberty, contract and sex work

The most common defence of legalized prostitution and pornography is on the grounds that it is not the business of the state to interfere with or regulate what are private relationships and behaviours, as long as those private matters do not cause harm to others. This distinction between public or common matters and the private sphere is, as we have seen, fundamental to modern liberalism, in both its free-market libertarian and its egalitarian forms. It underlies John Stuart Mill's argument against a paternalist state in *On Liberty*, in which he maintains that governments should intervene in the behaviour of individuals only to prevent actions of individuals that directly harm others (Mill, 1989a [1859]). Mill believed that people must be free to make their own choices about their self-regarding behaviour; paternalistic intervention by the state to protect them would only hinder them from developing themselves as free and autonomous individuals. This 'harm principle' has remained a standard by which to judge legislation in liberal democracies, and was invoked by the Wolfenden Committee in its recommendation to decriminalize homosexuality. Mill argued specifically that contracts for the sale of sex should not be prohibited, although he did think the state was justified in discouraging them (Mill, 1989a [1859]).

Liberals are suspicious of state intervention into private behaviour, even when it is supposedly for the good of those concerned, because they believe that society contains an unavoidable range of different views about what makes a good life. This, in itself, results from the co-existence of a plurality of moral, religious and cultural beliefs and perspectives. Political theory must accommodate the realities of a pluralist society. Liberal pluralists argue that, while people might adhere strongly to particular viewpoints or beliefs in their private lives, the nature of politics is that, in order to live together in a plural society, we must separate our private views of the good from the principles and rules we agree on across a range of view-points. Contemporary liberals often refer to this as giving the 'right' (meaning what is just and fair in the eyes of all) priority over the 'good' (meaning what is acceptable within the framework of deep or comprehensive moral values) (Rawls, 1993). Basic to Rawls' principles of justice and to Dworkin's egalitarianism, this distinction between the right and the good maps onto a liberal separation between the public and private spheres, with the public principles concerning what is right being separate from private beliefs about what is good. The reason the state should not interfere in private self-regarding actions, including sexual behaviour, is because public political action should be limited to matters about what is fair and just, which can be agreed by all, rather than what is moral and good, on which values will differ.

The liberal principle of non-intervention in private matters underlies three strands of arguments in favour of legalizing pornography and prostitution: the libertarian case based on individual freedom, liberal egalitarianism, and liberal feminism. In the case of pornography, libertarian liberals emphasize the right of individuals to free speech and expression, on the grounds not only of an irreducible plurality of views, but also because human autonomy and self-development requires that people choose and freely hold their own opinions (Mill, 1989a [1859]). This principle is most entrenched in the

United States, where, as we have seen, the First Amendment to the Constitution, guaranteeing freedom of speech and expression, has been held to cover more than mere verbal communication, and to include the expression of sexuality. Anti-censorship liberals invoke Mill to support their argument that individuals have the right to possess and enjoy whatever materials they choose, as long as they are not causing direct harm to others.

Ronald Dworkin cautions against treating pornography as a pure issue of freedom of speech, pointing out that pornography is not the expression of dissident political views. As much of it can be argued to be basic and repetitive, it is difficult to argue that the availability of more pornography will give people more choices, and increase their opportunities to be autonomous. So, the argument that free availability of pornography is necessary for full human self-development is hard to sustain (Dworkin, 1986). Dworkin suggests, instead, a rights-based argument in favour of the legalization of pornography: individuals have a 'right to moral independence', which authorizes them to make decisions about the morals by which they will live. This means that we cannot prohibit pornography on the grounds that people find it offensive or obscene, or think that it demeans or degrades others. This does not mean that some restrictions cannot be placed on it, in the name of the community good. But, ultimately, concerns about the common good cannot outweigh the individual right to moral independence.

The libertarian defence of prostitution is based on the individual right to contract. Libertarians argue that adults, in the absence of direct coercion, are able to make their own decisions to enter into whatever contractual relationships they wish – to sell sex or to make pornography for a fee – and that we should not prohibit certain kinds of contract because we think they are damaging to society or to individuals. These principles underpin the legalization of prostitution in the Netherlands. As we saw in Chapter 2, Robert Nozick takes this freedom of contract approach (Nozick, 1974). Nozick argues that human beings have property in themselves and, thus, are entitled to make whatever contracts for the use of their bodies and minds that they choose. Lars Ericsson makes a strong case along these lines for legalizing prostitution as free exchange on an open market (Ericsson, 1980). Ericsson argues that sexual services are no different from any other kind of service involving the body that might be sold (an argument also made by Martha Nussbaum). This counters the conservative argument that sex must be part of a marital relationship, but it also challenges more egalitarian and feminist arguments that sexuality is necessarily a deep and meaningful aspect of human personality. Ericsson dismisses this view as sentimental.

Naturally, the freedom of contract argument does not apply to cases where prostitutes or sex workers are forced into selling sex by threats of violence. Neither does it mean that, once a sex worker has contracted to sell sexual services, the client can do anything to the sex worker that he or she wishes. In cases such as this, libertarians argue that the proper approach is to criminalize the abuse or coercion, rather than the sex work itself. But what about cases where women resort to sex work because of economic hardship, or drug addiction, or pressure from husbands and boyfriends? As we have seen, feminist critics argue that consent in such cases is not meaningful. Libertarians are sceptical of such claims, and maintain that the state should assume that, if women are not forced to enter into contracts for sex work, then they do so freely. This reflects a long-standing way of thinking in liberal thought. The seventeenth-century philosopher Thomas Hobbes, one of the originators of social contract theory, argued that people could not escape their contractual obligations simply because they had agreed to contracts under duress – even contracts 'extorted by fear' are valid, writes Hobbes (Hobbes, 1962 [1651]). Modern law takes a more protective approach than Hobbes, and does not uphold contracts agreed to under duress. But the pressures of economic circumstances or personal relationships are not usually held to render contracts void.

The case for legal prostitution and pornography can also be made from a more egalitarian liberal perspective. Rawls defends state action to redistribute resources, but not to enforce any particular moral perspective. Rawls argues that public reason – by which he means public political debate based on common reasons – and state regulation should be limited to regulating matters that affect the reproduction and maintenance of political society over time. This, in practice, is a much more limited role than protecting particular cultural and social institutions. As long as political society continues, it is not the business of the state to enforce or ensure particular cultural values or customs, including those concerning family life or the relations between the sexes (Rawls, 1997). It is only cases where these practices or customs affect political society – say, the liberty and equality of sexes – that should be open to political debate and state regulation.

As we have seen, this is precisely the main argument made by MacKinnon: that pornography substantially contributes to women's inequality. Some egalitarian liberals claim that, because the sex industry impacts on gender equality, it is a fit subject for state regulation (Dyzenhaus, 1992). From this perspective, the legality of the sex industry depends on whether it could, indeed, be shown to impact on gender equality. Ronald Dworkin argues, however, that, even if such an impact can be shown, the right to freedom of expression outweighs it. As he points out, verbal claims that women are inferior to men would not be censored – even if they were made to an impressionable audience likely to believe them (Dworkin, 1991). In any case, defenders of censorship must show that pornography has a particular impact on women's equality as distinct from the media, advertising and other forms of public expression. MacKinnon's argument that men's negative liberty from censorship damages women's positive liberty to participate in public life runs up against a similar problem.

The liberal arguments we have examined so far are more interested in freedom in general, whether of contract or expression, than in sexual freedom in particular. Some theorists, however, in their defence of legal prostitution and pornography, have drawn on the relationship between sexuality, individuality and liberty. They argue that individuality includes a right to sexual expression and sexual autonomy (Altman, 2005). Joshua Cohen argues that pornography is important to the expressive interests of human beings (Cohen, 1996). We have an interest in expressing and articulating thoughts, attitudes and feelings on a range of matters of human concern. Much depends on how we view sex. As we have seen, conservatives see it as a demonstration of marital commitment, while others who take what Ericsson calls the sentimentalist view see it as an expression of love. If we view it, rather, as an expression of individual identity or autonomy, then we can have no justification for discriminating between different expressions of sexuality: pornography, sex outside marriage, homosexuality, prostitution, all are expressions of sexual autonomy. Our rights to them are qualified only in the usual egalitarian manner by respect for the rights of others.

Feminist arguments for sexual freedom

As the sex industry overwhelmingly involves women selling their sexual services to men, it is not surprising that many feminists argue that women are not truly free to make these contracts, and that the freedom of men to enjoy them is bought at the expense of the exploitation and subordination of women. However, feminists also make an equally strong case supporting the decriminalization of the sex industry. Their perspective is sometimes termed 'pro-sex', as opposed to anti-pornography or prostitution, but neither side in this debate admits to being 'anti-sex'. Their views of the liberatory potential of sex work for women, however, differ widely. Feminist libertarians believe that reinforcing and extending women's contractual rights in the market will increase their liberty. But many liberal feminists also defend the right of women to express themselves sexually through sex work. Wendy McElroy argues that women have been prevented from autonomous sexual self-expression, and that liberalizing pornography and prostitution allows them sexual freedom (McElroy, 1996). To insist that women are not truly free to decide to participate in the sex industry is to infantilize them, as they have been historically infantilized by a paternalist state. As feminist theorists acknowledge, this argument depends on the assumption that women are able to choose to enter the sex industry, and are not compelled by poverty or lack of alternatives.

Nussbaum examines what is required by free choice in the case of the sex industry – and, indeed, all employment (Nussbaum, 2008). She suggests that anti-sex work feminists who argue that women would not autonomously choose work that affected such an essential and intimate part of their identity are setting the bar of autonomy too high. Economic circumstances force many people to work at jobs they might not otherwise choose. (Marx claimed that all workers under capitalism lack autonomy, because they do not have full control over their labour and its products.) As do other egalitarian liberals, Nussbaum emphasizes the relationship between sexuality and autonomy, arguing that the ability freely to express oneself sexually is a key aspect of human flourishing. As we saw in Chapter 2, Nussbaum argues that legislation and policy should be judged by the degree to which they allow people to flourish as human beings, exercising central human capabilities (Nussbaum, 1999). We cannot assume, she warns, that only sex that is part of a loving, intimate and continuing relationship is required for human flourishing. Nussbaum concludes that if women who become prostitutes have sufficient central capabilities, there is no reason to be concerned as long as their rights as workers are protected. Similarly, Laurie Shrage suggests that, rather than criminalizing prostitution, the state should ban the exploitative labour practices that follow the sex industry, and allow sex workers to unionize (Shrage, 1994). For feminists who emphasize the effects of economic inequality, the real issue raised by prostitution is the lack of employment opportunities open to working women and lack of control over the conditions of their employment.

In practice, this is the position of the many prostitutes' and sex-workers' rights groups that have sprung up over the past three decades. Organizations such as the Californian group COYOTE (Call Off Your Old Tired Ethics) and the International Prostitutes Collective insist that their members have freely chosen their work, and that their working conditions should be protected in the same way as other workers. They maintain that abuse of women in the sex industry is not inherent in the work itself but is, rather, the result of the fact that women's rights as sex workers are not protected. As we have seen, this argument has influenced legislation in some countries, notably the Netherlands. Many sex workers have spoken up against feminist arguments such as MacKinnon's, and have asserted their free choice (Nagle, 1997). Anti-sex work feminists counter with studies showing that large numbers of prostitutes would leave the industry if they could. Men and women in many low-waged and unskilled jobs might evince a similar lack of enthusiasm about their work. All that we can conclude for certain is that women's experience of sex work varies widely: for some, it is liberating and empowering; for some it is just a job; while for others it is oppressive and degrading.

Box 5.2 Prostitution and pornography: competing norms and values

The debates over whether to legalize prostitution and pornography turn on different interpretations of some key norms: gender equality, liberty and the common good:

- **Gender equality**

Supporters of legalizing prostitution and pornography argue that women are entitled to make autonomous decisions about their sexual behaviour and expression in the same way as men. Women's inequality is due not to sexual expression, but to their position in the labour market. The best way to ensure equality is to prevent the exploitative practices that often accompany the sex industry, rather than the industry itself.

Opponents counter that both prostitution and pornography reflect and perpetuate the structural inequality of women, which is based on their sexual subordination to men.

- **Liberty**

Supporters of legalizing prostitution and pornography argue that individuals are entitled to enter freely into contracts to sell their sexual services – whether through prostitution, or the production and sale of pornography. Freedom of expression includes the right to free sexual expression, whether through the consumption of pornography or involvement in prostitution.

Opponents counter that prostitutes and women who make pornography do not freely choose their work, but are forced or manipulated into it by their lack of economic opportunities, and exploitative sexual relationships.

- **The common good**

Supporters of legalizing pornography argue that banning it amounts to censorship, and accords too much power to the state to establish and enforce morality.

Feminist opponents counter that pornography and prostitution legitimize wider sexual exploitation and violence. Conservative critics argue that they destroy traditional morality and the institution of the family.

Much of the liberal feminist case for legalizing the sex industry appeals to principles of liberty and individual rights. But many feminists are also concerned with the consequences for women of granting the state the power to censor sexually explicit materials. Historically, governments in almost all nations have been dominated by men and have reinforced male privilege, and women's movements have had to struggle against them to achieve basic civil rights. Sex roles, appropriate sexual behaviour for women, and the relationship between sex and reproduction have all been regulated: civil libertarian Nadine Strossen points out that, historically, the state has used censorship to prevent the publication of material providing women with information about sex, birth control and lesbianism – information that they can use to exercise control of their sexuality (Strossen, 1995). What is more, repressive regimes have banned political dissidence on the grounds that it is pornographic. Strossen concludes that state authorities cannot be trusted to make the best decisions concerning women's interests.

Conclusion

Debates over the sex industry have been particularly divisive for feminists over the past two decades – each accusing the other of effectively supporting the male exploitation of women, and ignoring the real experience of sex workers themselves. MacKinnon charged the Feminist Anti-Censorship Taskforce that opposed her anti-pornography ordinance with being the 'Uncle Toms' and scabs of the women's movement. Anti-censorship feminists claimed, in turn, that she promoted a Victorian view of sex, in which men are sexually rapacious beasts and women unwilling victims of their passions. It is impossible to imagine reconciliation between opposing camps as long as there is so much diversity in women's experiences of commercial sex and their interpretations of those experiences. A similar problem emerges with prostitution, where the Swedish and Dutch legislative approaches differ on the fundamental issue of whether women should be empowered in doing sex work, or empowered to escape it. In both cases, even many of those critical of sex work and its consequences for women's equality are sceptical about the capacity of the state to intervene positively to balance liberty and equality. We saw similar concerns expressed by some theorists in our discussion of distributive equality in Chapter 2.

In any event, the realities of globalization have recently begun to change the focus of activism and state policy on these issues. All feminists – and all liberals, conservatives and communitarians – agree that, whatever the case for legalizing prostitution by citizens, the rapidly growing trade in internationally trafficked women – and children – poses obvious threats to liberty, equality and human security. In the case of pornography, the rise of the Internet has made it more difficult to regulate the content of globally available sexually explicit images – and, at the same time, has made it easier for these images to be viewed in private. Here, the focus of governments in developed countries has shifted to children's access to Internet sex sites and to child pornography, an industry that crosses national borders, and where abuse and harm are indisputable. Global economic inequality has opened up the sex industry to large groups of vulnerable and easily exploited people. While states are responding by tightening law enforcement, we can also argue that international inequalities in wealth need to be tackled. We will look at this question directly in Chapter 10.

Chapter 6

Should Same-Sex Marriage be Legal?

While historians of sexuality have traced back ceremonies uniting homosexual couples for most of recorded history, in both western and non-western cultures, the demand that same-sex couples be allowed to marry formally has emerged only during the past couple of decades. Nevertheless, same-sex marriage has come to be one of the most controversial and divisive social policy issues in western countries. It raises questions concerning not only the rights of gay and lesbian people, and what is required for their equality, but also the status of marriage – an institution declining in popularity in many countries – and the relationship between the state and the institutions of civil society. Although public debate centres on rights to marriage, a range of different types of legally recognized and protected relationships has developed that various countries have adopted for same-sex couples, as a substitute for marriage. Often called 'civil unions' or 'domestic partnerships', these officially recognized relationships offer many of the same legal and economic rights and benefits that accompany marriage, including rights to property and inheritance, hospital visitation rights, rights to housing and insurance benefits and, in some cases, the right to adopt children. In some cases, they are also open to heterosexual couples that do not wish to enter into a formal marriage. These parallel institutions, which are much more commonly available than same-sex marriage and which tend to attract higher levels of public support, make this a complex issue from a political point of view, although as we shall see, most political philosophers who support civil unions or domestic partnerships also support same-sex marriage.

Only a handful of states have legalized same-sex marriage, but civil unions or domestic partnerships have become relatively common in Europe and in English-speaking countries. Denmark was the first to offer a legal institution parallel to marriage, when 'registered partnerships' legislation was passed in 1989. Similar legislation recognizing 'civil unions' followed in Norway, Sweden and Iceland, the Netherlands and France during the 1990s. Germany introduced registration for 'lifetime partnerships' for same-sex couples in 2001, and the United Kingdom passed the Civil Partnerships Act in 2005 (see Box 6.1). In 2000, the Netherlands became the first country in the world to offer full same-sex marriage, on the same terms as heterosexual marriage. Belgium extended civil marriage to same-sex couples in 2003, as did Spain in 2005. Outside Europe, the push for same-sex marriage has been mainly confined to English-speaking countries. It was legalized in Canada in 2005 and South Africa in 2006; in 2006, civil unions were introduced in New Zealand.

The issue has particularly mobilized and polarized public opinion in the United States, where the struggle over same-sex unions has been waged at both the federal and the state levels. In 1996, the Republican Congress

---

Box 6.1 The United Kingdom Civil Partnerships Act (2005)

Several states have opted to legalize civil unions, or a similar institutional structure for same-sex couples, rather than allowing them to 'marry', as such. While there is a higher level of public support for these structures than for actual same-sex marriage, many of those who oppose them claim that they are marriage by another name. The question of civil unions or marriage raises important issues concerning the scope of equality and justice, many of which were aired in the debate in the United Kingdom over the Civil Partnerships Bill, which became law in 2004.

- The government and supporters of the Bill, including the opposition Conservative Party, claimed that it allowed for equality for gays and lesbians, by prescribing the same economic and social rights for same-sex as for heterosexual couples – pension rights, access to hospital records, Inheritance Tax exemptions – and the same responsibilities, such as requiring maintenance payments for children in the event of divorce. Supporters claimed that justice requires that homosexual couples be accorded the same rights as heterosexuals.
- Conservative opponents of the Bill, such as the Christian Institute, claimed that it provided 'special rights' for gays and lesbians that were not equally available to others in committed but not sexual relationships, such as caregivers and dependents, or family members living together. They insisted that it was unjust to provide benefits for homosexual couples, but not to people who were not couples but were in long-term caring relationships. Opponents rejected the equality argument. They did not disagree with the general principle that 'like should be treated equally with like', but maintained that same-sex couples were not similar to heterosexual spouses.
- Some radical gay and lesbian groups, such as Outrage!, argued that, while civil partners would now be entitled to almost all the material benefits associated with marriage, the fact that their unions were not called marriages would mean they would be seen as second-class. Because it was a separate institution, civil partnerships could not be equal to marriage. 'Separate but equal', they pointed out, was discredited by apartheid in South Africa and segregation in the United States. According to this position, justice and equality required treating same-sex couples in the same way as heterosexuals.

passed (and Democratic President Clinton signed) the federal Defense of Marriage Act, which declared that marriage under federal law referred only to a union between two people of opposite sexes, and that the federal government need not recognize same-sex marriages performed by states. It also provided that states could refuse to recognize same-sex marriages performed by other states. The impetus for this was the possibility that same-sex marriage could be legalized in some states, either by judicial interpretation or by legislation. In 1993, in *Baehr* v. *Lewin*, the Supreme Court of Hawaii had declared that the restriction of marriage to heterosexuals might violate the equal protection clause of the Hawaiian state constitution. Since the Defense of Marriage Act, over half of the states in the USA, including Hawaii, have, by popular vote, passed amendments to their constitutions that limit marriage to unions between a man and a woman. A popular movement to introduce an amendment to the federal Constitution prohibiting same-sex marriage attracted the support of President Bush but, in 2006, the Federal Marriage Amendment that would have prohibited the recognition of same-sex marriage was ultimately defeated in Congress.

However, in 2003, the Supreme Court of Massachusetts ruled (in *Goodridge* v. *Department of Public Health*) that it was contrary to the state's constitution to restrict marriage to heterosexual couples and, the following year, marriage licences were issued to same-sex couples. Attempts to amend the state constitution to restore the traditional definition of marriage have been unsuccessful. While Massachusetts has been the only state to legalize same-sex marriages, others – New Jersey, Vermont, Connecticut, California and New Hampshire – have created legal institutions that explicitly offer the same rights and benefits as marriage to same-sex couples. In 2005, the California legislature passed a bill legalizing same-sex marriage. This was the first instance in the United States in which such legislation was passed, as the decision in Massachusetts had been made after judicial interpretation. However, the bill was vetoed by Republican Governor Schwarzenegger. In May 2008, the California Supreme Court ruled (*In re Marriage* cases) that same-sex couples could marry in the state but, the following November, California voters passed Proposition 8, which restricts the definition of marriage to a man and a woman.

The introduction of civil unions or same-sex marriage has been accompanied in every case by strong organized opposition to them on the part of conservative lobby groups – particularly religious organizations. In Spain, the Catholic Church declared the law illegitimate, and urged state officials to refuse to carry out same-sex wedding ceremonies. Britain's Anglican Church declared that those in civil partnerships were to be viewed as being in unsanctioned sexual relationships outside marriage. In 2003, the Vatican launched a worldwide campaign against gay marriage. Cardinal Ratzinger (later Pope Benedict XVI) called gay unions immoral and harmful. In the

United States, many evangelical groups, as well as the Roman Catholic Church, strongly oppose same-sex marriage but, while both the Catholic and many Protestant churches also oppose civil unions, a recent survey shows that a majority of individual Catholics and Protestants are in favour of these parallel institutions.

Same-sex marriage, and gay and lesbian rights

The question of same-sex marriage is a particular – and particularly controversial – case in the wider debate surrounding the rights of homosexual people. Since the Enlightenment in the seventeenth and eighteenth centuries, equal civil rights and liberties in western countries have gradually been extended to further groups of people – to working class people, women, and people of different races, ethnicities and religions. As members of these groups, gays and lesbians have enjoyed this extension of liberties and rights in most areas but have, until recently, been prohibited from freely and openly engaging in sexual relationships with the partners of their choice, and have been subject to prejudice, discrimination and exclusion on the grounds of their sexuality. Prohibitions against sex between men were widely in force until well into the twentieth century, although the law in most countries was silent on lesbians. Homosexual behaviour was regarded as evil, insane or sick. Historians have traced the way in which it has been characterized as both immorality – the result of bad choices – and psychological illness (D'Emilio, 1998). The American Psychiatric Association only removed homosexuality from its list of mental disorders in 1973, and, until 1990, it was listed by the World Health Organization as a mental illness. Most scientists now believe that homosexuality, as with heterosexuality, is the product of a combination of genetic, early psychological and environmental factors. Whatever the reason given for their sexual orientation, gays and lesbians were subject to discrimination and harassment on both private and public levels. Homosexual acts were only decriminalized in Britain in 1967, while the first American state to do so was Iowa in 1962. They are still illegal in about 70 countries today, most of which are in Africa or Asia.

While there continues to be strong conservative religious opposition to homosexuality, and controversy about recognizing the rights of gays and lesbians as a group, there is a fairly wide consensus in western democracies that private acts between consenting adults should not be criminalized. Even the conservative philosophers whose opposition to same-sex marriage is discussed later in this chapter argue that the value of allowing people to act freely is more important than the damage allegedly done to them by homosexual relationships. They conclude that the state should discourage, but not criminalize, homosexual behaviour (Finnis, 1980). At this level, much of the public debate about homosexuality is less a matter for politics than for personal ethics. But when the equal rights of gays and lesbians are disputed – in employment, for example, or in membership of associations, or to marry – then that debate becomes political.

The widespread acceptance – or, at least, toleration – of homosexuality as private behaviour is a result of the clear split between the public and private spheres of human action that has become fundamental to politics in western societies. The notion that human freedom depends on the existence of areas of activity that are cordoned off from state interference is distinctly modern, dating from the emergence of liberalism in the seventeenth century. In the classical world of ancient Greece and Rome, freedom meant men's ability to exercise their capacities as citizens and to take part in the development and administration of the laws that governed them. To be free was to be a citizen – a status denied to women and to those who had to earn their own living. Modern liberal philosophers have changed our view of freedom, so that we now more commonly understand it to mean the absence of restraints – both from others and from the state – on our actions. Thomas Hobbes wrote in 1651, in *Leviathan*, that freedom was the absence of 'impediments to motion' (Hobbes, 1962 [1651]). As we saw in Chapter 1, Isaiah Berlin described this absence of regulations and restrictions as 'negative freedom' (Berlin, 1969), and it has come to mean freedom from interference and regulation by others and by the state. It is what John Stuart Mill defended in his essay *On Liberty* (Mill, 1989a [1859]) and is a cornerstone of modern liberal democracies, shared by liberals and conservatives alike. As long as behaviour does not injure or cause harm to others, there is, at least, a presumption that it should be regarded as private and exempt from state control.

While individual liberty is now understood to protect sexual activity between consenting adults, irrespective of their gender, the question of same-sex marriage involves not only private action but, rather, state recognition of homosexual relationships. In this case, the state is called on not simply to accept or 'tolerate' private behaviour but, rather, to confer official recognition on private relationships, with all the practical and economic benefits that attach to being married. As we shall see, the argument in favour of same-sex marriage is still sometimes made on the grounds of personal freedom. Some libertarians see marriage as, essentially, a contract and therefore subject to the same rules of freedom of contract as any other. But most political philosophers agree that marriage is a public institution, and plays a special role in society – and that access to it cannot be considered in the same way as freedom to enter into other contracts. Many of the arguments on both sides of the same-sex marriage debate, as we shall see, depend on particular views of the meaning of marriage, and the role it plays in supporting individuals and social cohesion. Many who oppose same-sex marriage do so because of the negative effects they argue it will have on the institution of marriage. Many who support it do so because they claim it will have a positive effect both on marriage as an institution and on the broader society.

As we shall see, arguments made in favour of same-sex marriage are made on both deontological and consequentialist grounds. Deontological arguments focus on rights and equality, while consequentialist arguments look at the effects of marriage on gays and lesbians, and the broader society. Theorists who take this latter perspective argue that same-sex marriage will reduce homosexual promiscuity and promote more long-term committed and stable relationships, particularly amongst gay men. Moreover, it will help to reduce homophobia by normalizing gay and lesbian relationships, so that children grow up thinking of them as legitimate. Many consequentialists also argue that same-sex marriage would have positive consequences for marriage, redefining it away from its patriarchal origins. These deontological and consequentialist arguments cut across a range of philosophical perspectives. Some few philosophers take a strictly consequentialist approach. Richard Posner, for example, argues that moral philosophy provides no guide in deciding any claims about gay rights; rather, he argues, we should look only at the pragmatic consequences of same-sex marriage – such as a reduction in the spread of AIDS (Posner, 1997).

We will begin by briefly considering the libertarian argument on the grounds of personal freedom, before turning to liberal, feminist and communitarian perspectives in support of same-sex unions that take into account marriage's institutional role. The impact of redefining marriage to include same-sex couples is interpreted very differently by conservatives, who are sceptical of the value of redefining and reforming institutions with a long history in order to conform to recent ideas of what is just. Their scepticism is, ironically, shared by those on the opposite end of the political spectrum. Finally, we examine feminist and radical gay and lesbian theorists who argue that the movement for inclusion in marriage is a mistake. These leftist critics do not aim to exclude gays and lesbians from marriage but, rather, to challenge the whole institution as irredeemably patriarchal and hierarchical.

The freedom of contract argument

Marriage is, at one level, a contractual agreement between two people, made for the mutual purposes of sex, affection and support; thus, we might argue that any people able to make a contract should be able to enter into marriage as they would into any other contractual relationship. This would rule out marriage with children, who are not presumed to be sufficiently rational to enter into binding contracts. It would, however, permit marriage between same-sex partners, as well as between close relatives, and between several partners (polygamous and polyandrous marriages). Libertarian advocates of this position point out that the religious view of marriage as a divinely ordered institution, with special roles for husbands and wives, is irrelevant to civil marriage. In the civil ceremony, both parties are contracting equals, relating to each other not in terms of the conventional status of husbands and wives but, rather, as contracting parties (Eskridge, 2002). This radical view of marriage reflects a broader tendency in western societies towards seeing people as being, in a deep sense, defined by the contracts that they make, rather than the status or position into which they are born. The English legal theorist Sir Henry Maine described this as a shift from status to contract in the late nineteenth century (Maine, 1901), but it is also central to the critique of capitalism by Marx and Engels.

Not all libertarians, however, would be happy with this treatment of marriage as purely a matter of free contract. They might argue that a political theory of limited government and regulation relies on a healthy civil society, with institutions strong enough to provide the social support that the state should not. The family is obviously a key institution responsible for providing care for people in the absence of state welfare. This is not necessarily grounds for libertarian opposition to same-sex marriage; some libertarians, as do other liberals, argue that same-sex marriage is beneficial in that it extends family support to gays and lesbians, thus reducing demand on public resources. Andrew Sullivan, a self-described small-government libertarian conservative who is also gay, makes an even stronger argument along these lines. Sullivan argues that limited government requires a focus on personal responsibility and stable relationships, for homosexual as well as heterosexual people (Sullivan, 1995). On the other hand, libertarians, as do most conservatives, might argue that same-sex marriage would undermine the family and should be opposed on those grounds. In any case, the role played by marriage as an institution is key to most arguments on both sides of this issue.

Liberal arguments, rights and the role of marriage

If we recognize marriage as a basic social institution, we can argue on liberal grounds that access to it is essential to enabling individuals to live good lives that they have chosen for themselves. The most basic liberal argument for same-sex marriage is on the ground of equal rights – not only to enter freely into contracts, but also to participate in a fundamental social institution. The ancient Greek philosopher Aristotle established the basic principle of justice that similar cases should be treated similarly, and liberals assert that, because homosexual people are in almost all respects no different to heterosexuals, with the same needs, they deserve equal treatment at work, equal freedom from discrimination and of speech and association, and equal rights to participate in sexual relationships with other consenting adults. The same argument justifies their right to enter into marriage contracts – or, at least, recognized relationships that confer the same benefits as marriage. Ronald Dworkin argues that attempts to restrict the rights of homosexual people are just the extension of private prejudice into public policy (Dworkin, 1978). A fundamental principle of liberal equality is that people have the right to be treated equally by the government, that is, to have access to the same goods and opportunities as everyone else.

All but the most individualist of philosophers have recognized that marriage not only provides goods and opportunities essential to human happiness and welfare, but also – with the family – forms the environment in which people are socialized in the values of justice and equality. This also has a long heritage in liberal thought. In his defence of women's rights, John Stuart Mill argued that inequality between the sexes in marriage meant that the family promoted selfishness and exploitation: 'If the family in its best forms is, as it is often said to be, a school of sympathy, tenderness and loving forgetfulness of self, it is still oftener, as respects its chief, a school of willfulness, overbearingness, unbounded self-indulgence, and a double-dyed and idealized selfishness' (Mill, 1989b [1869]: 153). We discuss feminist criticism of marriage in more detail later in this chapter. But liberals have wanted to preserve the idea of the family as a 'school of sympathy', an institution in which (once women were made equal) the virtues of justice, responsibility and care could be taught. The family teaches children the virtues of mutual responsibility and sharing that they need in order to be good citizens. Admitting same-sex couples to the institution of marriage – particularly given that these marriages cannot, by definition, involve the exploitation of wives by husbands – can only increase the opportunity for this positive socialization to occur.

According to this argument, it makes no difference whether families are based on heterosexual or homosexual relationships: what matters is that they promote and reinforce the values that will nurture good citizens. As we saw in Chapter 2, John Rawls designed his two principles of justice in *A Theory of Justice* to regulate society as a 'scheme for mutual cooperation' (Rawls, 1971). While families are not subject to regulation in the same way as economic institutions, they are essential in that they ensure the orderly reproduction of society over time. As long as they fulfil this role, Rawls argues, there is no reason for the state to regulate family life. In a later essay, he explains that no particular form of the family (monogamous, heterosexual or otherwise) is required for a just society so long as the family is arranged so that it effectively nurtures and develops citizens, and does not threaten other political virtues (Rawls, 1997: 788).

Rawls sees disagreements about same-sex marriage and what counts as legitimate family as belonging to people's comprehensive systems of moral belief, which must, in a pluralist society, be separated from the 'overlapping consensus' between these systems of belief on the political values that all can share. In *A Theory of Justice*, Rawls based his principles of justice on the premise that they would be agreed to by all who did not know what their social or natural talents and disadvantages would be, who were reasoning from an 'original position' (see Chapter 2.) In his later work, Rawls shifts to the more realist justification that principles of justice should be those that can be commonly agreed to by people with diverse moral commitments (Rawls, 1993). So long as the family based on a same-sex union can effectively nurture and develop citizens, and foster values such as toleration and respect, it must be permitted irrespective of the private moral views of citizens who oppose it. If the state prohibits same-sex marriage, it is intervening to impose comprehensive moral views on citizens, rather than confining itself to commonly agreed political principles. The question as to whether families based on same-sex marriages do nurture and socialize children to become good citizens is an empirical one: while there has not been extensive research into this question, studies undertaken of children raised in same-sex families show that they present no harmful effects as a result (Eskridge, 2002).

Some liberals and feminists have argued that same-sex marriage will not only extend the right to participate in an institution that nurtures citizens for a just society, but will socialize children to be more just and egalitarian. Same-sex marriage is sometimes argued to contribute to the reforming of the family – a goal urged by liberals, feminists and male supporters of women's rights since the early nineteenth century. It is a central tenet of all varieties of feminism that marriage and family should involve a more equal distribution of rights and duties between men and women (Okin, 1989). Much has improved in this respect over the twentieth century. Previously, in western countries, women lost their independent legal identity when they married, as well as their rights to hold most property independently. They had fewer rights over their children than did fathers, and fewer grounds on which they could divorce their spouses than did men. They could not legally refuse their husbands sex: rape in marriage has only recently been recognized as a crime in most countries. As the feminist philosopher Susan Okin argues, justice was regarded as an inappropriate virtue for families, which were supposed to rely, instead, on the goodwill and mutual sacrifice generated by love and intimacy (Okin, 1989).

Some feminists argue that same-sex marriage, which does not rely on the different roles and expectations traditionally assigned to men and women, will free the institution of marriage of its associations with the subordination of women. Studies of gay and lesbian relationships show that they make fewer assumptions about gender roles and the division of labour than do heterosexual couples that live together (Blumstein and Schwartz, 1983). Robyn West claims that same-sex marriage has a better chance of reconstructing marriage as an egalitarian institution, in part because these relationships do not emphasize reproductive sexuality (West, 1998). West points out that the producing and rearing of children has traditionally been thought to foster the disposition to care for others, thus reducing selfish behaviour – an argument often made by conservative opponents of same-sex marriage. West suggests, however, that there is a selfish element to this care, as parents have a genetic interest in their children's survival. The mutual care of spouses for each other provides a more selfless model of care – though in this case, of course, the model offered would be to the broader society rather than to children in the family.

West's larger argument is that liberals should not emphasize freedom to contract and individual rights over the communitarian and communal nature of marriage. If we take too individualist a view of it, we ignore the entrenched inequalities of men and women as partners to the marriage contract. The issue of what is required for freedom of contract has been a controversial one for liberals. As we saw in the Chapter 5, Hobbes argued that anyone who entered into a contract could be assumed to consent freely to it – irrespective of whether they were coerced to do so by circumstances (Hobbes, 1962 [1651]. Since Mill, in the nineteenth century, liberals have recognized unequal power relations between different groups in society, and are now much more likely to look at the circumstances of parties to a contract when determining whether or not it is valid. In the case of marriage, the unequal gender expectations attached to men and women lead many feminists to conclude that neither the contract nor the institution is just.

The liberal arguments about the positive role of same-sex marriage discussed so far focus largely on its exemplary function – the way in which it models, for children and others, a more egalitarian partnership. But we can also look more directly at the positive role marriage plays in the lives of spouses themselves. Carlos Ball argues that human beings have certain basic needs that must be satisfied, and capabilities that must be exercised in order for them to lead 'lives that are fully human' (Ball, 2003). Martha Nussbaum makes a similar argument based on human needs, which we discussed in Chapter 2. We might see theories such as these as more detailed explorations of what is required for autonomy. Liberal philosophers such as Rawls and Dworkin justify their principles of justice on the grounds that they ensure that people can live autonomous, freely chosen lives that express their understanding of what is good. Ball's 'moral liberalism' requires the state to identify these basic needs and capabilities, and to ensure that they are met and exercised, in order for people to live autonomous lives. This, he argues, is different to Rawls' neutral liberalism, which, as we have seen, separates the right from the good, and which makes no judgement about what constitutes a good human life. In Rawls' view, principles of justice are those that are reasonably agreed across a diverse range of moral perspectives. As we have seen, he concludes that there is no justification for prescribing what families are legitimate, as long as they effectively nurture citizens. Ball thinks, however, that a stronger case for same-sex marriage can be made on the grounds that marriage is required for people to fulfil their needs and capacities for love, intimacy and mutual care – needs and capacities that are the same for gays and lesbians as they are for heterosexual people (Ball, 2003).

Any of these related liberal justifications for same-sex marriage, whether based on rights or the role played by marriage, might bring defenders into conflict with the views of more traditional and conservative minority cultures. There is no more consistency on this controversial issue among the plurality of cultures in any society than there is within the dominant culture itself. As we saw in Chapter 3, liberal multiculturalists argue that cultural rights should be recognized because of the role cultures play in guaranteeing the autonomy of individual members, and the rights of cultures must always be subordinate to basic individual rights and freedoms. Minority cultural opposition to gay and lesbian rights – including same-sex marriage rights – should thus not be permitted to prevail over the individual rights of gays and lesbians. A liberal defence of minority cultural rights would not mean a rejection of the rights of gays and lesbians to marry.

We should note, finally, that all the liberal arguments canvassed above in favour of same-sex marriage are also consistent with supporting civil unions, or other state-recognized relationships that carry the same rights and benefits as marriage. The point of marriage is to support long-term committed and caring relationships between people with equal standing, and civil unions or partnerships carry out that same role. But there is no liberal argument for restricting the term 'marriage' to heterosexual couples, and liberals who support civil unions tend to see these pragmatically as a short-term policy solution until such time as public support has accumulated for same-sex marriage (Eskridge, 2002). The strongest argument along these lines is made by the consequentialist theorist Posner, who concludes that, although same-sex marriage would have overall positive consequences, because there is insufficient public support for extending actual marriage to same-sex couples, civil unions should be adopted instead (Posner, 1997).

Communal values and moral argument

Where liberals see marriage and family as institutions that help to develop a disposition towards justice, communitarians go further and emphasize the moral commitments to the common good that are developed in the family. Underlying this argument is their broader claim that what is 'right' cannot be separated from what is 'good' in political discourse, and that controversial political questions, such as that of same-sex marriage, cannot be settled politically without considering moral arguments. This is clearly distinct from Rawls' neutral liberalism – according to which, political principles should be drawn from what is commonly held in an overlapping consensus between moral views. Michael Sandel, who represents one strand of communitarian thinking, argues that the government cannot remain neutral between various 'competing conceptions of the good'. Our conceptions of the good inevitably shape our 'thin' political principles. Moral discourse, Sandel argues, plays an important role in political debate (Sandel, 1996).

Same-sex marriage should, thus, be defended not on the grounds of individual choice or equal rights but, rather, 'in the name of the intrinsic value or social importance of the practice it protects' (Sandel, 2005: 126). We might invoke at this point all the commonly agreed benefits of marriage: security, stability, and mutual care – goods that can benefit gay and lesbian as well as heterosexual couples. In the civic republican tradition, on which communitarians draw, which was very influential on the founders of the United States, marriage plays an important political role as well. As the fundamental social unit of the republic, it binds citizens together by mutual affection, modelling the egalitarian and mutual relations that citizens were to have with one another.

As do West and Ball, Sandel points out that to defend same-sex marriage on the grounds of state neutrality towards private goods leaves prejudices and negative attitudes towards homosexuality unaddressed. This issue arose in the 2003 US Supreme Court case *Lawrence* v. *Texas*, in which the Supreme Court struck down a law criminalizing homosexuality in Texas. Reversing an earlier case, the Supreme Court decided that intimate sexual conduct was protected by due process under the Fourteenth Amendment to the Constitution, but the majority also cited the positive benefits that flow from homosexual relationships. As Sandel points out, Justice Scalia's dissenting opinion in that case pointed out that, once the Court rejected moral disapproval of homosexual behaviour as a legitimate ground for criminal sanction, it would be difficult to justify the prohibition against same-sex marriage (Sandel, 2005: 143).

If we accept that same-sex marriage must be defended by moral arguments about the good that it accomplishes, it also becomes possible to argue that it should be prohibited as 'immoral'. It is for this reason that some liberals prefer to defend their case using rights or, as does Ball, human needs and capacities. Conservative communitarian arguments are sometimes made against same-sex marriage, on the grounds that it offends popular morality. Perhaps the strongest case along these lines was made by Lord Devlin, a British High Court judge and legal theorist, in response to the Wolfenden Report of 1957. This was the report of a British government appointed committee commissioned to investigate the law on homosexuality and pros-titution (see Chapter 5, p. 93). It recommended the decriminalization of homosexuality on the grounds that the law should not intervene in the private lives of citizens, or attempt to enforce particular moral views about private conduct. Devlin argued that society was acting to protect itself and its children, so that it could be reproduced in the same form over time. His argu-ment is vulnerable to the same criticism made of multiculturalists discussed in Chapter 3: that it assumes that cultures are not internally contested, and are constantly developing and changing. This is one of the responses made to Devlin by the liberal philosopher H.L.A. Hart, who pointed out that if 'soci-ety' included a complex of moral views, these were constantly changing and therefore could not be protected. If, on the other hand, one took what he called a more 'conventional' view of society, assuming a common moral code, there was no evidence that a practice commonly regarded as immoral or disgusting could be seen to threaten it (Hart, 1963).

Conservative opposition

Conservative opposition to same-sex marriage also reflects different philo-sophical perspectives. Conservatism itself is a difficult political term to define, as it encompasses different positions in various real-world political debates. Libertarians, who are opposed to state regulation, are often referred to in political debate as conservative. Same-sex marriage involves deeply held convictions about sexual morality and, unsurprisingly, elicits a range of strong conservative responses. Some religious conservatives, such as Finnis, oppose same-sex marriage on the grounds that it is inherently immoral and contrary to natural law (Finnis, 1980). As we saw in Chapter 5, natural law theorists believe that God's laws for the universe and for human society are made known to human beings through their reason, and are expressed in human nature. Reasoning properly, as well as following their natural moral instincts, people will follow what is good, and perfect their natural inclinations. The new natural law theorists claim that homo-sexuality is contrary to natural law, and opposed by human instinct and reason, except where these have become corrupted. They argue that tradi-tional marriage (required for the legitimate expression of heterosexuality) is a natural and divinely ordered institution, with the purpose of procreation, which results in 'one flesh' – a kind of mystical union between the sexes. Homosexual sex, by contrast, is claimed to be non-procreative, selfish and contrary to nature's purposes. It prevents gay and lesbian people from participating fully in human community. While most natural law theorists do not argue for the criminalization of homosexuality, they strongly oppose same-sex marriage.

Liberals of all varieties would respond that, in a pluralist society such as our own, it is no longer possible to appeal to a single shared moral code based on religious doctrine. We see this fundamental idea expressed, for example, in Rawls' argument that political principles must be supported by a consensus among a range of different moral viewpoints. In the light of this, the conservative philosopher Roger Scruton makes a parallel case that aims to avoid the religious basis of natural law, and to rely on nature itself – on what he sees to be the innate differences between the two sexes. Heterosexual intimacy forces people to confront difference or otherness, while homosexuality is narcissistic (Scruton, 1986).

Many conservatives concentrate their arguments instead on the alleged negative consequences of same-sex marriage – for heterosexual marriage and for children. Conservatives claim that same-sex marriage weakens the special nature of marriage, and diminishes the strong commitment it requires (George, 2003). It suggests that non-procreative sexual expression has the same social value as procreative sex. Thus, it offers a damaging lesson to children in general, and perverts the natural development of children raised by gay and lesbian families. Critics have responded to this that, if we accept the argument that procreative sex should be privileged and protected over recreational sex, we should disallow contraception and marriages between infertile or older people (Macedo, 2003).

These arguments follow from the particular and special character and role ascribed to traditional marriage. But some conservative arguments focus less on the substantive role nature of traditional marriage, and more on its importance as a long-standing institution. Some conservatives allow that, while unions between gay and lesbian people should entitle them to the same legal rights, privileges and protections as marriage, their recognized relationships should not be marriages as such, simply on the grounds that the historical nature of marriage as an institution should not be radically changed. This argument is sometimes made by gays and lesbians themselves, who see marriage as a potentially oppressive institution. We discuss this position in greater detail later in this chapter. However, it also reflects a conservative scepticism about change – particularly about large-scale change to institutions made in the name of political principles or ideals. Conservatives often argue that the beliefs and institutions that exist might be presumed to be of value because they might be long-standing, and have stood the 'test of time'. This position was set out as a fundamental principle by the eighteenth-century British political theorist and politician Edmund Burke, who used it to help justify his opposition to the French Revolution (Burke, 1955 [1790]). Following Burke, later conservatives have argued that institutions are valuable because of the stability they afford to human lives, and that they should not be challenged in the name of abstract ideas about justice.

With respect to same-sex marriage, some conservatives point to the controversial nature of the issue, uncertainty as to the consequences of legal change, and the need to reform slowly and cautiously (Rauch, 2004). John Witte Jr sets out this position:

> For nearly two thousand years, the Western legal tradition reserved the legal category marriage to monogamous, heterosexual couples who had reached the age of consent, who had the physical capacity to join together in one flesh, and whose joining served the goods and goals of procreation, companionship and stability at once ... In the face of such a long and venerable tradition, we would be wise to exercise some humility before declaring our current arguments ineluctable and some patience before rushing to radical legal change. (Witte, 2003: 45)

Radical opposition to marriage

There are some gay and lesbian theorists who feel that marriage is such a patriarchal and inegalitarian institution that it cannot be reformed and revised to accommodate same-sex relationships. This position reflects the more radical feminist critique of marriage. These theorists argue that emphasizing marriage as a political issue is locking gay and lesbian people into conforming to traditional institutions that have historically been hostile to them (Card, 1996; Warner, 1999). Marriage, as an institution, depends on conventional understandings of gender, and privileges monogamous relationships (the very reason that liberal and communitarian supporters of the family advocate extending it to gay and lesbian couples). According to this argument, the demand for gay marriage is crushing the potential of gay and lesbian relationships to achieve greater freedom for those in them and to present a fundamental challenge to the social order.

Other lesbian and gay critics have challenged this, arguing that same-sex marriage will not only give gays and lesbians the right to participate in a traditional institution but, rather, will change the definition of what counts as a family (Calhoun, 2000). They cite research that suggests that lesbian and gay relationships are more egalitarian and less based on traditional roles than heterosexual marriage (Ball, 2003). They maintain that the institution can be reformed from the inside, and does not necessarily reflect patriarchal roles and attitudes.

Finally, we also find scepticism about marriage, and the degree to which it can be reformed, in the Marxist socialist critique. Socialists have contended that the traditional family unit underpins capitalism – an argument first made, as we saw in Chapter 5, by Marx's collaborator Engels in his *The Origin of the Family, Private Property and the State* (Engels, 1948

[1884]). Engels argued that monogamy developed not to express the romantic love between individuals, but to cement what he referred to as the victory of private property over original, naturally developed common ownership. Marriage appears as the subjection of one sex by another and, historically, has existed side by side with prostitution. Engels predicted, in 1871, a social revolution in which the economic foundations of monogamy would disap-

---

Box 6.2 Same-sex marriage: competing norms and values

The key norm shared by both sides in the debate over same-sex marriage is equality. Supporters also invoke justice – and opponents, the common good – to support their arguments:

• **Equality**

Supporters of same-sex marriage argue that gay and lesbian couples should be treated equally to heterosexuals. Like should be treated equally with like, and long-term and committed homosexual relationships are no different to long-term and committed heterosexual unions. There is no principled ground for civil unions rather than same-sex marriage: supporters accept civil unions as a compromise, recognizing the historical association of marriage with different-sex couples.

　Opponents maintain that the gender of parties to a couple does make a significant difference, and that same-sex couples should not be treated in the same way as those of different sexes.

• **Justice**

Supporters maintain that justice requires that the state does not discriminate against gays and lesbians, and confers the same rights on them as it does heterosexual couples.

　Opponents counter that justice cannot require the recognition of relationships that are contrary to the common good.

• **The common good**

Supporters argue that allowing same-sex marriage will encourage more gay and lesbian couples to commit to exclusive long-term relationships – thus strengthening social stability.

　Opponents insist that homosexuality is destructive to traditional morality and to the institution of the family. While most accept that it should be tolerated as private behaviour, they argue that to recognize homosexual relationships officially will damage the common good.

pear, as the individual family ceased to be the economic basis of society (Engels, 1948 [1884]). Marx himself argued that simply allowing more people to have access to bourgeois liberal rights – we might include the right to marry at this point – would not bring about equality or freedom. In *On the Jewish Question*, Marx distinguishes 'political' emancipation from 'human' emancipation (Marx, 1978 [1843]). The former would be achieved by granting equal political rights to all. But political rights, Marx argued, were premised on the idea that people were in competition with one another, and required protection for themselves and their property, both from each other and from the state. Human emancipation allowed all to live together as full members of a community, sharing resources based on need. Although Marx does not refer specifically to marriage, we can conclude that relationships designed to protect exclusivity and private property would be incompatible with human emancipation. We should, however, note that, despite their critique of traditional marriage, Marx and Engels were not sympathetic to homosexuality. While Marx did not write explicitly on the subject, he was critical of fellow socialists who were homosexual. Engels condemned 'the abominable practice of sodomy' in ancient Greece (Engels, 1948 [1884]).

Conclusion

The debate over same-sex marriage in countries that have not yet passed legislation is unlikely to diminish. As more and more states pass legislation allowing either for marriage or for parallel institutions such as civil unions, gay and lesbian groups elsewhere can argue that – at least, in western democracies – recognizing same-sex unions has become an established norm. Those governments who have refused to introduce changes have pointed to the relative unpopularity of same-sex marriage with their voters. In fact, popular opposition to same-sex marriage is slowly declining in western countries, while support for civil unions is rising. In the United States, for example, a Pew Research Center independent poll in 2006 found that 35 per cent of respondents favoured same-sex marriage, while 54 per cent favoured recognized civil unions. This figure had risen from 45 per cent three years earlier. Moreover, there is evidence of a generational change of attitude. The same poll found that 53 per cent of adults under 30 supported the legalization of same-sex marriage – a result replicated in other surveys. In Australia, where federal law recognizes neither same-sex marriages nor civil unions, an independent poll in 2007 found that 57 per cent of people favoured same-sex marriage, while 71 per cent supported civil unions.

Most western countries are likely to adopt legislation allowing civil unions, because these tend to be favoured in public opinion over marriage. This strategy allows governments to avoid conservative opposition to radical institutional change. But it also reflects the declining popularity of marriage itself in many western countries. In 2005, the marriage rate had declined in the United States by 50 per cent since 1970, while, in Britain, the marriage rate in 2005 was at the lowest level since records were first kept in 1862. As the private and social goods that flow from marriage become increasingly associated with other forms of exclusive intimate relationships, conservative arguments about the special status of heterosexual marriage are likely to be less relevant to gay and lesbian claims for state recognition and support.

Chapter 7

Should the State Prohibit Abortion and Euthanasia?

Abortion and euthanasia are not only deeply divisive political issues in many countries; they are, as Ronald Dworkin writes, the great moral issues that bracket life in earnest (Dworkin, 1993). The questions of when life begins, and when it may end, appeal to our moral convictions, our religious and spiritual beliefs, and our cultural traditions. They also require us to think about what the role of government should be in deciding and imposing answers to moral questions. Philosophical arguments about both abortion and euthanasia range across all these issues: our focus is on the political dimensions of these issues, although, as we shall see, it is not possible to separate them completely from moral arguments

The issues we will consider include:

- The role of the state in imposing policy where there is moral disagreement.
- The ways in which individual rights justify various arguments for and against both abortion and euthanasia.
- The tension between individual rights and communal obligations.
- The implications of gender difference and inequality.

Many of these problems arise in both abortion and euthanasia, and in both cases the role of physicians is an important aspect of the debate. However, there are also crucial differences: abortion as an action or procedure is performed on, or done to, the pregnant woman and the foetus – as one side in this controversy claims, to two living beings. Euthanasia, however, is an action performed on, or done only to, the patient. This has important consequences for the kinds of arguments made in each case. In addition, feminist arguments play a key role in the abortion issue, while they are not central (although, as we shall see, they have been made) in the case of euthanasia. For these reasons, we will consider these issues separately. We begin with abortion, comparing some of the legal approaches countries have taken to this issue.

Abortion law

It was only in the nineteenth century that many western countries began to regulate abortion by statute. Before then, laws had reflected a complex and changing range of religious attitudes and concerns about the broader social good. In the ancient world, the practice was prohibited by the doctors' Hippocratic Oath, but the Athenian philosophers Plato and Aristotle both argued that it was sometimes justified in the interests of the common good. Plato advocated abortion for what we would now see as eugenic reasons, when the parents were considered too old for childbearing (Plato, 1981 [Third century BCE]). Aristotle, who argued that the soul entered human foetuses only at 40 days after conception, or 90 in the case of girls, viewed abortion before this stage as an acceptable method of limiting the size of families and populations (Aristotle, 1981 [Third century BCE]). Neither philosopher was concerned with the individual rights of either the pregnant woman or the foetus.

Early Christian theologians focused on the morality of the act itself, rather than its social consequences, and gradually adopted the view that abortion after 'ensoulment' – when the soul was thought to enter the foetus's body – was murder. This position was set out by the medieval Christian philosopher St Thomas Aquinas (Aquinas, 1952 [written 1265–74]), and is a view still very influential on Christian thinking today. The Catholic Church continued to make a distinction between abortions performed before and after ensoulment, usually set at 40, 80 or 116 days of gestation, and coinciding with 'quickening' – when the pregnant woman senses the movement of the foetus. Before the nineteenth century, the Church's position was that abortions before quickening destroyed only potential human life and, thus, were a sin – but not such a serious one as to justify excommunication. It was only in 1869 that Pope Pius IX forbade all abortions without exception.

Laws in most countries reflected the distinction between before and after quickening, penalizing only later abortions, until the nineteenth century. From this period on, most western countries enacted laws to prohibit abortion at any stage, unless required to save the life of the pregnant woman. By this point, arguments appealing to the rights and concerns of women were a key factor in the debate. The tightening up of laws was promoted not only by religious conservatives, but also by social reformers concerned about threats to women's health posed by the procedure, which, because of its social stigma, was more likely to be performed in unsanitary conditions by untrained and exploitative practitioners. This meant that doctors supported regulation, as it enabled them to gain control over abortion. But several prominent nineteenth-century feminists also opposed the practice on the grounds of women's health, and because they believed that it made women more vulnerable to what was perceived as aggressive male sexuality. The early feminist Mary Wollstonecraft blamed abortion on the fact that men had socialized women to be weak and irresponsible (Wollstonecraft, 1995 [1792]).

It was also an alliance of social reformers and medical professionals that helped to liberalize abortion law in most western countries from the 1960s. Today, abortion is most strictly regulated in a few countries where the influence of the Catholic Church is strong; it is prohibited without any exceptions in Vatican City, Malta, Nicaragua, Chile and El Salvador. African, Asian and Latin American countries tend to have stricter provisions about abortion, some restricting it to cases where the mother's life is in danger. Canada is exceptional in that it has no laws concerning abortion – only regulations imposed by the provinces on how, where and by whom the procedure is performed. Most European countries allow it more freely in the early stages or first trimester (three months) of pregnancy, although some countries impose restrictions, such as medical certification concerning the likely dangers of the pregnancy, counselling and waiting periods. Most European countries are far less permissive when it comes to later abortions. In France, for example, abortions are permitted until the tenth week of pregnancy, with counselling and an enforced waiting period; after this point abortion is illegal unless it is to protect the health of the mother or when the foetus is severely deformed.

Britain's legislation is more liberal in that it does not have a first trimester cut-off date for legal abortion, but less liberal in that health reasons must be given to justify the procedure. The Abortion Act of 1967 made abortion legal in most cases of pregnancy of fewer than 28 weeks, as long as two physicians certified that the pregnancy posed a risk to the life or physical or mental health of the woman or her family greater than the risk of terminating it. Past this date, abortion was permitted only to prevent serious permanent injury to the mother's mental or physical health, to save the mother's life, or where the foetus was likely to be severely physically or mentally handicapped. This was later amended to 24 weeks, and there have recently been calls for the limit to be lowered to 20 weeks, particularly since advances in medical techniques have reduced the age at which babies might survive premature birth. In Britain, as in other western countries where a danger to physical or mental health must be shown to justify abortion, these grounds tend to be interpreted broadly, so that abortion is freely available. Recent surveys show that approximately 75 per cent of Britons support a woman's right to an abortion in all or most cases. Abortion is not permitted, however, to select the sex of a child (see Box 7.1).

Because abortion raises issues of women's rights, sexual equality, the protection of life and the role of religion in public life, it has been almost universally controversial. But in no country has it been so divisive and, at times, violent as the United States. Until the 1970s, the practice was regulated independently by each state, nearly all of which prohibited abortion, although some granted exceptions for pregnancies caused by rape and incest, those that threatened the life of the mother, and cases where the foetus

Box 7.1 Abortion and sex selection

The entrenched divide between pro-choice and pro-life groups falters on the issue of abortion to select the sex of a child. In some cases, this is done to select female embryos, which will not be affected by serious genetic disorders carried on the male Y chromosome. But, in many countries, the practice reflects cultural norms that value male, rather than female, children. Abortion for sex selection is practised in many developing countries, but is particularly common in China, India and South Korea, where it has contributed to an imbalance in the sexes: more boys are born than girls. Ultrasound and abortion for sex selection are illegal in China and India, although these laws are not strongly enforced. Abortion for reasons of sex alone (without medical grounds) has also become an issue involving South and East Asian communities in the United Kingdom (where it is banned), the United States and Canada.

Opponents of abortion rights reject all abortions, including those undertaken for the purpose of sex selection. But the position is more complex when it comes to supporters:

- Strong liberal and feminist supporters of abortion rights argue that women's rights to control their own bodies, and to decide whether or not to support and nurture a developing foetus, must outweigh moral concerns about any particular reason to have an abortion. While feminists see sex-selective abortion as evidence of gender inequality, the individual freedom and autonomy of pregnant women are the most important concerns. However, it might be particularly important to ensure that the decision to abort is freely made by the woman herself in sex-selection cases, and is not imposed by male family or cultural authorities.
- Sex-selective abortion poses more of a challenge for arguments that offer a more limited defence of abortion, on the grounds that the value of a pregnant woman's life is greater than the sanctity of developing human life. If the state has a legitimate interest in ensuring that decisions about life and death are treated as morally serious, we might argue that a preference for one sex over another is not morally serious – is, in fact, morally indefensible – and might not serve as a ground for abortion.
- Sex-selective abortion is most problematic from the critical perspective on sexual inequality and abortion. We might argue that the practice reveals the ways in which abortion rights are necessitated by, and reinforce a system of, gender inequality. The continued subordination of women as a group is maintained, ironically, by invoking the rights of individual women 'to choose'.
- As this practice is most prevalent in western countries within cultural minorities, it raises some of the issues concerning cultural rights and gender equality that we discussed in Chapter 3. Those who argue that gender equality takes precedence over cultural norms are likely to support banning sex-selective abortions while on the other hand they might conclude that a woman's right to self-determination must ultimately guarantee her right to an abortion.

suffered a serious abnormality. In 1973, however, the landmark Supreme Court case *Roe* v. *Wade* established that no legislation could prevent abortion in the first trimester of pregnancy. Regulation was permitted in later stages, and abortion could be prohibited in the last trimester. The Supreme Court held that the Fourteenth Amendment to the United States Constitution, guaranteeing that no one be deprived of life or liberty without due process, implied a natural right to privacy. The Court held that this right, although not enumerated in the Constitution, had been established by earlier decisions, and protected a woman's right to terminate a pregnancy until the foetus had developed to the point at which the state had an interest in protecting it as human life. This point was fixed at the beginning of the third trimester, by which time the foetus was viable (it could live outside its mother's uterus). After this point, abortions could be banned by the states, except when necessary to preserve the health or life of the mother. The Court declined to rule on when after conception human life began, but concluded that the foetus was not at any point a person with rights.

The subsequent Supreme Court decision in *Planned Parenthood* v. *Casey* in 1992 affirmed *Roe* v. *Wade*, but replaced the trimester scheme with the point of viability. This, and later cases, have also legitimated various restrictions imposed by state legislation on the right to choose abortion before foetal viability, including requiring counselling, a waiting period, and parental notification for minors. In 2003, President Bush signed into a law the Partial Birth Abortion Ban Act, which prohibits a particular procedure used sometimes in late pregnancy. In 2007, the Supreme Court determined in *Gonzales* v. *Carhart* that the Act did not impose an undue burden on a woman's Constitutional right to an abortion. But, in general, abortion is more easily available at a later stage in pregnancy in the United States than it is in Europe.

Since *Roe* v. *Wade*, the pro-choice (in favour of abortion rights) and pro-life (opposed to legal abortion) groups in the United States have waged a fierce battle over this issue. During the 1980s and 1990s, extremist pro-life groups picketed and attacked abortion clinics, in some cases killing medical staff. Access to abortion has become the single biggest defining and mobilizing issue for American feminists, and Congressional and Presidential candidates are assessed in terms of their attitude to *Roe* v. *Wade*, and their views on whether Supreme Court justices should be chosen on the basis of their support of or commitment to overturning the decision. It is no coincidence that, uniquely in the United States, the debate has centred on the role of the Supreme Court and its interpretation of the Constitution. In most other countries, the focus of the abortion issue is on legislation. Even some commentators who support legalized abortion have been critical of the way in which policy in the United States has been imposed by the judiciary rather than being subject to democratic deliberation and debate, and many critics have suggested that this is the reason for the particularly polarizing nature of the controversy in the United States (Glendon, 1987). Americans themselves are divided on the issue of abortion: poll results differ considerably depending on how the question is asked, but most results show that the majority of people support the right to abortion in the first trimester, although they approve of regulations such as waiting periods. Support for the right to abortion diminishes as pregnancy advances beyond the first trimester.

Morality and politics

Contemporary debates about abortion centre on the conflict between the duty of the state to protect human life and people, on the one hand, and the rights of women to make decisions about their own bodies and lives, on the other. The issues involved here are clearly moral, religious and biological, as well as political. Political philosophy cannot solve the problem of where life begins, or what the status of human life is before birth. But it can help us to think about implications of the fact that considerable disagreement exists over whether or not the foetus is a person, or a form of human life, and, if it is, over how to balance any rights it might have with those of the pregnant woman. Moreover, we might argue that, even if abortion is considered to be immoral, there is an important distinction between holding this and concluding that it should be illegal. As we shall see, this distinction appears also in the debate over euthanasia. Naturally, those who oppose abortion argue that it is immoral and must also be prohibited. We will consider these arguments first. In public debate, this case is made by political conservatives; the prochoice position is associated with liberals. But the fundamental claim of antiabortion philosophers is *ontological*: it is based on what the foetus actually *is* as a living being. Ontological questions form part of many political debates, but they do not necessarily imply any particular political agenda. (For example, the ontology of communitarianism sees human beings as embedded in, and constructed by, a network of social relations, rather than separate or atomistic individuals, but communitarian political philosophers can take conservative or radical political positions.) Much of the debate around abortion focuses on the ontological status of the foetus, although, as we shall see, some supporters of abortion rights concede the argument that the foetus is a person, defending the practice on other grounds.

The foetus as a person and the case against abortion

The strongest argument against abortion is made on ontological and moral grounds. It is the position of the Roman Catholic Church, the Anglican

Church and most evangelical protestant groups, as well as some philosophers and scientists without religious affiliation, that the foetus is a human person, with the same fundamental right to life as human beings who have been born. The foetus is not just a potential person or a form of human life but, rather, a human person. Once this has been established, opponents of abortion conclude that it cannot be permitted, either at all or with few exceptions, as it involves the taking of an innocent person's life. The most commonly advanced natural law argument advanced is that on conception, a human being comes to exist, with both its own soul and its distinct genetic identity (Lee and George, 2005). It is this individual soul and, in secular terms, this unique genetic identity that defines a human being, rather than, for example, being independent, or autonomous, or visible, or a member of any social community (Noonan, 1970). Other philosophers have emphasized different aspects of the foetus that, in their view, identify it as a person. Catholic philosopher Germain Grisez acknowledges the power of arguments based on community membership when he maintains that it is membership in the human species that defines a human person (Grisez, 1970). The secular claim proposed by Don Marquis is that foetuses are human persons because they have futures in the same way that we do (Marquis, 1989).

All these theorists share in common the belief that, while foetuses are not capable of all the specific rights that children and adults possess (just as children are not entitled to all the rights of adults), they have a right to life in virtue of what they are (Lee and George, 2005). This takes precedence over other claims, including that of the pregnant woman to rights over her own body, as these rights do not allow her to damage innocent others. Some who hold this position take the view that abortion to save a woman's life may be permitted as the killing is in self-defence, although others counter that even in this case abortion is unjustified, as the foetus does not intend to harm the woman. Once the pro-life case has been made, that abortion is immoral because it involves killing an innocent person, it follows that it must be illegal: since Hobbes' defence of state power in the seventeenth century, the fundamental role of the modern state has been understood to be protecting the physical security of its members (Hobbes, 1962 [1651]).

Self-ownership and bodily rights

Even if the foetus has the moral status of a person, we can make a libertarian defence of abortion rights, on the grounds of a pregnant woman's rights over her body. This is in fact one of the strongest feminist arguments in favour of abortion rights, as I discuss on page 137. The more general case for self-ownership is made by Robert Nozick, who argues that our most fundamental property is in our own bodies; that we have rights over our bodies and rights to use them to exercise our capacities for self-realization (Nozick, 1974). No one has the right to use another's body against their will (Rothbard, 1998). This invokes a commonly held fundamental premise of all liberalism: the Kantian principle that individuals cannot be used as the means to others' ends (Kant, 1993 [1785]). Even if a foetus is a person, a pregnant woman is not obliged to nurture or support it within her own body. This position justifies abortion before viability – although, after that point, we might conclude that the foetus, once expelled from the woman's body, would have to be sustained alive.

Distinguishing human life from personhood

Several philosophers who defend abortion rights have made the ontological case that, while the foetus is undoubtedly living, and is entitled to respect, it is not a human person with rights. As they point out, this accords with our intuitive sense of things: we do not treat foetuses, especially early on in pregnancy, in the same way as babies – an early miscarriage is not mourned in the same way as the death of a child. On the other hand, abortion seems to be importantly different from, for instance, the surgical removal of a tumour. Some rely on the distinction between human life and full personhood to distinguish early and late abortions. Jane English argues that there is no single definition of the person, and no group of agreed necessary and sufficient characteristics for personhood. 'Person' is a cluster of features – some biological, some psychological, some rational, some social, some legal (English, 1974). These characteristics develop at different rates – not all are present at birth, and a later foetus exhibits more of them than does an early-stage foetus. The conservative legal philosopher Mary Ann Glendon describes with approval the legal approach taken in most European countries, where the gravity of abortion is expressly recognized in legislation, and abortion rights are generally freely accorded in the early stages of pregnancy but restricted shortly after the first trimester. This reflects, she argues, a commitment to the sanctity of developing human life, and acknowledges that, while it may be acceptable to terminate a pregnancy in the early stages, as the foetus develops it must be accorded respect similar to that accorded a person (Glendon, 1987).

Utilitarian philosopher Peter Singer builds his case for abortion rights by arguing that the foetus is a member of the human species, but is not a person. Utilitarians argue that the policy and legislation should promote the greatest welfare of individual persons; consequently, if the foetus counts as a person, abortion in most cases (excepting those where there is grave foetal abnormality) cannot be justified. Singer defines sentience as an essential aspect of being a person – a definition that excludes foetuses (Singer, 1993). On the other hand, once the foetus has developed to the neurological point of being able to feel pain, abortion methods that are excessively painful to it cannot be justified. Singer has made the controversial argument that newborn babies also do not have the same full rights as older children and adults – a case also made by Michael Tooley, who argues similarly that the foetus is a member of the human species, but not a human person. A human person, Tooley claims, must have a concept of the self as the subject of experiences over time – a capacity not reached until an infant is a few months old (Tooley, 1972).

Mary Ann Warren defends abortion, but counters these claims about infanticide by emphasizing not only the developmental character of a foetus or newborn, but also the way in which it is viewed by others. Birth is the point at which human beings cease to be completely dependent on the body of the mother, and become members of the human community, able to be cared for as a 'known and socially responsive individual'. Before birth, and particularly before sentience, the foetus is entitled to only modest moral status, which can be overridden by the moral claims of the pregnant woman. Its moral status increases with development: the more advanced in development it is, the more likely it is to be sentient, and the more it invokes feelings of recognition and mutual responsibility in us, other members of its community (Warren, 1997).

Dworkin attempts to use this distinction between human life as a broad category and an individual person with rights and interests to find common ground between the pro-choice and pro-life camps (Dworkin, 1993). Dworkin describes two different kinds of objection to abortion:

1 Foetuses have the same rights and interests as other human beings – including the right not to be killed. This is what he calls the *derivative objection*, because it derives from the rights and interests that all human beings, including foetuses, are alleged to have as persons.
2 The foetus is human life, and thus shares in the intrinsic, innate and sacred character of all human life – although it is not a person with the same rights and interests as children and adults. This is the *detached objection*, because, unlike the derivative objection, it does not depend on rights and interests of the foetus as a person.

It is the detached objection, Dworkin argues, that really underlies most pro-life arguments. Once this is understood, we see that opponents and supporters of abortion rights can agree on the crucial claims that, generally, human life deserves respect and, specifically, that the foetus is a form of human life deserving of respect. Both sides accept that something – although not an individual person with rights and interests – is alive at the point of abortion and can be destroyed, and that it is a pity that it is destroyed. Where they differ is how they strike the balance between the respect due to the foetus, and that due to the pregnant woman, and other members of the family affected by the pregnancy. This detached objection seems to explain the fact that opinion polls in the United States regularly report that majorities of Americans surveyed think that abortion is taking human life, but majorities also favour limited rights to abortion.

As Dworkin suggests, it is also possible to make pro-choice arguments that appeal to the value of human life – arguments that emphasize the value of the life of the pregnant woman, and of the lives of other children in the family, when weighed against that of the early foetus. Some feminists, as we shall see, emphasize these arguments rather than arguing, against the derivative view, that the foetus is not a person with interests and rights. Interesting evidence in support of this is provided by one of the best-known accounts of the reasoning of a group of pregnant women who were considering abortions. In the 1970s, after the *Roe* v. *Wade* decision, feminist psychologist Carol Gilligan interviewed a group of pregnant women who were considering having abortions (most went on to do so). She found that when they talked about what they should do, they did not refer to rights that they or their foetus might have; rather, they emphasized their concerns about what kind of life and prospects they could provide for a child, the importance of caring for others in their families and their responsibilities to make something of their own lives (Gilligan, 1982).

Understanding the foetus as human life, but not a human person, allows us to accept the value of life but still defend the right to abortion in some, if not all, cases. The life of the foetus must be balanced against that of the mother, and of others who will be affected by the birth of the child. The state can recognize that the sanctity of life is contestable, and leave people to make their own decisions about protecting it in the early stages of pregnancy, and about balancing the protection of foetal life with the quality of life of the mother and other family members. As the foetus develops, its life becomes more worthy of protection. As this suggests, Dworkin thinks that the approach of *Roe* v. *Wade*, distinguishing the right to abortion in early pregnancy from later stages of pregnancy, is appropriate. But restrictions and regulations on abortion, if designed to make pregnant women aware of the sanctity of life, can also be defended. As Dworkin puts it, the state has 'a legitimate interest in maintaining a moral environment in which decisions about life and death are taken seriously and treated as matters of moral gravity' (Dworkin, 1993: 168). Restrictions, such as those considered in the 1992 Casey Supreme Court decision in the United States, must be judged by whether they conform to this requirement, or if they impose an undue burden on women's rights.

Women's rights and the feminist defence of abortion

Much of the philosophical debate about abortion focuses on the status and claims of the foetus, rather than its essential and intimate relationship with the body of the pregnant woman. What feminists remind us is that the foetus uniquely exists inside the body of another human being, drawing all its sustenance from her body without her express consent or, even, possibly, her intent. Many of the arguments about abortion (including some made by feminists) proceed by analogies – between the foetus and a baby or an animal, between pregnancy and temporary illness, between killing someone in self-defence and abortion. The fact is that pregnancy is a unique condition, posing particular difficulties for western philosophy, which holds as a fundamental assumption that human beings are physically separate and distinct. This assumption is deeply related to our beliefs about individuality and autonomy. Feminist arguments take a range of approaches to dealing with the bodily reality of pregnancy, and the need to balance the obligations we owe to a foetus against the rights and interests of pregnant women. As we shall see, feminists build on both the libertarian and liberal arguments we have discussed above.

The strongest (and most libertarian) feminist argument asserts that women have a right to full and equal personhood, which includes the right to control their own bodies and maintain their bodily integrity (Cornell, 1995). Whatever the ontological status of the foetus, and whatever its point of development, it cannot take precedence over this right. Other feminist philosophers emphasize the claim that the foetus is a form of human life, but not a human person with rights. More specifically, it is a form of life that cannot be seen as separate from and independent of the woman's body. As Margaret Little points out, the pregnant woman's body is not just housing for the foetus – it physically makes it what it will become (Little, 2005: 28). The foetus does not simply grow in the uterus – it must develop, and that development requires the active contribution of its mother's body. While the foetus is indeed a potential human being, its ability to reach its potential depends crucially not only on a passive environment, but also on the actions of the woman as an autonomous agent. The foetus makes extremely personal and intimate demands on its mother's body, and both pregnancy and motherhood create enormous obligations and fundamentally change personal identity. Are women obliged to provide what Little calls 'gestational assistance' to the foetus and to take on these obligations? Little concludes that, while the early foetus has value as human life in progress, it does not have the same value as the person who must work to ensure that such progress occurs. Abortion is not a decision to destroy but, rather, not to create – to withdraw physical support from a life that would not have existed without the woman's physical support in the first place (Little, 2005). By the same argument, a more advanced foetus later in pregnancy has greater value, and, as the pregnant woman has already made more investment in it, it is less justifiable for her to withdraw gestational support.

Judith Jarvis Thomson also focuses on the physical sacrifices required by pregnancy in her famous and influential analogy about abortion rights (Thomson, 1971). Thomson starts from the position of accepting, purely for argument's sake, that the foetus is a person from the moment of conception, with full rights to life. She argues that, even so, a pregnant woman is no more obliged to use her body to sustain and nurture it than anyone would be to sustain and nurture a stranger dependent on them for life support.

Thomson asks us to imagine a hypothetical situation: you wake up one morning to find yourself in bed attached to a famous, unconscious violinist. He has been found to be suffering from a fatal kidney ailment and needs kidney support, and you alone have the right blood group to help him. You have been kidnapped, and your circulatory system has been plugged in to the violinist. The director of the hospital tells you that they did not know this was being done but, now that it was done, you must accept it. However, this state of affairs will only last nine months. After that, the violinist will have recovered from his illness and can be unplugged from you. Do you have to accept this? As Thomson argues, both our moral intuitions and laws answer 'no'. The violinist undoubtedly has a right to life, but he has no right that you should be forced to use your body to keep him alive.

Thomson's analogy suggests that the pregnant woman did not in any way contribute to her situation – which is clearly the case with rape. But what if the woman voluntarily engaged in sex, with or without contraception (which, after all, she knows may fail)? In Thomson's second analogy, 'people seeds' drift around in the air like pollen; you open a window and one drifts in and takes root in the carpet. You do not want children, so you buy good screens for your windows, but one is defective, and a seed makes its way in. Are you responsible because you should have foreseen that the screen might be defective? But what if you took all reasonable precautions? In this case also, Thomson concludes, nobody is morally required to make the large sacrifices required to keep someone else alive for nine months, and then to nurture and raise them after birth. No country's laws require that we give long stretches of our lives to sustain others. At most, the woman might have the obligations of a 'minimally decent' (as distinct from 'good') Samaritan to carry a pregnancy to term, if it is almost over, and provided she is not sick or seriously discomfited. Of course, this argument does not justify killing a foetus that has reached viability, if it can be removed and survive outside its mother's body.

Care and our duties to others

Many of the objections made to Thomson's analogy rest on her assumption that killing the foetus is the same as withdrawing support from it. From a public political perspective, however, the more interesting responses focus on the duties we owe to others. As we have seen, we can argue for abortion rights on the grounds that weighing up the value of human lives – those of the foetus, the mother and other family members – leads us to conclude that the best way of respecting the value of human life is not to continue with the pregnancy. This recognition of the interrelationship between the pregnant woman, the foetus and others in the family is what is missing in Thomson's argument, according to many critics from both the pro-life and pro-choice sides of the debate. Conservatives and some communitarians argue that her analogy fails to recognize the special relationship between the pregnant woman and her foetus, and the special moral obligations that pregnancy produces. Conservative philosopher Francis Beckwith argues that moral obligations are not necessarily voluntary (Beckwith, 1998). In addition, Thomson's argument, as with others based on women's rights to bodily integrity, does not take into account the sentiments and claims of fathers who wish their foetuses to survive. The survival of families – and of social structure – depends on the fact that familial relationships produce moral obligations in us – particularly to dependents such as children and the elderly. Of course, as we have seen, feminists also make the communitarian argument that obligations and duties to the child that would eventually be born, and to other family members, are what motivate some women to choose abortion. Gilligan's study of pregnant women found that some were concerned about their responsibilities to their existing children, while others without children expressed their concern about the permanent nature of motherhood, and whether or not they could responsibly take on those obligations.

Abortion and sexual inequality

As we saw earlier (p. 128), some nineteenth century feminists opposed abortion on the grounds that its purpose was only to ensure that men would continue to have free sexual access to women, without worrying about consequences. Some contemporary feminists, while not opposing abortion rights, are similarly sceptical about the degree to which they will advance women's equality – viewing abortion as, rather, a symptom of sexual inequality. Adrienne Rich wrote that, in a society in which women voluntarily entered into sexual relationships, with freely available and completely reliable contraception, there would be no abortion issue (Rich, 1986).

Nevertheless, an egalitarian liberal case is often made for abortion rights, on the grounds that requiring women to continue with unwanted and unplanned pregnancies denies them equal status as citizens (Rawls, 1997). Catharine MacKinnon relies on a deeper analysis of sexual inequality in her defence of abortion rights (MacKinnon, 1983). She argues that the approach taken by the United States Supreme Court in *Roe* v. *Wade*, based on the right to privacy, only reinforces women's exploitation and inequality, while appearing to grant them equal rights with men. The alleged constitutional right to privacy emphasizes the idea that there exists a private sphere, distinct from the public, that is immune from state regulation and that is open to the unrestricted exercise of power. Such an idea has been used to exploit women, by ignoring the abuse and exploitation that goes on in private, particularly in the family. MacKinnon maintains that we cannot separate pregnancy from the private sexual relations that cause it. Women do not control the terms of sex. Often, she asserts, they are raped and coerced – and, even if the act itself is voluntary, the system of meanings around sex, and male and female roles in it, are not. If women do not use contraception, that is because to do so appears as though they are taking control of sexuality from men, and acting in an inappropriately unfeminine manner.

By emphasizing privacy, and the limited role of the state, the Supreme Court in *Roe* v. *Wade* left the disposition of power between the sexes as it was. Men's domination of women is undisturbed, while the availability of abortion rights is meant to signal to women their equal autonomy – despite the sexual inequality that produced their unwanted pregnancies in the first place. MacKinnon concludes that abortion rights must be accompanied by a critique of gender inequality. Ironically, her position is similar to that of conservative feminist Mary Ann Glendon (Glendon, 1987). Both offer a critique of the liberal language of rights – MacKinnon from radical feminism, and Glendon from a conservative and communitarian perspective. The latter argues that the privacy doctrine of *Roe* v. *Wade*, and abortion on demand, should be replaced by the more limited availability offered by European states, but that this should be accompanied by a large-scale review of laws that bear on maternity and child-raising. Maternity leave, child care, paternal child support and welfare assistance must be adequate to support women as equals while they are raising children, and should reflect the strong commitment of the state to families.

Dealing with the divide over abortion: pluralism and toleration

As long as opponents of abortion insist that the foetus is a full human person, innocent and possessing rights (making what Dworkin calls the derivative objection), no compromise on the issue seems possible. In fact, forceful resistance to abortion providers appears justified and necessary. We might claim that, given the plurality of views on abortion, the state should not regulate it, but should allow people to make their own decisions about whether or not to choose to abort – in the same way as, for example, the law allows people to decide whether or not to smoke or to drink alcohol. Liberals have adopted this general approach since John Stuart Mill argued, in the nineteenth century, that the state should not intervene to prevent actions that do not affect others (Mill, 1989a [1865]). This position is not satisfactory, of course, for those who insist that the foetus is a human person who must be protected in the same way that a child or adult is protected by the state – neither would it answer the concerns of those who support only limited abortion rights.

Rawls' political liberalism is built on a similar liberal view about the relationship between politics and private morality. Rawls argues that political values – those defining justice and the basic legal and political structure of society – refer to different subjects and problems than do private moral values. Political values must be independent of comprehensive moral views, philosophies or religions, in the sense that they must be capable of being agreed to across a range of different moral perspectives (Rawls, 1993). Personal moral issues are not appropriate subjects for political debate – what Rawls calls public reason (Rawls, 1997). (We should remember though, that Rawls did not define abortion as a private issue.) A similar principle underlies the separation of religion from politics that is enshrined in the constitutions of some countries – most notably the United States separation between Church and State, but also France's principle of *laïcité* (state secularism). Prominent Roman Catholic political leaders in the United States who are personally opposed to abortion on religious grounds have concluded that it is inappropriate for the state to impose their views on those who disagree.

The pro-choice case is based on the idea that the government may not enforce a moral view about the beginning of life over the private capacities of people to choose their own moral principles and ways of life. In practice, Canada is the only country to take the approach of imposing no legislative restriction on abortion, but the United States Supreme Court's privacy doctrine is based on the same refusal to regulate what it sees as private moral decisions. Michael Sandel suggests that the continued controversy over abortion highlights the futility of liberals' attempts to separate private moral issues from public political decisions, and to maintain the neutrality of law on moral questions (Sandel, 2005). Moral issues such as the status of life before birth must be argued out in public debate, rather than bracketed or left in the hands of unelected authorities such as the courts.

Euthanasia

The term euthanasia is from the Greek, and literally means 'dying well', or a good death. In practice, it has come to mean medical assistance to bring about death – either by administering lethal drugs, or ceasing to provide essential means of life-support. Euthanasia covers a range of practices but, in this chapter, we will restrict it to voluntary physician-assisted suicide, which has recently become the subject of widespread controversy in many countries. (The term voluntary euthanasia is sometimes used interchangeably with physician-assisted suicide, although it generally means that the physician performs the act of ending life, rather than assisting the patient to do so.) We will exclude, for example, eugenic practices, such as the killing of disabled newborns in the ancient world, and the Nazi programme of putting to death the mentally and physically infirm in 1930s and 1940s Germany. Providing the means to help someone take their life is expressly prohibited by the Hippocratic Oath and has been sanctioned in western societies for most of human history, although the prohibition on unassisted suicide arose with Christianity. Suicide itself, in ancient Greece, was judged generally in terms of its effects on the social duties and obligations of the suicide, while the Roman Stoics believed that the ability to choose death when life had become unbearable was a fundamental expression of human freedom. Both Christian and Jewish laws forbid physician-assisted suicide, and there are very few defences of the practice through most of western history until the twentieth century.

For most of the twentieth century, euthanasia was associated with the murderous eugenic policies of fascism, and it is only relatively recently that popular movements have emerged and attempted to liberalize the law against voluntary, physician-assisted suicide. It remains illegal in the great majority of countries. The first government in the world to legalize the practice was the Northern Territory in Australia in 1996 – four cancer patients ended their lives with medical assistance before the law was overridden by federal legislation the following year. The Netherlands, Belgium and the American state of Oregon (see p. 144) currently have the most permissive legislation: in Belgium, physician-assisted suicide has been legal since 2002, and, since 2005, pharmacists have been allowed to supply drugs for euthanasia to physicians. Euthanasia was effectively legalized in the Netherlands in 2002, formalizing a long-standing practice of not criminalizing doctors who performed euthanasia in limited circumstances. The Dutch legislation is widely supported by the country's medical profession and by the general public, and there are movements to introduce similar legislation in other European countries. Switzerland allows anyone, including non-physicians, to assist in a suicide – as long as they do not actually themselves administer the drugs or perform the act causing death. Assistance short of this is a crime only when the person assisting acts from selfish motives. The law applies also to non-citizens, and people from many countries have travelled to Switzerland to end their lives.

In the UK, active intervention to help someone die is a criminal offence, but the British law distinguishes between acting and refraining from acting, and people can demand to have life support removed. The courts have recognized the delegated rights of family members to make this decision when the patient is not conscious. A series of cases in the 1990s established that doctors were justified in withholding treatment from newborns that were so disabled that they would not be able to have any quality of life. This decision was applied to adults in the 1993 case of *Airedale NHS Trust* v. *Bland*, involving a young man who was in a persistent vegetative state since being crushed in the Hillsborough soccer stadium disaster in 1989. His parents and the NHS sought permission to cease providing him with artificial hydration and nutrition, and permission was granted by the High Court and the House of Lords. Active assistance to die, however, continues to be illegal. In 2001, Diane Pretty, a British woman suffering from terminal motor neurone disease that left her severely disabled, sought a court ruling that would allow her husband to help her end her life. The case went to the High Court and the House of Lords, both of which refused to allow her husband to assist her, on the grounds that legislation clearly forbade mercy killing. She then appealed to the European Court of Human Rights, on the grounds that the law infringed her human rights, but her case was dismissed. She died naturally shortly afterwards. The Pretty case galvanized into action lobby groups both in favour of and against euthanasia. A Bill permitting Assisted Dying for the Terminally Ill was rejected by Parliament in 2006. It appears that this distinction between withholding support and actively intervening remains widely supported among British doctors, despite changes to legislation in European countries.

The legal situation is similar in Canada, where court cases have established the right of a patient to refuse treatment, but have prohibited assistance. In 1993, in a very high profile case, Sue Rodriguez, who suffered from Lou Gehrig's disease, sought Court permission to kill herself with the assistance of a doctor. She was unsuccessful, but went ahead anyway with anonymous physician help. In 2005, a Right to Die with Dignity Bill was introduced into the Canadian Parliament, but was unsuccessful.

The United States similarly distinguishes between allowing people to die and assisted suicide. The right to refuse medical treatment has been recognized by the Supreme Court, which interprets it to mean that legal guardians of people unable to consent can refuse medical treatment. In *Cruzan* v. *Director, Missouri Dept of Health*, in 1990, the Court held that if there was clear and convincing evidence that the person had not wished to remain alive in such a state, life support could be removed. How controversial this position continues to be is clear, however, from the recent Terri Schiavo case. In 1990, Schiavo, a young woman in Florida, collapsed for unknown reasons and lapsed into a coma. She was diagnosed as being in a persistent vegetative state and, in 1998, her husband and legal guardian petitioned the court to have her feeding tube removed, on the grounds that before her illness she had expressed a desire not to continue living if she were ever in a vegetative state. Her parents opposed the request and a protracted court battle began, eventually involving the state government in Florida, the federal Congress and President Bush. All attempted – ultimately unsuccessfully – to override the decisions of several courts that Schiavo's husband was entitled to order his wife's feeding tube to be removed.

Physician-assisted suicide remains illegal in most states. But, in 1994, following a state referendum, Oregon passed the Death with Dignity Act, which allowed doctors to assist in suicides under specific and controlled circumstances. A patient with a terminal illness that is expected to kill them within six months is permitted to request a prescription for a lethal dose of medication. The request must be confirmed by two witnesses, one of whom cannot be a family member or physician of the patient, or a legatee to the patient's estate. The request must then be confirmed by another physician. The patient must then wait at least 15 days, and then make a second request for the prescription. He or she must be in sound mind. The Bush Administration tried to prosecute doctors acting under the law on the grounds that they were illegitimately prescribing controlled substances, but the Oregon legislation was upheld by the Supreme Court in 1993, in *Gonzales* v. *Oregon*. Nevertheless, the Supreme Court has refused to strike down laws that prohibit physician-assisted suicide. In 1997, the Supreme Court heard two cases, *Vacco* v. *Quill* and *Washington* v. *Glucksberg*, involving physician-assisted suicide – in both cases, the Federal Court of Appeals had overturned legislation preventing assisted suicide. In these, two groups of physicians argued that the statutes of New York and Washington State preventing assisted suicide were in violation of the equal treatment provision of the Constitution, because terminally ill patients were allowed to refuse treatment and choose to die, but could not authorize a doctor to end their life. The *Vacco* and *Glucksberg* cases established that there is no constitutional right to die, and that a clear distinction exists between killing and letting die.

Where abortion raises questions about the rights of individuals to end other human life, the central issue of euthanasia is whether individuals are entitled to end their own lives. Arguments in support of euthanasia fall into two broad categories:

1 The liberal case that autonomy and liberty require that we be permitted to determine the end of our own lives.

2 The utilitarian case, which argues that the consequences of allowing voluntary physician-assisted suicide are more positive than insisting that the patient continues living until death comes naturally.

In both cases, supporters must overcome the difference generally relied on in law between allowing someone to die and actively intervening to bring about their death. The philosophical case against legalizing euthanasia also takes two corresponding forms:

1 Some critics argue that liberty and autonomy do not extend to deciding when our lives should end, and that our obligations to others and to our communities must override our personal wishes to die.
2 The more common secular argument against euthanasia, however, depends on consequences, and focuses explicitly on the role of physicians and others who assist.

Critics argue that if voluntary physician-assisted suicide were allowed, a 'slippery slope' would be established, which would lead to people who did not want to die being pressured to do so by their families and doctors.

Autonomy, liberty and the right to die

Supporters of physician-assisted suicide argue that autonomy – the right to make choices and determine the direction and shape of our own lives – includes the right to choose the manner of our own deaths. People have dramatically different ideas about death, and the state, physicians or relatives should not be entitled to impose their ideas on others. As John Harris argues, making someone die in a way others approve, but that the person dying believes to be a horrifying contradiction of his or her own life, is a form of tyranny (Harris, 1995). Similarly, Dworkin argues that forcing people to live when they genuinely want to die causes serious damage to them (Dworkin, 1993). Individuals have what Dworkin calls 'critical interests' in living the kind of life we choose ourselves, and to live on suffering when we would prefer to die runs counter to our critical interests. Several countries, as we have seen, recognize this insofar as patients have the right to refuse medicines and life-saving treatments. Underlying this position is the belief that individual life is valuable because of its value to the person living it, rather than because all human life is sacred. It is this latter view that justifies opposition to abortion, as we have discussed.

But liberal philosophers have also argued that autonomy requires not only allowing people to die by not acting or stopping acting – ceasing to provide life support – but also assisting people to end their own lives. One way of defending this on grounds of autonomy is to argue that individuals should be allowed to delegate the right to end their lives to others, as they are entitled to delegate other rights. We might also think, as Harris does, that killing is wrong because it involves depriving somebody of what they value and want – their life. When a person does not value or want their life, killing them or assisting them to die cannot be wrong (Harris, 1995). James Rachels argues that the crucial issue involved in these cases is the intentional termination of the life of one human being by another (Rachels, 1986). This applies equally whether a physician is turning off a life-support machine or administering an injection.

The argument from autonomy cannot be used to defend any form of non-voluntary euthanasia, and those who make it usually require strict conditions to be observed – all of which are designed to ensure that the decision to die is, indeed, freely made. These conditions typically include the requirement that the patient be suffering from a terminal or extremely incapacitating condition, or be suffering great pain for which no cure or acceptable pain relief is available, and that the request to die be discussed with physicians, and be made more than once, over a period of time.

A clear statement of the liberal autonomy-based argument for physician-assisted suicide is found in an amicus curiae ('friend of the court') brief submitted to the United States Supreme Court in 1997 in the cases of *Vacco* v. *Quill* and *Washington* v. *Glucksberg* (Dworkin *et al.*, 1997). The brief was written by six senior American political philosophers: John Rawls, Robert Nozick, Thomas Scanlon, Ronald Dworkin, Judith Jarvis Thomson and Thomas Nagel. The philosophers based their argument in support of physician-assisted suicide on the grounds that individuals have the right to follow their own moral convictions at the end of life. (They also argued that, in Constitutional terms, individuals have a liberty interest protected by the Fourteenth Amendment, similar to that granted to pregnant women seeking abortions.) They argued further that there was no important difference between these cases involving active physician assistance and the earlier case of Cruzan, in which the Supreme Court had recognized the right of patients to refuse life-saving measures. The crucial characteristic is the desire of the patient to die, rather than whether it is an act or an omission that is required in order to cause death. The philosophers conceded that no doctor should be forced to help a patient end their life. They also addressed the second argument made by the federal government in the *Vacco* and *Glucksberg* cases, concerning the consequences of allowing physician-assisted suicide, and this aspect of their argument is examined later in this chapter.

The limits of autonomy and the value of 'bodily life'

There are two key elements to the case against euthanasia on the grounds of autonomy:

1 Individual autonomy cannot override the intrinsic value that all human life has, even the bodily life lived in a vegetative state, or life lived in suffering and pain.
2 Individual autonomy cannot override the duties of care and justice that we owe to our families and communities.

Christians have argued along these lines that life is a gift from God, and does not belong to the individual who lives it. Sandel points out that both Kant and Locke, who placed individual autonomy at the centre of their philosophies, rejected a right to suicide on the grounds that only God could end life. Locke thought that, because the right to life is inalienable, we cannot end it any more than we can send ourselves into slavery, and Kant thought that suicide meant treating ourselves as means (Sandel, 2005). As Dworkin has shown, a widely held and similar secular view holds that human life is intrinsically valuable and sacred. Natural law philosopher John Finnis argues along these lines that human bodily life is an intrinsic and basic good, rather than being an instrumental good – valuable because of what the individual living it can do (Finnis, 1995). It follows that even a person living in a vegetative state or in pain remains a human person with full intrinsic value – just as, according to this line of argument, an early human embryo is a person with full human value.

The argument that suicide, in general, is a betrayal of our duties to others is long-standing. We can see this clearly in the case of duties to family members, but we might also argue, more broadly, that suicide means opting out of the duties and responsibilities we owe to our broader community. Communitarian critics have argued that physician-assisted suicide would mean abrogating the duties that we owe to care for the dependent and needy, and assuming that only autonomous and independent individuals have lives worth living (Sandel, 2005). Feminist philosopher Susan Wolf has argued that the emphasis on individual autonomy and rights fails to recognize that people are embedded in social networks and relations of dependency. A focus, instead, on the context and history of the patient, and on his or her relations with his or her care-givers would allow us to explore alternatives to dying, and focus on improving care (Wolf, 1996).

Utilitarian arguments in favour of assisted suicide

Perhaps the most obvious argument in favour of physician-assisted suicide is utilitarian: those who are ill and suffering, and wish to end their lives, will have their desires satisfied, and be able to end their physical pain and their psychological frustration and helplessness. A utilitarian argument draws no distinction between allowing someone to die by withdrawing life support (as in the *Cruzan* case in the United States, and *Bland* in Britain) and intervening medically to bring about death. As Singer argues, once we have decided that death is justified, what counts is how painless and easy that death should be for the patient, rather than whether it is brought about by acting or ceasing to act (Singer, 1993).

Once we look beyond the suffering individual, however, it might seem that the consequences of allowing the practice are potentially very damaging, in that someone who does not really wish or choose to die might be persuaded to do so. Given this, the safer or more conservative approach might appear to be to ban the practice. But this assumes, as the philosophers' brief to the Supreme Court points out, that a person who is forced to stay alive against their will is not damaged by this. Rather, the brief argues, preventing people who are mentally competent from ending their lives, when they believe that to continue living contradicts all the principles by which they have lived, 'grievously and irreversibly harms such people', doing them a terrible injury (Dworkin *et al.*, 1997). From a feminist perspective, we might add that this damage is particularly likely to be experienced by women, who are socialized to accept suffering by a long cultural history of women's self-sacrifice (Davis, 1998).

Moreover, as Singer argues, there is no reason to think that allowing physician-assisted suicide would lead to a 'slippery slope' descent into involuntary or forced euthanasia (Singer, 1993). Opponents of the practice often cite the eugenics policies of the Nazis as a cautionary warning about where physician-assisted suicide might lead. But there is no relationship between these cases. The Nazi euthanasia programme was designed with goals of racial purification in mind, rather than relieving individual suffering. In fact, lines between different types of euthanasia can easily be drawn, as has been the case in history. The ancient Greeks exposed infants but did not kill innocent adults. In any case, given that surveys of doctors show that some do assist in suicides unofficially (Meier *et al.*, 1998), supporters point out that legalizing the practice would subject it to greater scrutiny, thus ensuring that decisions to die are not made under pressure.

The consequences of legalizing physician-assisted suicide and the 'slippery slope'

Some opponents of physician-assisted suicide concede that, in individual cases, the wish to die might be interpreted as an expression of the patient's

Box 7.2 Abortion and euthanasia: competing norms and values

Debates over abortion and euthanasia debates are generally distinct, and much of the controversy around abortion centres on the specific issue of foetal personhood. But they also raise competing interpretations of some key norms and values:

• Liberty and autonomy

Supporters of rights to abortion and voluntary euthanasia argue that individuals must have the freedom to make decisions about their own bodies and their own lives. This includes the right to terminate an unwanted pregnancy and to end life.

Opponents counter that individual liberty and autonomy are not absolute rights, but must be limited by concern about the social consequences of choices, the duties we owe to others, or higher principles of natural law.

• Equality

Equality is a key norm in the abortion debate. Supporters argue that women cannot be equal to men unless they are allowed the choice about whether or not to continue with pregnancy. Radical critics argue that women are not equal in sexual relations and, thus, it is doubly unfair to require them to bear the burden of unwanted pregnancy.

Opponents deny that preventing abortion affects women's equality.

• The role of the state

Libertarian supporters of abortion rights argue simply that women own their own bodies, and the state has no right to intervene in decisions about them. Similarly, libertarian supporters of the right to voluntary euthanasia insist that the state has no right to intervene in decisions to end life.

Other more egalitarian liberals argue, with respect to abortion, that the aim of government must be a just society, which protects the rights and freedom of women to choose pregnancy, rather than a society based on a common comprehensive moral code.

Critics contend that the state must protect the foetus as it protects the lives of citizens. Here, legalization is a failure of the duty of the state to protect. In the case of euthanasia, critics fear that legalization will ultimately accord the state too much power to direct and control the end of life.

autonomy, and therefore a good to them as individuals. Nevertheless, the social consequences of a public policy legalizing the practice would be so damaging that they would outweigh the good of allowing it in particular cases. On utilitarian grounds, therefore, the practice ought not to be legalized.

One danger of legalizing euthanasia might be that decisions to die would not be autonomous – that unscrupulous people, or even well-meaning family members and physicians, might try to persuade the ill to suicide, against their real wishes. In addition, removing the prohibition against killing might have a powerful symbolic effect, allowing others to argue that it is legitimate in other cases – a slippery slope argument. Arguments about the scarcity of medical resources might be used to justify recommending euthanasia to the long-term ill. Voluntary physician-assisted suicide would soon lead to involuntary euthanasia, where the ill or disabled are killed without request. Some critics argue that this is what has happened in the Netherlands since physician-assisted suicide was legalized (Keown, 1995).

Those who take this position do not always insist that the law should punish doctors who, in individual cases and out of compassion, assist patients to die. Tom Beauchamp warns that we should not assume that there is a close fit between a moral justification for a doctor assisting death and a public policy that allows this (Beauchamp, 1996). One option here would be to continue the practice that currently exists, whereby physician-assisted suicide is prohibited, but authorities selectively fail to enforce prohibitions where there is clear agreement between everyone concerned that euthanasia was morally justified (Velleman, 1992).

Conclusion

Because it involves other human life, whatever its status, abortion raises issues importantly different to euthanasia. Yet, it is no coincidence that those who support abortion rights tend also to support a right to voluntary physician-assisted suicide. Liberal philosophers who emphasize individual autonomy argue that the rights and liberties of the pregnant woman to decide her own identity and to shape her own life override the respect that is owed to developing human life, at least in the early stages of its development. This is essentially the justification for abortion rights in early pregnancy in both the United States and other countries. Similarly, the argument for autonomy requires that that we respect the right of individuals to choose, freely and without coercion, to end their lives. While earlier liberals such as Kant and Locke rejected suicide, secular liberalism does not assume that human life is the gift of, and remains ultimately the property of, God.

The cases against abortion and euthanasia are, however, importantly different. While opponents of abortion do often claim that the procedure is damaging to women, the main argument against abortion turns on the status of the foetus as a human person, with full individual rights. There is no means satisfactory to both the pro-choice and pro-life sides of the argument to determine whether or not the foetus is a person, simply because there is no agreed full set of criteria for what makes a person (rather than a form of human life). In the case of euthanasia, however, claims about the possible negative social consequences of legalization are much more commonly made than arguments about the limits of autonomy. The difference between these issues is also a difference between two different models for the ways in which political decisions are made. Because arguments about negative effects can be responded to by attempting to control those effects, public deliberation about euthanasia – at least, in the form of voluntary physician-assisted suicide – is likely to continue. In the case of abortion, despite the attempts of those such as Dworkin to find common ground, policy will reflect not deliberative decision-making but, rather, the success of one side or the other on the competitive stage of electoral politics.

Chapter 8

Should Offensive Speech be Regulated?

Freedom of speech is a widely accepted central principle in liberal democracies, but debates regularly surface over its limits. Should it encompass all speech – even that which attacks fundamental democratic or egalitarian principles? The paradox of this liberal right is that it allows people to call into question the very political system that guarantees it, and all other rights. The growing pluralist and multi-ethnic nature of democratic societies from the last century onwards, and the increase in claims by ethnic and cultural groups for collective rights, which we discussed in Chapter 3, have led to new challenges to freedom of speech. Should it extend to curtailing the liberty with which people make statements and claims, or use names and epithets to insult or vilify others on the basis of their race, gender, ethnicity, religion or sexual orientation?

This question was forcefully brought home to liberal democratic states in late 2005, when a Danish newspaper published a series of twelve editorial cartoons satirizing Islam and the Prophet Mohammed. At first, Danish Muslim organizations protested, and then demonstrations spread amongst Muslim immigrants in western countries, as the cartoons were reprinted around the world. Muslim activists targeted Danish embassies, boycotted Danish goods, and protested outside the embassies of other countries that had published the cartoons. While most protests were actually peaceful, by February 2006 there were increasing threats of violence both in Muslim countries and in the west, and demonstrations became violent. Over 100 people were killed. The response of western governments was mixed: British, European and American leaders maintained the right to freedom of speech, and condemned the violence; though, as the situation escalated, they increasingly conceded that the cartoons were, indeed, offensive. Western media organizations insisted on their right to publish material satirizing religions, claiming that Christianity was subject to satire without restriction. Public opinion in western liberal democracies was generally critical of Muslim immigrants for allegedly failing to understand western norms and values around freedom of speech, and for placing loyalty to their religion above their civic commitments to their newly-adopted home countries.

The cartoons controversy reflected deep social anxieties about immigration and assimilation. But it also raised the issue of whether freedom of speech was an absolute right, or whether it should be constrained by the demands of cultural pluralism and sensitive relations between majorities and minority ethnic and religious groups. As we shall see, most liberal democracies balance a general commitment to freedom of speech with restrictions on statements that are designed to provoke hatred or resentment on the basis of membership in particular minorities. The Danish cartoon case called into question the extent of these restrictions, and the legitimacy of the balance, making clear how different it looks from the perspective of members of minority groups. Many defenders of the cartoons felt that they were mild and inoffensive, while Muslims argued that they deeply insulted their religion.

In this chapter, we examine the way political philosophy deals with the problem of offensive speech. This is a broad category, but we will focus on two of its most controversial forms:

1 Speech that offends members of minority groups.
2 'Hate speech', which is designed to stir up hatred against minority group members.

Hate speech is almost always offensive to its targets; however, not all offensive speech is designed to incite hate, as we shall see when we consider the Salman Rushdie case. Offensive speech, broadly understood, is only one aspect of freedom of speech. We have already examined the related issue of pornography in Chapter 5, and we will consider freedom of speech and other civil liberties in the context of the terrorist threat in Chapter 9. Our discussion also relates to the more general claims of minority cultural groups that were examined in Chapter 3. In this chapter, we focus on what happens when the claims of minority groups to equal rights and recognition come up against well-entrenched western rights to freedom of speech.

Most European countries – as well as Canada, Australia and New Zealand – have passed legislation criminalizing speech that amounts to the vilification of racial and ethnic and, in some cases, other groups. This has been, in part, a response to the rise in xenophobia and race-related tensions that countries with large immigrant populations have experienced since the 1980s. States must balance their commitments to human rights under the United Nations Declaration on Human Rights, which specifies the right to freedom of expression, with the requirements of the International Convention on the Elimination of all forms of Racial Discrimination (CERD). CERD, which entered into force in 1969, requires states under Article 4 to:

> declare an offence punishable by law all dissemination of ideas based on racial superiority or hatred, incitement to racial discrimination, as well as

all acts of violence or incitement to such acts against any race or group of persons of another colour or ethnic origin, and also the provision of any assistance to racist activities, including the financing thereof.

European Union members agreed in 2007 to make incitement to hatred or violence against a person on the basis of race, ethnicity or colour a criminal offence across the EU. European states also follow Article 10 of the European Convention for the Protection of Human Rights and Fundamental Freedoms, which guarantees freedom of speech as essential to the development of democracy. The European Court has interpreted this to mean that some restrictions to speech might be necessary in a democratic society, and that this includes the right to restrict hate speech directed against religious, racial and ethnic groups.

The balance that states strike between guaranteeing free expression and preventing the expression or incitement of racial hatred tends to depend on the historical place of freedom of speech in their legal systems, and on the national history of minority treatment. In countries with relatively recent constitutions, free expression tends to be interpreted in the light of recent history. The German Basic Law stipulates that freedom of speech is limited by, among other factors, 'the inviolability of personal honour'. This has been interpreted to include the honour of groups, and the expression of hatred against a minority is a criminal offence. Nine European countries, including Germany, Austria and France, have passed laws that make denial of the historical fact of the Holocaust a criminal offence. These have been upheld by the European Court of Human Rights as a justifiable limit on freedom of expression. In 2006, author and Holocaust denier David Irving was sentenced to gaol in Austria under this legislation, based on a speech he gave in 1989. More general legislative prohibitions on racial vilification tend to be interpreted to reflect the continued relevance of freedom of speech as a basic principle. Denmark, Norway and Sweden, for example, all prohibit hate speech, defined as speech that threatens or insults groups defined on the basis of race, ethnicity, religion and sexual orientation. In Denmark, however, the Public Prosecutor held that the anti-Muslim cartoons did not constitute a criminal offence, because they dealt with matters of public interest. The right to freedom of speech must be taken into account, he concluded, when assessing whether or not a violation of the Criminal Code had taken place.

The dominance of freedom of speech is even more marked in the United Kingdom, where it is a fundamental principle in the light of which others must be interpreted. The British commitment dates from the religious conflicts and Civil War of the mid-seventeenth century, when freedom of expression was famously defended by the poet John Milton in his pamphlet *Areopagitica* (1644). Increased racial diversity in Britain as a result of post-World War II immigration has meant the balancing of this fundamental right with the need to prevent racial and ethnic conflict. The Race Relations Act of 1976 and the Public Order Act of 1986 made 'incitement to racial hatred' an offence. The limitations of this legislation, which addressed only racial and not religious groups, became apparent in the Salman Rushdie case. In 1998, Rushdie, an Indian-British author, published the novel *The Satanic Verses*, which contained an unflattering depiction of a character modelled on the Muslim prophet Mohammed. The issue in this case was offence to the sensibilities of a group, rather than incitement of hatred towards them. Muslims condemned the book as blasphemous, and protests broke out against Rushdie and his publishers in the United Kingdom and abroad. In February 1989, the Supreme Leader of Iran, the Ayatollah Khomeini issued a *fatwa* calling for the death of Rushdie and his publishers.

Political leaders and the press in Britain and abroad strongly defended the right to publish the book. As in the Danish cartoons case nearly a decade later, Muslim immigrants were criticized for failing to integrate and subscribe to western values such as freedom of expression. They countered that it was unjust that Sikhs and Jews but not Muslims were protected from ridicule aimed at inciting racial hatred. Moreover, blasphemy laws in Britain protected Christianity (as defined by the Church of England) but no other religion (Parekh, 1990: 57). This was rectified in 2006, when the Racial and Religious Hatred Act was passed, making the intentional incitement of religious hatred an offence. As with all UK legislation, the Act must be interpreted in the light of the Human Rights Act (1998) guarantee of freedom of expression.

Some religious groups have been among the strongest critics of laws that limit speech critical of religion. These laws cover not only the criticisms of sceptical secularists, but also attacks by some religions against others, as we see in a recent case testing offensive speech regulation in Australia (see Box 8.1).

In Canada, freedom of speech is protected under the Charter of Rights and Freedoms (1982). Canadian legislation on offensive speech protects more groups than similar laws in other countries: advocating genocide or inciting hatred against any particular group – defined as being based on race, ethnicity, colour, religion or sexual orientation – is a criminal offence under the Criminal Code. The law provides exceptions for cases of truth, matters that are the subject of public debate, and religious doctrine. Freedom of speech is protected under the Canadian Charter of Rights and Freedoms (1982), which guarantees freedom of expression. The Canadian Supreme Court considered the relationship between these racial hatred provisions and constitutionally protected freedom of speech in the 1990 case *R. v. Keegstra*, in which a high school teacher was charged with promoting hatred towards Jews. The Court upheld the constitutionality of the Criminal Code provisions, finding that the prohibition against hate speech was aimed at 'fostering harmonious social relations in a community dedicated to equality and

Box 8.1   The Catch the Fire Ministries religious vilification case

In 2001, the Australian state of Victoria passed the Racial and Religious Tolerance Act, prohibiting the vilification of people on the grounds of their race or religion. The express objects of the Act were to promote the full and equal participation by all Victorians 'in a society that values freedom of expression and is an open and multicultural democracy'. In March 2002, two Christian pastors from Catch the Fire Ministries spoke at a public information seminar for Christians on Islam. The Islamic Council of Victoria brought a case against them, claiming that the intent of the speech had been to vilify Muslims, rather than to convey information. An administrative tribunal held that the pastors had breached the Act. The State Supreme Court allowed an appeal, and the case was eventually settled by mediation.

- The initial judgement against the pastors provoked a storm of protest from both Australian and American religious liberties groups, who argued that the men were simply reporting what the Koran said and formulating a Christian response to Islam. Epithets and insulting names were not used. The Islamic Council responded – and the Administrative Tribunal agreed – that, nevertheless, their comments had misrepresented, ridiculed and insulted Islam.
- The Tribunal held that it did not matter that the remarks made about Islam might have been true, what counted was that they could be interpreted as vilifying. This opened up the possibility that no objective standard of vilification or offence existed, and that any speech critical of another religion could potentially be proscribed under the Act.
- The decision also suggested that what counted as public religious discussion could be narrowly defined. The Tribunal held that the pastors did not act reasonably and in good faith, and, hence, the seminar could not be protected as religious discussion.
- The outbreak of protest in response to this case, both within Australia and externally, suggests that there is much less support in liberal democracies for limiting speech that offends on religious grounds than there is for limiting racist offensive speech.
- This case provoked a strong popular movement for repeal of the Act on the grounds that it causes division and tensions in a multicultural society – the very same problem that the legislation was introduced to address.

multiculturalism'. It followed that speech did not have to lead directly to violence in order to be exempted from protection; it was enough that it caused damage and harm to its targets, and caused racial, religious or ethnic tensions within broader Canadian society.

Quite a different approach has been taken in the United States to the regulation of offensive speech. The United States has no legislation against racial vilification or incitement to racial hatred because of the crucial role of the First Amendment to the Constitution, which states that 'Congress shall make no law ... abridging the freedom of speech, or of the press.' The United States signed, but never ratified CERD, because of its concerns about the implications of Article 4. Because the Supreme Court is charged with interpreting the Constitution in the United States, much of the American debate concerning freedom of speech centres on its decisions. While some regulation of speech has been upheld if it applies generally, the courts have rejected both content based restrictions of speech (those that target, for example, particular racist content) and viewpoint based restrictions, which prohibit only the expression of a particular viewpoint (such as white supremacy or anti-Semitism). Apart from the well-recognized cases of 'falsely shouting fire in a crowded theatre', established by the Supreme Court in *Schenck* v. *United States* (1919), personal libel and obscenity (see Chapter 5), the only class of exceptions comprises those cases where the speech prohibited is considered by the Supreme Court to be 'fighting words' likely to result in immediate violence. This was established in 1942 by the Supreme Court in *Chaplinsky* v. *New Hampshire*, which held that fighting words (in that case, 'damned fascist') did not have enough social value to justify protection under the First Amendment. The social interest in order and morality outweighed the interest in freedom of speech. Initially, this line of reasoning led the Court to refuse protection to hate speech. In the 1952 Supreme Court case of *Beauharnais* v. *Illinois*, an Illinois law that made it illegal to publish or exhibit any material that suggested that a group of people was criminal or otherwise immoral on the basis of their race, colour, creed or religion, was declared to be constitutional. The Court described speech of this kind as a group libel, which was dangerous to the peace and well-being of the state, and not protected by the First Amendment.

Beauharnais v. *Illinois* has been undermined, however, by subsequent cases. The landmark decision is the 1978 Supreme Court case of *National Socialist Party of America* v. *Village of Skokie*, where the Supreme Court held that an American Nazi group was entitled to march through the suburb of Skokie in Chicago, an area with a large population of Jewish Holocaust survivors. The fighting words exception of *Chaplinsky* v. *New Hampshire* was restricted to personally insulting epithets that were likely to lead directly to violence, and held not to apply in this case. The *Skokie* decision affirmed that the First Amendment protected free expression of even extremely offensive and unpopular views. In *Brandenburg* v. *Ohio*, a 1969 case involving the Ku Klux Klan and anti-Black and anti-Semitic speech, the Supreme Court held that the state cannot punish inflammatory speech unless it immediately incites lawlessness. The US Supreme Court's position is similar to that of legislative provisions in other democracies, in that speech can be regulated because of its consequences. The difference is that it requires that those consequences include an immediate violent response, rather than the promotion of hatred or ill feeling against groups.

The issue of freedom of speech resurfaced in the United States in the 1980s and 1990s with the proliferation of university and college campus speech codes, which prohibited speech offensive to particular groups – usually racial or ethnic. Universities justified the codes on the grounds that offensive speech encroached on the equal rights of minority students to their education, and that regulation was necessary to ensure a civil environment in which all students were equally able to learn. Some prohibited only action, but many extended to speech that victimizes or stigmatizes individuals on the basis of their race, ethnicity, religion, sexual orientation or other group affiliation. Civil liberties groups opposed the codes, arguing that freedom of speech was essential to academic endeavour, and that racist speech should just be combated by more speech in opposition (Downs, 2005).

The most fundamental problem raised by legislation and court cases dealing with offensive speech is how to balance liberty with other political values. Offensive or hate speech is often referred to as a hard case, because one of the common defences of freedom of speech – that the exchange of ideas enables us to discover the truth – might seem to apply less to this kind of expression. This is what the United States Supreme Court meant in *Chaplinsky* v. *New Hampshire* when it described offensive speech as having low social value. Critics argue that hate speech is an exercise in the freedom of its perpetrators at the expense of the equality of its targets. It also pits the individual liberty of speakers against a common good, or against democratic politics.

As we shall see, the contested balance between liberty and equality reflects debates between libertarian and egalitarian political philosophers, as well as disputes over the meaning of equality:

- Should egalitarians focus on ensuring that everyone has an equal legal right to speak, or on making sure that everyone feels equally included and worthwhile, and therefore able to speak?
- Underlying this is the question of what poses the greater danger to individual freedom: the law, or the opinions and attitudes of others?

We might also see offensive speech as a problem in reconciling individual rights with a common good, such as social cohesion. Should individual rights always take precedence over considerations of the social good, or do these rights in fact depend on shared moral beliefs?

Offensive speech also raises the question of whether we should value an abstract right to freedom of speech independently of the effects, both psychological and social, that it might have. Arguments in favour of freedom of speech are both deontological (in that they appeal to what is right) and consequentialist (Scanlon, 1972), while most arguments for regulation focus on the negative consequences of offensive speech. Because freedom of expression continues to be such a centrally important value in liberal democracies, even those who allow exemptions for offensive speech because of its damaging effects require the state to consider whether or not the circumstances and nature of the speech justify prohibiting it as offensive. And those who argue against exemptions for offensive speech often concede its negative social effects but argue that to make exceptions for it might lead to eroding the central principle of free speech. We have examined similar 'slippery slope' arguments with respect to euthanasia in Chapter 7. We begin by outlining the civil libertarian argument against prohibiting offensive speech. We then turn to the various arguments in favour of limiting speech. Most of these are based on the effects of offensive speech on the good of the community, or on individuals or the groups to which they belong. Because of these negative consequences, critics argue, such speech is of low value and does not deserve protection. A few scholars go further and challenge the deontological defence of freedom of speech, arguing that it is mistaken to talk in terms of a fundamental right to freedom of speech.

The civil libertarian argument against regulating speech

The argument against regulating speech is based on the fundamental liberty of the individual and on the positive consequences of freedom of speech for both the individual and the community. Freedom of speech is good for society because it produces more vigorous debate and engagement, in which good and true ideas are more likely to emerge and to attract supporters. But it is also essential to individual freedom and autonomy – our capacity to direct and shape our own lives. We must all choose and commit to our own beliefs and values and, if the state regulates the expression of our opinions, it prevents us from expressing who we truly are. The eighteenth-century German philosopher Immanuel Kant argues along these lines that the public use of reason is essential to individual autonomy (Kant, 1991 [1784]), and this has become a fundamental tenet of modern liberalism.

Kant is addressing legal prohibitions on freedom of speech. John Stuart Mill, who published his famous and influential defence of freedom, *On Liberty*, in 1859, is concerned not only with the dangers of state censorship, but also with the censoring powers of public opinion, which deters people from developing their own views. Mill defends freedom of speech because it will strengthen true opinions and weaken the false, and because it is essential to individuality. Mill argues that being freely able to express oneself is an essential part of being a free and autonomous individual: 'It is desirable ... that in things which do not primarily concern others, individuality should assert itself. Where not the person's own character, but the traditions or customs of other people are the rule of conduct, there is wanting one of the principal ingredients of human happiness, and quite the chief ingredient of individual and social progress' (Mill, 1989a [1859]: 57). Freedom of thought and expression is necessary for individuals to develop their own selves. We might call this 'expressive liberty'. It is this relationship between freedom of speech and individual autonomy that Rawls has in mind when he describes freedom of expression as one of the basic liberties guaranteed equally to all by his first principle of justice (Rawls, 1971).

In addition to guaranteeing individual autonomy, Mill contends that freedom of speech would lead to the discovery and acceptance of the truth: 'But the peculiar evil of silencing the expression of an opinion is; that is robbing the human race; posterity as well as the existing generation; those who dissent from the opinion [expressed] still more than those who hold it. If the opinion is right, they are deprived of the opportunity of exchanging error for truth: if wrong, they lose, what is almost as great a benefit, the clearer perception and livelier impression of truth, produced by its collision with error' (Mill, 1989a [1859]: 20). Opinions that are true should be able to be expressed. Those that are false will only be proved so and discredited if they are subject to public debate. And, in the case of opinions that are partly true and partly false, open debate is required to sort out the truthful from the false elements. It is this position that underlies the common contemporary argument that offensive speech is best countered not by censoring, but by more speech – so that debate and discussion ensues in which the better opinion (or the truth) is likely to triumph (Sunstein, 1995).

If freedom of speech were to cause direct harm to others, such as in cases of incitement to violence, it could not be defended from a liberal perspective no matter what its relation to autonomy and truth. After all, the purpose of the state for liberals is fundamentally to protect our security and safety. Some supporters of the regulation of hate speech do cite the harm it does to its targets, as we shall see later in this chapter. But liberals are careful to restrict harm to damage that is direct, and which is to the interests of individuals, rather than to their sensibilities or feelings. As we saw in the liberal case against regulating pornography and prostitution, merely being offended by speech or conduct is not enough to justify banning it (Hart, 1963). According to Mill in *On Liberty*, the only justification for state intervention or regulation is to prevent the individual from directly harming others (Mill, 1989a [1859]). Mill's views, we should note, assume that our sentiments and feelings are not deeply related to our identities as moral beings. As Kant puts it, individuals deserve respect because they are agents who can make moral choices, and choose their ends – their purposes, goals and affiliations in life (Kant, 1993 [1785]). It is not those purposes, goals or affiliations, in themselves, that are worthy of respect. Our feelings can be hurt without hurt being done to our real selves.

Critics might argue that, while encouraging full and fair public debate is necessary for true and good ideas to defeat wrong and bad ones, this does not apply in the case of offensive speech. This speech makes no arguments or reasoned claims, and we might conclude that it is of little social value. Civil libertarians respond that speech that deals with political matters, or issues of public concern, including race relations, cannot be considered low value, even if it is offensive (Sunstein, 1995). This, as we have seen, was the approach taken by the Danish authorities in the case of the cartoons, and has been followed by the courts in the United States, Britain and Australia. It was the basis of the Supreme Court's decision in the *Skokie* case.

Civil libertarians also point out that restrictions on speech might be used to ban public expression by, or from the perspective of, minorities targeted by offensive speech. Freedom of speech, particularly concerning public matters, has been an important tool for minority groups to use in making their political case, a point often made about the Civil Rights movement in the United States. Banning the speech of oppressed minorities in the past made it more difficult for them to make, and garner support for, their political cases (Karst, 1990). Gays and lesbians, for example, have been persecuted when they 'come out' and declare their sexuality openly (Rubenstein, 1994). From this perspective, the chief threat to individual liberty is the state representing censorious majorities, and it is dangerous to grant it the power to make judgements about which speech should be tolerated and which should not. The state is not a neutral and objective institution, and might ban speech necessary to the freedom and autonomy of just those minorities who demand a ban on the offensive speech of others. A similar argument can be made along Marxist lines, as is discussed later in this chapter.

While civil libertarians are suspicious of allowing the state to determine whether speech is legitimate or not, they do not necessarily oppose – indeed, most support – the goals of inclusiveness and equality that critics of offensive speech support. As Kent Greenawalt concludes, direct commitment to positive values of equality and prohibitions against discriminatory behaviour, rather than speech, are better ways for governments to show their support for equality than silencing speakers (Greenawalt, 1995).

Freedom of speech and good self-government

So far, we have focused on the defence of freedom of speech from the perspective of both individuals and minority groups. But it is also important, as we have seen Mill argue, from the wider social perspective of the requirements of a democratic society. Most obviously, democratic government requires public debate and discussion, and restrictions on freedom of speech might easily be seen to obstruct that process. (We consider a counter-argument made on the same grounds in the next section.) Ronald Dworkin suggests that free speech is necessary because it ensures that everyone has an equal chance to influence the political process, the laws and mores under which they live (Dworkin, 2000). Sexists and bigots do not have the right to have their views institutionalized, or even respected, but they do have the right to express them (Dworkin 1996). Dworkin addresses the difficult balance between liberty and equality by arguing that freedom of speech is justified on egalitarian grounds: everyone has an equal right to be heard and to participate in and influence politics. This includes what Dworkin calls 'the right to ridicule'. According to this view, the Danish cartoons should not have been censored; although, as he points out, this does not mean that every newspaper had a duty to print them, as they were available on the web. Free speech does not mean the public has the right to see whatever they want wherever they like (Dworkin, 2006). From this perspective, freedom of speech protects individuals not only from the imposition of state-sanctioned official views, but also from the 'tyranny of the majority' – the chief danger of democratic politics, at least as Mill saw it. It also, as Robert Post argues, allows citizens to feel that they are participating in the legislative and policy-making process, and this ensures that laws are perceived as legitimate (Post, 1991).

Democratic self-government and the case against offensive speech

While Dworkin believes that citizenship entails the right to express whatever unpopular views we may choose, other liberal philosophers distinguish between speech that is necessary for democratic politics, because it contributes to democratic deliberation – the reasoned, public and inclusive discussion of political issues, and speech that subverts or undermines deliberation. Political philosophers today increasingly understand politics in democracies as a deliberative process, rather than a competition for political power between elites representing organized interests (Cohen, 1989; Dryzek, 2000; Gutmann and Thompson, 1996). This view emphasizes the way in which political views are shaped, influenced and changed as a result of public debate. Some speech, we might argue, prevents or corrupts everyone's ability to participate in democratic deliberation. This is certainly true of personal libel, which is proscribed speech, and of 'fighting words', which are likely to provoke immediate violence. We might also argue that offensive speech prevents democratic deliberation by undermining the equal respect of citizens. If we take this position, we agree with Mill that the most important threat to individual freedom comes not from the state, but from other citizens. The threat here is not necessarily the power of a majority, however.

Even the hateful speech of a few can undermine the self-respect of minorities. Moreover, such speech often does not contain reasoned arguments or claims, and so will add nothing to the search for the truth.

Some American legal and political philosophers have developed these arguments to support a distinction between speech that deals with matters of public concern and should be protected under the First Amendment, and non-political speech that could be restricted if there were a social interest in doing so. This distinction is recognized in other democracies that exempt matters of public concern from hate speech laws. While the arguments described in this section focus on the United States' Constitution, the issues they raise about the relationship between democratic society and free speech apply much more widely. As we have seen, the European Convention for the Protection of Human Rights has been interpreted to allow restrictions on speech, as they are necessary to sustain a democratic society.

Alexander Meiklejohn argued that the First Amendment was designed not to maximize individual autonomy but, rather, to protect the speech necessary to serve common needs by ensuring that citizens would make good democratic decisions (Meiklejohn, 1965). The state should function as a 'parliamentarian', setting the rules for open and fair debate. Owen Fiss claims similarly that it is a mistake to see the First Amendment as a guarantee of individual autonomy: its purpose is, rather, to enable the public debate necessary for collective self-determination (Fiss, 1996). In order to carry this out, the state must be able to manage the terms of public engagement. It might legitimately restrict some speech in order to enhance the relative voice of others, because the key aim of politics is to achieve a rich and informative public dialogue. Citizens must therefore have access to all the options, and be able to judge and make decisions. Insulting speech interferes with the speech rights of minorities, discouraging them from participating in the deliberative activities of society. Members of minority groups withdraw into themselves and are effectively silenced (Fiss, 1996).

A similar argument is made by Cass Sunstein, who also interprets the purpose of the First Amendment as being the protection of popular sovereignty and democratic government (Sunstein, 1995). Free speech concerning political or public matters is necessary to deliberation, because people will only be able to consider alternative views if they are exposed to a diversity of opinions. But this does not necessarily mean that non-political speech must be protected so carefully. Sunstein points out that much free speech now available is trivial and sensationalized, rarely dealing with public issues in depth. Dissenting views rarely get a hearing – not because of legal limits on freedom of speech, but because commercialization dominates the market of ideas and opinions. Government regulation of speech might therefore be justified precisely in order to promote free speech as part of a deliberative democracy. The rules for regulating speech should be:

- Do any regulatory rules promote greater public attention to public issues?
- Do they allow a diversity of viewpoints to be heard?

While Sunstein allows that it is difficult to define what constitutes political speech, he argues that we can distinguish between hate speech that consists simply of epithets and name-calling, and hate speech that makes an argument – however prejudiced that argument might be. The former is clearly 'low value speech', and should be amenable to regulation, while the latter should be protected, however offensive or injurious to the self-esteem of targeted groups it might be. Again, this distinction is reproduced in national laws (such as those in Denmark) that allow otherwise prohibited hate speech if the speech deals with matters of public concern. It means that arguments alleging, for example, the natural inferiority of people of colour or women would be protected under freedom of speech, while public taunting with racist or sexist names would not. This is despite the fact that these forms of expression might be equally offensive to a person of colour or a woman.

Freedom of speech 'rights' versus the community 'good'

The case we have considered for regulating offensive speech on the basis of good self-government and deliberative democracy draws our attention back to the relationship between speech and the community in which it is heard. Communitarian theorists take this a step further by arguing that freedom of speech can only be meaningfully discussed in terms of the moral values of the community, rather than the rights of the individual. This is part of a broader challenge to the liberal emphasis on individual rights over communal under-standings of a common good. Communitarians argue that rights-based liber-alism is mistaken in its ontology (its view of what the person is) and, consequently, misunderstands the way individuals act in politics. 'Political liberals' understand that individuals are members of communities with shared conceptions of the good, but they believe that people might bracket or set aside these moral values in public life, committing instead only to more minimal political values, such as individual rights. Rawls sets out this view when he argues that his principles of justice are those shared across overlap-ping conceptions of the good (Rawls, 1993). Communitarians do not accept this separation between what is politically 'right' and what is morally 'good' (MacIntyre, 1981, Sandel, 1982). Michael Sandel argues that the debate over freedom of speech demonstrates the relationship between rights and the goods which rights protect (Sandel, 2005). Free speech absolutists try to sever the link between the right and the good by protecting freedom of speech independently of the moral value of what is expressed. American courts express this in their rejection of content-based restrictions on speech.

Once we recognize a connection between moral discourse and freedom of speech, we might go on to argue, from a communitarian perspective, that rights of free speech should be balanced against the moral values of the community. These considerations were explicitly taken into account by the Canadian Supreme Court in *R. v. Keegstra* (1990), and led the Court to uphold a hate speech law banning speech inconsistent with Canada's commitment to equality and multiculturalism. Opinions and positions are not to be treated equally – those consistent with broader social purposes and values merit protection, while those subversive of societal values do not. Content-specific restrictions on speech can thus be justified, and liberal democratic societies might prohibit the racist speech of Nazis, for example, but not the expression of civil rights protesters. We might note that arguments against the absolute nature of freedom of speech that appeal to the way a community good shapes and gives meaning to free speech could potentially justify more extensive restrictions than the racial vilification laws on the books in most western states. They allow the state to take into consideration the values of specific communities in a historical context when considering offensive speech. We might, thus, justify legislation against Holocaust denial because, although it is not explicitly racial vilification, it could be said to contradict any reasonable conception of a good enshrined in a state that has, in the past, been guilty of supporting the persecution of Jews and other minorities. In the case of campus speech codes, we might argue (as did universities) that a supportive environment promoting learning for people of all ethnicities and races is a fundamental good in university and college communities. Insulting speech that compromises this basic value might therefore be proscribed. (In practice, the courts have focused, instead, on whether or not direct harm is caused to individuals by offensive speech.)

Up to this point, the discussion has assumed that the interests of minorities must be balanced with a fundamental right to free speech. But what if there is no such fundamental and absolute right? Stanley Fish has controversially made this case (Fish, 1994). Freedom of speech, in Fish's view, is not an ideal to be balanced against a community good – rather, it is a weapon used in the conflict between competing goods and aims, which is the basis of politics. In *There's No Such Thing as Free Speech ... And It's a Good Thing Too*, Fish argues that free speech is not independently valuable but, rather, is a political prize: 'Free speech is just the name we give to verbal behaviour that serves the substantive agendas we wish to advance' (Fish, 1994). We have already noted that all legal jurisdictions recognize exceptions to free speech, including libel, incitement to violence and fighting words. Fish argues that affirmations of freedom of speech are defined by the inevitable exceptions for which they provide. Where people stand on freedom of speech, and the exceptions they are willing to recognize, reflect their conception of the good. Thus, campus hate speech codes can be defended on the

grounds that learning is the substantive purpose of the university, and freedom of speech, while advanced as a value, is tolerated only as long as it is
compatible with learning. The alternative to an absolute guarantee of freedom of speech, Fish concludes, is politics: the struggle over different moral
conceptions and over the right to define what is and is not acceptable in a
given society. It is a mistake to put our faith in 'apolitical abstractions' such
as freedom of speech.

Fish's argument, that free speech is a counter for supporters of one moral
view or another to use in politics, is, in itself, ideologically neutral, but it has a
family resemblance to Marx's critical view of the relationship between liberal
rights and freedoms and political power. Marx's *On the Jewish Question* was
written in response to the demand by Jews that equal civil rights be extended
to them (Marx, 1978 [1843]). He argued that civil rights and liberties, including freedom of speech, could lead to political emancipation for minorities, but
could not break the stranglehold of the system of property relations over society and individual lives. Civil liberties would be used as a tool by the property
owning class to reinforce their power, under the guise of applying equally and
universally to everyone. It was only when the real power relations generated by
unequal ownership of property and capital had been changed that civil rights
and freedoms would really be available equally to all. Marx's analysis also
parallels the critical argument made against pornography as a form of speech
by feminist theorist Catharine MacKinnon (MacKinnon, 1995). As we saw in
Chapter 5, MacKinnon contends that freedom of speech impacts differently,
depending on the relative power of the group speaking. Those who are relatively powerful will be able to use free speech to maintain their position, and to
enforce the inequality of others. We discuss MacKinnon's work in greater
detail later in this chapter.

Free speech versus the recognition of cultural minorities

The communitarian case, that freedom of speech must be in the service of the
moral good of the community, also underlies multiculturalist concerns about
offensive speech. From this perspective, pluralist societies committed to
recognizing and respecting the rights of cultural minorities might be justified
in banning offensive speech, because it fails to treat cultural minorities as
equal members. Bhikhu Parekh has argued that this was behind the angry
Muslim response to Salman Rushdie's *The Satanic Verses* in Britain in 1989
(Parekh, 1990, 2006). Muslims felt that their concerns about how their religion was represented were not taken seriously in British society, and that this
reflected broader attitudes of marginalization. They pointed out that the fact
that the offence of blasphemy only applied to Christianity suggested that
other religions were not equally legitimate and worthy of respect.

It is apparent from this that freedom of speech in this situation was not an absolute right, but was meaningful in a material social context, in which some people were able to take advantage of it, and some were not (Parekh, 1990). The Rushdie affair clearly demonstrated that demands for freedom of speech must be understood within their political context. Those who criticized British Muslims for not subscribing to western civil liberties went on to suggest that Muslim immigration to Britain should be reduced because immigrants were failing to assimilate. This tapped into a xenophobic, anti-immigrant discourse that had emerged in the 1970s in Britain, and reflected deep suspicions and tensions between the majority and minority ethnic groups. Similarly, hate speech cases in the United States and other pluralist democracies have led to protests and unrest on the part of minority ethnic and racial groups – most notably in the Danish cartoons case. The Canadian Supreme Court recognized the threat posed by hate speech to multicultural equality in *R. v. Keegstra*. These are societies and cultural environments quite different to those faced by Mill when he justified free speech to protect the eccentric and intellectual individual in the much more homogeneous society of mid-Victorian Britain.

Parekh argues that the crime of libel, a well-recognized exception to freedom of speech, should be extended to group defamation (Parekh, 2006). In most countries, libel applies when the individual reputation of the target has suffered damage, rather than the reputation of the group to which he or she belongs. But, as Parekh points out, libel is a crime not because it injures the feelings of the victim but, rather, because it damages his or her public reputation and social standing. It is a social crime. The reputation and social standing of races, ethnic and other groups can also suffer as a result of insulting speech, and this affects individuals because they are, as communitarians argue, socially embedded: their sense of self-worth and self-respect depends partly on the standing of their communities. Communal libel is objectionable, Parekh argues, because it is a form of social and political exclusion, a declaration of hostility against a social group. These are the arguments used to justify the laws in many countries against racial vilification and inciting racial hatred. There is no reason, Parekh contends, why these laws should lead to a slippery slope extension of controls on freedom of speech. Personal libel laws have not done so, and the distinction between libel and fair critical comment should be easy to maintain in practice.

Offensive speech and personal harm to group members

Underlying concerns about the damage offensive speech does to cultural groups and communities inform the argument that such speech damages individuals. A powerful case can be made for prohibiting offensive speech on the grounds that it injures both its targets and others who belong to the same group. We have already examined one of these arguments, in the anti-pornography writings of feminist philosopher Catharine MacKinnon (MacKinnon, 1995). As we saw in Chapter 5, pornography is defended in the United States on the grounds that it is free expression protected under the First Amendment. MacKinnon argues that pornography causes real harm to women, by legitimizing violence and sexual abuse. Where it is freely available, men are more likely to abuse women, and women live in fear of male abuse and come to internalize assumptions about their inequality, and about the legitimacy of sexual exploitation. Hate speech can be seen as causing psychological harm in similar ways to its targets. These arguments were made in the *Skokie* case, and are one of the reasons used to justify the racial vilification laws in many western states. MacKinnon contends that because words cause this direct damage, they should not be treated by the law as if they functioned differently from actions (MacKinnon, 1995).

A critique of offensive speech has been developed along these lines in the last couple of decades by critical race theorists – an important new movement that emerged in legal scholarship, and has been influential on political theorists (Matsuda *et al.*, 1993). Critical race theorists are sceptical about claims to objectivity, neutrality and colour-blindedness on the part of the law. They contend that, instead, legal principles and rules, as well as the legal system, reflect racial inequality. The experiences of racial minorities are crucial because, from them, we can gain an 'experiential knowledge' that provides a basis for analysing law and society: it allows us to see the lived experience of racism (Matsuda *et al.*, 1993). Critical race theorists argue that the experience of victims shows that a general attack on a racial group is experienced as a direct and personal attack by members of that group. (This supports the communitarian claim that people feel their identities and self-esteem are, in part, dependent on the status of the communities to which they belong (Taylor, 1994).) Victims of 'vicious hate propaganda' experience physiological symptoms and emotional distress, 'ranging from fear in the gut to rapid pulse rate and difficulty in breathing, nightmares, post-traumatic stress disorder, hypertension, psychosis and suicide' (Matsuda *et al.*, 1993: 24). Matsuda *et al.* contend that the victims of hate speech are restricted in their personal freedoms. They live in fear. In order to avoid offensive speech, they have to quit their jobs, drop out of university and leave their homes. Minorities must also watch their own governments intervening to support hateful speakers, an experience that further alienates them from the societies in which they live. The damage done by hate speech is overwhelmingly done to its targets. But it also impacts on the majority: those who are associated with minorities are also damaged and made to feel inferior.

From the perspective of minorities, we see that offensive speech is 'assaultive speech', which silences, intimidates and subjects victims to

---

Box 8.2 Regulating offensive speech: competing norms and values

Much of the debate around regulating offensive speech turns on different inter-pretations of rights, freedom and autonomy, and the common good:

- **Rights**

Supporters of regulation argue that members of minority groups who are the targets of such speech have rights not to be harmed by offensive speech – partic-ularly speech that incites racial hatred.

Public argument against regulating offensive speech often cites the fundamen-tal individual right to freedom of expression.

- **Freedom and autonomy**

Supporters of regulation argue that freedom of speech is never absolute and is always subject to some limits (for example, speech that incites violence is not protected in liberal democracies). Our freedoms must be compatible with the freedoms of others – and the freedom and autonomy of the speaker must be balanced with the effect that the speech has on the autonomy of its targets.

Opponents of regulation argue that freedom of expression is fundamental to human liberty and autonomy. Moreover, being able to express one's view in public and to participate in public debate and conversation are essential aspects of being a free citizen.

- **The common good**

Supporters of regulation argue that offensive speech – particularly hate speech – alienates minorities, and exacerbates racial and religious tensions. It prevents open and democratic deliberation about politics. Some argue also that unre-stricted freedom of speech is damaging to the moral values that hold a society together.

Opponents of regulating offensive speech argue that the circulation of a full range of views and opinions is necessary for a healthy society. Censorship stifles social change and progress, and, while hate speech might not contribute substantively to this end, allowing the state to prohibit it will ultimately allow it to gag the expression of views favourable to minorities.

---

psychological and physical trauma. Those who use such speech are 'racist assailants' (Matsuda *et al.*, 1993). If we follow MacKinnon's argument, there is no reason to distinguish racist speech from actions that might be prohibited by law. In practice, critical race theorists accept a distinction between assaultive speech and statements of opinion about the alleged inferiority of a specific racial group. The key element justifying prohibition is the expression of hatred, or calls for persecution. This is the standard adopted by most democratic societies in their anti-racial vilification laws.

Conclusion

While the commitment to freedom of speech continues to occupy a central role in the constitutions of liberal democracies – and is affirmed in all major international human rights documents – an international norm or principle is gradually emerging that exempts speech expressing or inciting racial hatred, vilification or persecution from protection in most cases. The United States is unique in remaining outside this consensus. Most countries balance freedom of speech with concerns about promoting equality, democratic government and multiculturalism, thus reflecting the new political realities of increased ethnic, cultural and religious pluralism in liberal democratic nations. When Mill published his famous defence of freedom of speech in 1859, he was not speaking to a nation composed of large and mobilized cultural minorities able to make public claims for equality.

As we have noted throughout our discussion, this new norm provides only for a balance. Anti-racial vilification laws do not allow the banning of offensive speech in most cases, if it is held to refer to matters of public or political concern: they did not prevent the Danish cartoons controversy. For some who support the regulation of offensive speech, it is tempting to try to find the perfect legislative wording that would prohibit hate without encroaching on individual expression or vital public debate. Critics of free speech absolutism remind us, however, that political principles and values do not operate in an ideal world. They are inextricably part of, and reflect, the real-world political context of plurality, difference and the competition for power. As we saw in both the Rushdie and the Danish cartoons case, the controversy over offensive speech was only part of a deeper divide about the role and status of Muslim minorities in western societies. Governments and courts cannot pre-empt or avoid this, or any, debate about cultural pluralism, either by regulating or by refusing to regulate speech.

Chapter 9

Should Civil Liberties be Restricted in Responding to the Threat of Terrorism?

Since the terrorist attacks of September 11, 2001 in the United States, a raft of new measures designed to control and prevent terrorism has been passed into law in democratic states. The United States Patriot Act, passed shortly after the attacks, has been among the most controversial, but similar legislation has been enacted in the United Kingdom and other European and Commonwealth countries. To varying degrees these anti-terrorist laws extend the powers of governments to monitor citizens; they make customary legal protections granted to those accused of criminal acts unavailable to individuals accused of involvement in terrorism, and they further restrict the rights of foreign nationals. Some legislation has also created new criminal offences around expressing support for terrorism, and belonging or giving money to groups that might be associated in any way with terrorism.

In the immediate aftermath of September 11, there was strong popular support – particularly in the United States, but also in other countries – for governments to do 'whatever it takes' to reduce the threat of terrorism. As a result, laws were passed in haste and with little debate. But, in the years since, there have been increasing concerns about the ways in which they infringe civil liberties by extending the powers of the state and restricting individual freedom – the cornerstone of liberal democratic societies. In this chapter, we examine whether or not diminishing civil liberties is justified by the threat of terrorism. We begin by surveying some of the key anti-terrorist measures that have been introduced by national governments, and then explore the different ways in which philosophers have analysed and evaluated the relationship between public security, the threat of terrorist violence, and rights and liberties. In some ways, this raises a familiar and long-standing political problem. Balancing individual rights with security for all is a fundamental challenge for modern democratic societies; underlying, for example, the way criminals and those accused of crimes are treated, the way the state responds to protest demonstrations, and whether or not citizens should be permitted to own guns. But it has become particularly pressing since the September 11 attacks.

Specific legislation on terrorism already existed before 2001 in a range of countries that had direct experience of terrorist violence, including the United States, Israel, the United Kingdom, Germany, France and Italy. The scale of the 2001 attacks was characterized as unprecedented, however, and the anti-terrorist legislation that followed them was justified in terms of the need to protect liberty and democracy, and national ways of life. There was strong pressure on the American Congress from the Bush Administration to pass emergency measures to deal with the threat. The USA Patriot Act was signed into law in late October 2001. Its provisions, which affect civil liberties, fall into three categories:

1 Those expanding surveillance of citizens.
2 Those diminishing the rights of non-nationals.
3 Those dealing with support for terrorist groups.

Among the most controversial of its provisions were those that modified the Foreign Intelligence Surveillance Act, expanding the powers of the state to undertake surveillance of citizens, without judicial oversight. The Act empowered the FBI – without a court order, and with only the authorization of a 'national security letter' issued by the FBI itself – to search telephone and email communications, medical, financial and other records of anyone suspected of involvement in terrorism. State officials were authorized to conduct 'sneak and peek' searches of homes and businesses well in advance of obtaining warrants that notified the subjects of their searches. The FBI was empowered to demand that books, papers or records used or produced by individuals under investigation for involvement in terrorism, be made available by third parties – a provision strongly objected to by public libraries. Roving wiretaps were permitted, which allowed the FBI to conduct wide-ranging and open-ended searches of electronic communication. Both sneak and peek searches and roving wiretaps were declared unconstitutional by the US District Court in 2007 in *Brandon Mayfield* v. *USA*.

The Patriot Act also tightened laws around immigration and the rights of non-nationals. Foreign nationals deemed by the Attorney General to be engaged in any activity dangerous to United States' security can be detained for seven days before they are arrested or deportation proceedings are begun. If they cannot be deported, they can be detained indefinitely. In the third category of restrictions on civil liberties, the Act creates an offence of 'domestic terrorism', which, according to the American Civil Liberties Union, threatens to define protesters as terrorists if they engage in activities potentially dangerous to life. It broadened the range of organizations that could be designated as being terrorist and provided for the detention of anyone, citizen or foreign national, who contributes money to even the peaceful activities of any group designated as terrorist. Providing expert advice and assistance to such organizations was declared to be illegal. This provision was found by the US Court of Appeals (in *Humanitarian Law Project et al.* v. *Gonzales*, 2005) to be contrary to the First Amendment's protection of freedom of speech.

There has been strong opposition from civil liberties groups to all of these measures and, more generally, to the extending of the powers of the executive branch of government, without judicial oversight. Some proposals were abandoned after public outcry – including the Total Information Awareness Program, and the Terrorist Information and Protection System, which would have allowed the systematic collection and analysis of mass information about individuals, and which would have encouraged people to inform on the apparently suspicious dealings of their neighbours. In another controversial extension of executive power, a Presidential Military Order issued shortly after the attacks allowed for the detention, without trial, of terrorism suspects and enemy combatants, suspending habeas corpus (the right of citizens not to be detained without a court warrant, long recognized in liberal democracies and protected by the United States Constitution). Foreign nationals have been held at the US Naval Base at Guantanamo Bay, Cuba. The Supreme Court subsequently upheld the constitutional right of US citizens to seek habeas corpus, even if detained as unlawful combatants (*Hamdi* v. *Rumsfeld*, 2004). In 2008, in *Boumediene* v. *Bush*, the Court extended this right to non-citizens.

Many of the Patriot Act's controversial provisions were due to expire at the end of 2005 but, at this point, the Administration and their supporters in Congress argued to make them permanent, on the grounds that the United States was engaged in a continuing war on terrorism. Despite considerable opposition from civil liberties groups, the Act was reauthorized that year and again in 2006, with those provisions not overruled by the courts remaining intact. Further measures were added, including providing the death penalty for terrorists, new measures to combat the financing of terrorism and new powers for the Secret Service. There have been some attempts at ensuring oversight: the Intelligence Reform Act of 2004 created a Civil Liberties Oversight Board in the executive office of the President. But the Board has no independence, and has only limited ability to gather information about matters for which it is responsible.

Anti-terrorist legislation existed in the United Kingdom prior to 2001, as a result of the experience of IRA terrorism. The Prevention of Terrorism Act, which gave emergency powers to the police, was passed in 1974, after the Birmingham pub bombings killed 21 people. It was renewed several times and, in 2000, the Terrorism Act recognized that anti-terrorist measures were to be permanent. After the September 11 attacks, the Anti-terrorism, Crime and Security Act was signed into law in December 2001, only a month after it was introduced to Parliament. The most controversial aspect of the British legislation concerned detention of non-nationals: the Act provided that any non-British citizens suspected of involvement in terrorism could be indefinitely detained and deported. This suspension of habeas corpus effectively renounced Article 5 of the European Convention on Human Rights (ECHR), which specifies that no one is to be deprived of their liberty unless they are brought before a court. The British government invoked Article 15 of the ECHR, which exempts states from their obligations under the Convention 'in time of war or other public emergency threatening the life of the nation'. It was the only signatory to the Convention to rely on this provision to justify anti-terrorist legislation. In 2004, the Law Lords considered in *A (FC) and Others (FC)* v. *Secretary of State for the Home Department*, a case in which a terrorist suspect had been detained without trial for two years, and held that the detention provisions did violate the ECHR. There was no observable state of emergency existing in Britain. Moreover, the law was discriminatory, as it applied only to aliens, and not to British citizens suspected of involvement in terrorism. This section of the Act was replaced in 2005 with the Prevention of Terrorism Act, which replaced detention in prison with control orders that allowed for extensive conditions to be placed on the movements of suspected terrorists, amounting to a form of house arrest. These could be applied to British citizens and non-citizens alike. But, in 2007, in *Secretary of State for the Home Department* v. *JJ and others*, the High Court found that these orders also amounted to a deprivation of liberty contrary to Article 5 of the ECHR.

In the same way as the Patriot Act in the United States, British legislation provides for increased surveillance: the secret services or police were empowered to request any information from government agencies necessary to pursue or investigate suspected terrorists. The police could also demand physical checks from individuals to ensure their identity – for example, fingerprints. Telephone companies and Internet providers had to retain data on communications. Further restrictions on civil liberties were imposed by the Terrorism Act (2006), which followed the London bombings of 7 July 2005. This Act made it an offence to glorify or encourage terrorism, and extended the period a suspect could be held without trial to 28 days. An attempt to extend this to 42 days in the Counter Terrorism Bill of 2008 was voted down by the House of Lords. Nevertheless, the United Kingdom has the longest period of pre-charge detention of all liberal democracies. (See Box 9.1.)

Other European countries passed anti-terrorist legislation in the wake of the 2001 attacks. The Council of Europe Convention on the Prevention of Terrorism (2006) created three new offences:

1 Public provocation to commit a terrorist offence.
2 Solicitation of others to commit a terrorist offence.
3 Providing training in terrorism.

Box 9.1 The United Kingdom Terrorism Act and the detention of Rizwaan Sabir

The impact of the UK's anti-terrorist measures upon civil liberties – and academic freedom – was demonstrated in the recent arrest of a student and an administrator at the University of Nottingham. In 2008, Rizwaan Sabir, a Masters student in international relations, was researching terrorist tactics, and downloaded the Al Qaida training manual from a publicly available United States Department of Justice website. He then sent it to a colleague, an Algerian national, who worked as an administrator on campus, to print out. Sabir was arrested under the Terrorism Act, and held for six days in prison without charge, while he was interrogated. He described his experience as 'psychological torture'. His colleague was re-arrested on immigration charges and scheduled for deportation. This case raises several of the civil liberties issues that we are concerned with:

- Sabir's download of the manual was reported to the police by the university. A few months previously, he had been involved in a protest by Palestinian students and supporters against Israeli policy in the West Bank. The University had also reported him to the police then, and he had been arrested. As a result, there were further protests by students claiming that the university was breaching rights to free speech. Sabir's subsequent arrest for downloading the Al Qaida manual raises concerns that anti-terrorist measures can be used to clamp down on rights to freedom of speech and lawful protest.
- It also raises questions about the role of the University and other institutions in informing on their staff. The University defended itself as being under a duty to report 'material of this nature' to the police. The Minister for Higher Education denied that the government wanted staff or students to spy on their colleagues.
- Sabir was a Pakistani-British student and a Muslim. Investigating police officers allegedly commented that he would never have been arrested had he been 'a young, blonde Swedish PhD student'. Critics charge that the racial profiling used in terrorist investigations amounts to racial discrimination.

All these provisions were, however, made explicitly subject to the right to freedom of expression protected in the ECHR. France and Germany, both of which passed security packages of exceptional anti-terrorist measures in late 2001, have, together with the United Kingdom, been singled out by human rights groups for their curbs on civil liberties. Legislative changes allowed personal records such as bank accounts to be monitored, and required Internet service providers and phone companies to keep records. Law enforcement officials were given greater power to conduct searches. Neither France nor Germany introduced substantial changes to immigration, or the rights of non-nationals. France's anti-terrorist emergency measures expired automatically in 2003 but, in 2005, legislation was passed that vastly increased the power of the state to conduct electronic surveillance, including closed-circuit cameras, the recording and monitoring of Internet activity, and the retention of data that must be supplied to the state. The period of detention of terror suspects without charge was increased to six days, and the crime of 'associating with miscreants' was created – which critics claimed would criminalize those who frequented the same cafes as suspected terrorists.

Anti-terrorist laws in Australia and Canada have similarly been singled out by critics for their impact on civil liberties. In Canada, the Anti-terrorist Act was rushed through in December 2001, and includes several provisions that critics have argued are contrary to the Canadian Charter of Rights and Freedoms. As well as increasing the surveillance powers of the police, the Act allows terrorism suspects to be arrested and held without charge for up to 72 hours, and authorizes judges to compel witnesses to testify in secret. Its controversial 'motive clause' defined as a terrorist act any crime committed with ideological, religious or political motives. The Ontario Superior Court struck down this provision in 2006 on the grounds that it violated the Charter of Rights and Freedoms. Unlike the US Patriot Act, the Canadian legislation provided for judicial review of surveillance orders and for some more controversial provisions to expire after five years. Nevertheless, critics complained that it was over-broad, and would define illegally striking workers or peaceful anti-globalization protesters as terrorists. Thus, it threatened what some critics have called the politics of associational life in Canada (Schneiderman and Cossman, 2001).

Australia passed the Anti-Terrorism Act of 2005, in response to bombings that killed a number of Australians in 2002 and 2005 in Indonesia. The Act allows for the detention of individuals considered to be able to provide information about a terrorist offence, whether or not they were suspected of being involved themselves. Disclosing that an individual had been detained was made a crime. Control orders issued without judicial review allow restrictions on individuals suspected of involvement – on their free movement, their association with others (including their lawyers,) and their movements – including the wearing of tracking devices. It is a crime under the law to praise a terrorist act, or to urge others to attempt to change the law by illegal means, or to provide funds for any aspect of a terrorist organization without enquiring into its purposes. Police were empowered to request information from any source about any named person – professional privilege did not apply. Critics have complained that the Australian legislation does not have the same provisions for parliamentary and judicial review as its British counterpart. This was particularly dangerous, given that Australia has no constitutional bill of rights, or any legislative charter of rights.

Liberty and security: framing the debate

In Chapter 8, we looked at the relationship between freedom of expression for individuals, on the one hand, and various ideas about what constitutes a good society, on the other. As we saw, powerful arguments for regulating individual free expression are made on the grounds that unrestricted offensive speech threatens the fundamental democratic and egalitarian character of a society. In the case of anti-terrorist legislation, the very survival of a society is invoked to legitimize arguments for diminishing individual rights and freedoms. What are the liberties under threat here? As we have seen in our survey of national legislation, they include freedom of movement, expression and association, as well as rights that establish how individuals are to be treated by state authorities: rights to privacy, to be treated with due process, and the right not to be detained without trial. David Luban distinguishes between powers, or substantive liberties – the right to do something, such as join a group or visit a website – and protections, which are liberties from state mistreatment (Luban, 2005). In this chapter, however, we will follow the convention of grouping these together as civil liberties. This concept covers both freedoms and rights, in the sense that individuals have rights to be free from various forms of state interference or mistreatment. John Rawls takes a similar approach when he argues, at the beginning of *A Theory of Justice*, that all citizens are to have an equal right to the basic liberties (Rawls, 1971).

We begin by acknowledging common assumptions. All those involved in the debate over terrorism and security in democratic societies recognize the importance of civil liberties. Even those who defend restrictions claim that their ultimate purpose is to preserve freedom and democracy in some broader sense. Similarly, political philosophers in liberal democracies share in the common popular condemnation of terrorist attacks, and agree that states must take some measures to protect their citizens. The question at stake is whether these measures should include restricting civil liberties on the grounds of maintaining national security. In public debate, this issue is usually framed in terms of the need to 'strike a balance' between individual liberty and security. As we shall see, however, several political philosophers have criticized the applicability of the idea of balancing. Critics focus also not only on the restrictions themselves, but on the way in which they were passed into law. Many anti-terrorist laws have been accused of being formulated and pushed through in haste, so that they were not subjected to appropriate scrutiny by lawmakers and the public (Haubrich, 2003).

We begin by examining arguments that support security measures despite the restriction of civil liberties that they involve. The most commonly made case here is consequentialist: that the consequences of terrorism are so damaging that restrictions on liberties, while unfortunate, pale by comparison. But scholars also argue that these restrictions are necessary in order to maintain the very political system and order on which liberty depends. We then turn to critical perspectives, some of which also emphasize consequences, focusing on the dangers that follow from allowing states to gain more extensive powers. As we shall see, however, critics also argue that fundamental human rights and liberties are at the basis of all systems of order, and that therefore there can be no legitimacy in a political system that denies them. Some argue more specifically that the security measures are unjust because they impact differently on different groups. Both sides of this debate require us to think about the purpose of the state, and the relationship between justice and order, both of which are perennial and central questions of political theory.

State power and the protection of citizens

Before the terrorist attacks of September 11, 2001, the relationship between liberty and security had not been a central concern in recent western political theory. Both liberal philosophers and their critics had, for the most part, focused on the relative rights of individuals, civil associations and the state, but had assumed the relationships between them to operate within the context of a stable and secure society. Rawls limits his principles in *A Theory of Justice*, for example, to well-ordered societies and, in the later *The Law of Peoples*, restricted his scope to peaceful, legitimate and non-expansionist governments (Rawls, 1971, 1999). One of the effects of the attacks and their political aftermath has been to bring questions about security back into normative political theory. Most political philosophers have responded to this by asserting the fundamental importance of civil liberties. But some have defended restrictions on liberties on the grounds of the protective role of the state. From this perspective, all normative political arguments presume the need for a secure state, because it is only in the context of civil order that we can develop principles of justice.

From the emergence of the modern state, which historians date from around the seventeenth century, the power and authority of government have been justified on the grounds that it is essential to maintaining order and stability. It is in the interests of individuals to agree to a concentration of power in the hands of the state in order to protect their security, as they would be unable to protect themselves effectively on their own. Social contract theorists of the seventeenth and eighteenth centuries suggested that individuals come together in a 'state of nature' to form government, in a social contract made in order to ensure their own protection. The pre-eminent theorist of this position is Thomas Hobbes, who wrote during the English Civil War – the bloody struggle between Parliament and the Royalists. In his *Leviathan*, published in 1651, Hobbes describes human life in the state of nature, without government, as being dominated by each individual's insecurity and constant fear of others. Under these conditions, life was, as Hobbes famously put it, 'solitary, poor, nasty, brutish and short' (Hobbes, 1962 [1651]). Only the establishment of a single and all-powerful authority would protect individuals from each other, and allow them to live free from fear, and to cooperate, work together, make contracts, and develop civilization and order. But the state would only be able to offer this protection if it could command absolute obedience. Hobbes argued that individuals must obey all of its commands, with the sole exception being for those that were contrary to self-preservation. Individual self-protection and preservation were the reasons for which the state had been formed in the first place and, if it threatened them, individuals were not obliged to obey.

The idea that civil liberties and rules of justice only apply in the context of a secure society is not restricted to a Hobbesian defence of absolute state power. The eighteenth-century philosopher David Hume argued that justice was a matter of mutual advantage; when law and order had broken down, or survival was at stake, its principles ceased to apply (Hume, 1983 [1751]). During the debate over the Constitution of the new United States in the late eighteenth century, Alexander Hamilton wrote: 'Safety from external danger is the most powerful director of national conduct. Even the ardent love of liberty will, after a time, give way to its dictates' (Madison *et al.*, 1987). The late American Supreme Court Chief Justice Rehnquist expressed this idea in 2000, when he said that, in times of war, the laws speak 'with a muted voice' (Rehnquist, 1998: 225). As we have noted, some international agreements, such as the ECHR, include provisions that they do not apply at a time of national emergency, when the very cohesion and security of the state is under threat.

From this perspective, as Benjamin Barber observes, the terrorist attacks of September 11 undid the social contract, at least in the United States, bringing Americans back to a state of nature, characterized by fear, where liberty meant unacceptable risk (Barber, 2003). Anti-terrorist laws represent the state's response: an assertion of power in order to protect both individual liberties and the common good. We might note that these extended state powers can be justified equally as well on the grounds that they are designed to protect communal moral discourse and social networks, as well as individual rights. As Jean Elshtain argues, civil security is essential for all other goods to flourish (Elshtain, 2003). If certain limited civil liberties must be sacrificed in order to ensure security, the trade-off is worthwhile, as no liberties and rights could be guaranteed without it. Richard Posner insists that rights are not absolute but, rather, depend on security (Posner, 2003). Posner even advocates what he refers to as civil disobedience, arguing that public officials should, if they think it necessary, refuse to follow human rights rules designed to restrain the state. The difficulty is in determining, as Posner argues, the point at which the expansion of a right would detract more from public safety than it would add to personal liberty, and when restricting a right would detract more from liberty than it would add to safety. Nevertheless, the task of the courts is to determine that point (Posner, 2006).

The dilemma of how to balance rights with security is avoided if we accept the consequentialist argument most commonly heard in public debate: that the damage caused by terrorism is so terrible, that protecting people from future attack obviously outweighs any discomfort caused by restrictions on civil liberties. Those who take this position might invoke the benefits of state action as described by the late eighteenth-century utilitarian philosopher, Jeremy Bentham. Bentham argued that the most important objective of legislation was security, so that individuals could enjoy the fruits of their labour (Bentham, 1931 [1802]). From this position, he criticized the various protections of English common law that had grown up to protect the individual against the exercise of state power. Such measures could not be legitimate if they hindered the state in protecting individual security. Bentham's concern was with criminal law; he argued, for example, that the state would be justified in arresting a criminal to prevent him from committing a future crime (Bentham, 1931 [1802]).

As critics point out, restrictions on civil liberties imposed by anti-terrorism legislation might be quite substantial to the minorities of citizens who must endure them. For many in the majority, the measures have very little practical effect. We discuss these concerns about unequal burdens imposed by anti-terrorist measures later in this chapter.

The dangers of state power

Hobbes wrote during a period of civil upheaval in England, in which the greatest source of danger to individuals came from their fellow countrymen. This is reflected in his reliance on the peacekeeping power of an absolutist state. But once peace was restored and, as the state subsequently became entrenched, and increased its power and influence over individual lives, it came to be seen as a greater threat to individuals. Liberal theorists from the eighteenth century onwards relied more on the political philosophy of John Locke, who saw the state as an impartial umpire in disputes among citizens, rather than an absolutist authority. (For an alternative interpretation of Locke's view of the state, see p. 186.) Locke's citizens retain the rights to life, liberty and property that they had in the state of nature, rather than surrendering all except self-preservation to the state. He established what Judith Shklar has called the liberalism of fear: the idea that liberalism is primarily concerned with protecting individuals from state coercion (Shklar, 1989). The worst evil is physical cruelty and the most dangerous force is an all-powerful state. For these reasons, state power must be limited (Locke, 1988 [1690]). In practical terms, what is to be feared, according to Shklar, are the extra-legal, secret and unauthorized acts of public officials. The only way to check these is by subdividing political power so there is always scrutiny and oversight of state action.

Concern about state encroachment on individual liberties has continued to be a central focus of liberal philosophy since Locke. In the nineteenth century, John Stuart Mill defended individual liberty against state interference (Mill, 1989a [1859]). But for Mill and more recent liberals, the security of citizens has been treated as a settled question. Some critics suggest now that even those who take a Lockean rather than Hobbesian approach must acknowledge that personal safety is a prerequisite of liberty. Tamar Meisels poses this as a question: How should Lockean liberals respond to a Hobbesian state of war (Meisels, 2005)? If we see state power as threatened by terrorism, with the result that individuals are at risk from each other (a description of the effects of terrorism that many liberal critics would challenge), then we can defend abrogating some civil liberties for reasons of expedience in times of national emergency. Preventive detention without trial for a specified period can be justified, on the grounds that it takes some time to amass evidence against suspected terrorists. But, Meisels argues, national emergency cannot justify giving up procedural liberties that deal with how the state treats us – for example, our right to be free from torture. From a Hobbesian point of view, these rights are essentially to do with self-protection, and therefore are never handed over to the state. From a Lockean perspective, the state is inherently limited and cannot compel us by force to implicate or harm ourselves (Meisels, 2005).

Some philosophers insist that even terrorism on the scale of the 2001 attacks does not amount to a Hobbesian 'war of all against all' (Goodin, 2006). Robert Goodin points out that there was no breakdown of law and order on September 11, and no social breakdown. We might add, in fact, that there was evidence of considerable social cooperation in Manhattan in the aftermath of the attacks, not the least of which was the selfless performance of their civic duty by public officials such as fire-fighters. Terrorism does not return people to a pre-social contract state of nature. It leads, rather, to a war of 'some against all', which, as Goodin argues, produces fear, but does not justify on Hobbesian terms the exercise of absolutist power by the state (Goodin, 2006). Rather, governments promote that fear by their own actions, in order to reinforce their own power.

On a more specific level, critics of state power, including several who defend emergency measures against terrorism, argue that, even if we accept the Hobbesian position, there is no justification for restrictions on civil liberties to continue on a long-term, or even semi-permanent basis (Ackerman, 2006; Ignatieff, 2004; Meisels, 2005). As the British Law Lords observed in

2004, there is no evidence that Britain is in a state of emergency, and we might conclude the same of other democracies. Emergency powers, once institutionalized, reinforce the powers of the state over citizens (Dworkin, 2002). For these reasons, Bruce Ackerman proposes for the United States a limited 'emergency constitution' that allows the President to make executive orders to deal with terrorist emergencies, but subjects these to legislative review (Ackerman, 2006). Michael Ignatieff argues that some restrictions on civil liberties are an unavoidable lesser evil. Because they are morally questionable, however, they must be 'strictly targeted, applied to the smallest possible number of people, used as a last resort, and kept under the adversarial scrutiny of an open democratic system' (Ignatieff, 2004: 8). Recognizing that any state of emergency must be only short-term is particularly important, given that it is almost impossible to show that restricting civil liberties has actually caused a diminished threat from terrorism (Waldron, 2003). Even if states experience a reduction in terrorist attacks after introducing restrictions, this could be brought about by other, less controversial measures, such as increased security at borders.

The democratic process and checks on executive power

Critics of anti-terrorist measures often point to the way in which they were passed into law, and the degree to which they are subject to review. As we have seen, many countries rushed to introduce laws curtailing civil liberties after September 11, and this meant that they were subject to no process of public deliberation about them, and little legislative debate. The Patriot Act was passed only six weeks after it was introduced to Congress, despite the major changes it brought about in the American government's surveillance powers, and in the legal rights of anyone suspected or accused of terrorism (Leone, 2003). Critics who protested in the United States were told that they were giving aid and comfort to the enemy, and subjecting others to risk of a further attack. Similar criticism was made of the rush to pass legislation in the United Kingdom and in Canada.

As we discussed in Chapter 8, when we considered the impact of hate speech on public debate and discussion, the democratic political process requires debate, discussion and public participation. A climate of fear, desperation and hate is not conducive to open and thoughtful consideration of the relationship between liberty and security. As do many critics, Ronald Dworkin has argued that the American Congress did not consider the implications of the Patriot Act sufficiently closely; neither did it insist on sufficient legislative and judicial review of its provisions once enacted (Dworkin, 2003). Goodin goes further along these lines and suggests that states are themselves guilty of a kind of terrorism in inducing and promoting fears in the populations out of all proportion to the actual risk of terrorist attack. They then use these fears to push through legislative programmes that would never be agreed were the populations less panicked, thereby promoting their own interests (Goodin, 2006).

The absence of adequate provisions for legislative and judicial review of anti-terrorist measures in much of the legislation passed since 2001 points to a troubling increase in the power of the executive branch of government over the legislative and judicial arms. In democratic societies based on the parliamentary system, we tend to think of the legislature as the most important branch of government – it is there that popular sovereignty is embodied, and the executive is drawn from the legislature. In presidential systems such as that of the United States, the Constitution provides for power to be shared between the legislative, executive and judicial branches. The balance between them is designed to prevent any single one becoming too powerful, particularly the executive arm of government, which is responsible for carrying out the law. There is less of a formal separation between the branches of government in parliamentary democracies, but in these systems the executive is responsible to the legislature, and the judiciary reviews its actions.

Legislative responsibility and judicial review check abuses of power by the executive, by promoting at least some degree of openness, publicity and democratic accountability. Civil libertarian Alan Dershowitz relies on this argument in his controversial defence of the right of the state to use torture to extract information about terrorist activities and plans. States should only have such a right, Dershowitz argues, when authorized by judicial warrants (Dershowitz, 2002). This will ensure that decisions to torture – which Dershowitz views as inevitable – are not made and carried out in secret: if they must be authorized by the courts, there will be greater scrutiny of each case, and more reluctance to allow torture. The courts in both the United States and the United Kingdom have often, in the past, deferred to executive decisions concerning what is a legitimate infringement of civil liberties. One of the most notorious of these cases in the United States was the Supreme Court's decision in *Korematsu* v. *United States* (1944), upholding a Presidential executive order to intern Japanese-Americans during World War II.

The fundamental role of liberties

The arguments we have considered so far against restricting civil liberties for security all assume that liberties must be balanced against the role of the state in guaranteeing personal security. But we might also argue that individual liberty, autonomy and rights are so important that state action that threatens them cannot be justified for any reason. According to this view, individuals should be understood, fundamentally, as more than bodies that can be hurt; rather, they are moral agents. As the eighteenth-century German philosopher Immanuel Kant puts it, people are 'ends in themselves', morally valuable for their own sakes, and defined by their ability to decide on and carry out moral purposes (Kant, 1993 [1785]). Our ability to function as moral actors making autonomous decisions is protected by the guarantee of civil liberties: the basic liberties of expression, movement, association, and the other protections that ensure that the state respects our rights. As a result, these rights, liberties and protections are fundamental. Dworkin expresses this as 'rights are trumps', which means that a presumption exists that rights will take priority over considerations of consequences (Dworkin, 1984). Libertarian philosopher Robert Nozick takes an even stronger view of the non-negotiability of rights, arguing that they impose 'side constraints' on the actions of others, which means that they set limits to what is morally permissible (Nozick, 1974). We might note that the conception of rights advanced in this case has to be strong, because the potential damage done by terrorist action is so great that concerns about consequences might easily outweigh rights and liberties.

Liberals who take this position are strongly critical of measures the state has introduced to combat terror that infringe civil liberties. These include not only obvious breaches of rights such as torture, but also many of the provisions we surveyed at the beginning of this chapter: the power to conduct surveillance of citizens, to detain suspects without trial and to deny them access to due process and proper legal representation, and to criminalize support for the lawful activities of groups that could be classified as terrorist. Dworkin argues that these measures are immoral because they breach basic human rights – rights that are independent of the state and do not depend on state security. We have them because we are human, not because we are citizens, law-abiding or otherwise (Dworkin, 2003). It is not appropriate to speak of balancing these rights with security, as they cannot be bartered away for any purpose. As Dworkin points out, ordinary criminals retain basic rights in their dealings with the state no matter what threat they pose to citizens: we do not abandon these rights because of concerns about state security (Dworkin, 2002). In war, where the parties are not bound to respect the civil liberties of their enemies (a case where rights do not completely trump consequences), most nations nevertheless accept that there are rules that regulate what states are permitted to do, particularly in their treatment of civilians. (It was to avoid these rules that the Bush Administration declared the prisoners at Guantanamo Bay to be enemy combatants rather than prisoners of war.)

Dworkin's reference to civil liberties in wartime does point to the fact that, even if we do not think in terms of consequences, we tend not to regard rights and liberties in absolute terms. The state can override an individual's rights, for example, to protect the rights of others (Dworkin, 1978). In practical terms, liberal democracies have agreed that rights and liberties can be limited for national security, territorial integrity or public safety, a caveat expressed in Article 15 of the ECHR.

The selective impact of anti-terrorist measures on minorities

A further problem with restricting civil liberties to maintain a balance with security is that those measures that have been introduced operate selectively. They are more likely to have an adverse affect on non-citizens, and citizens who belong to ethnic minorities originally from Muslim states, who are regarded as being more likely to be involved in terrorist activities. Racial profiling has been controversially employed in both the United States and the United Kingdom in investigating possible terrorism. After the July 2005 bombings in London, the British Transport Police chief constable said that his officers would not 'waste time searching old white ladies'. In the United States, Dworkin claims that no American who is not a Muslim, and has no Muslim connections, is in danger of any government surveillance or action (Dworkin, 2003). Detention without trial has been imposed disproportionately on non-citizens in both the United States and the United Kingdom, although the courts in both countries have now ruled against these discriminatory provisions.

Jeremy Waldron argues that the balance being struck is, thus, not between security and liberty, but between the security of the majority on one hand, and the liberties of minorities on the other (Waldron, 2003). This is much harder to justify, given the fact that, in liberal democracies, every person's life is held to be intrinsically and equally valuable and worthwhile. Equal treatment and non-discrimination are widely recognized principles of human rights, expressed in the principle that the law applies equally to everyone. We see this embodied, for example, in Rawls' first principle of justice: everyone has the right to equal basic liberties. Restricting the liberties of some for the security of others amounts to an unequal distribution of liberties (Moeckli, 2008). We might point out that members of minority groups also benefit from the protection offered by security measures. But benefits for all are still traded off against the rights of a few.

It is much easier to take a utilitarian approach emphasizing the value of security when only the rights of minorities are threatened (Luban, 2005). Cass Sunstein points out that the fact that the burden of restrictions falls overwhelmingly on minorities is an important reason why governments have not encountered more opposition in pushing them into law (Sunstein, 2005). Where restrictions fall equally on all, they are much more likely to be subject to public debate, and citizens will be forced to consider the realities of the actual risk that they are introduced to counter. As the political economist and theorist Friedrich Hayek argued, when restrictions to liberties apply to everyone, it is reasonable to conclude that they will be kept to a minimum (Hayek, 1962). Sunstein advocates judicial review of all restrictions on liberties, and argues that the courts should be relatively lenient in allowing restrictions that apply equally to everyone, because they can be assumed to have already undergone public scrutiny and approval (Sunstein, 2005). Restrictions of liberties that apply only to minorities, however, should only be permitted if the benefits to all are clear and significant, and the costs to the few are minor. We might express this in terms of Kant's dictum that moral principles should be universalizable (Kant, 1993 [1785]) or, as contemporary theorists put this idea, that they should be capable of being impartially defended to others. This would require politicians and citizens to think about the balance between liberty and security in each specific measure, and would make any decisions reached more legitimate (Moeckli, 2008). It would not necessarily rule out profiling if there was a clear link between ethnicity and involvement in terrorism, but it would require us to defend that link, and to think about its limits – about characteristics other than ethnicity and religion that also tend to be shared by terrorists.

Security and liberty: a critical perspective

Most of our discussion to this point assumes that liberty and security are fundamentally opposed and competing values in liberal democracies. Some recent theorists who take a more critical perspective on security studies argue, however, that security and liberty are intertwined, and that the liberties of individuals have always been circumscribed by the state's drive to protect itself and its interests. Mark Neocleous argues that the liberal defence of civil liberties has long been subordinate to a justification of the right of government to act unilaterally when matters of national interest are at stake (Neocleous, 2007). Neocleous points out that even Locke, whose defence of a limited state we discussed earlier (pp. 180–1), allowed that the state had the 'prerogative' to take action where necessary to protect national security. And, as we have seen, subsequent philosophers defending liberty have continued to acknowledge the fundamental importance of security as the grounds on which liberty rests. This is also the position of contemporary defenders of, at least, limited restrictions on civil liberties, such as Meisels.

Neocleous concludes that restrictions on civil liberties to combat terrorism do not express the necessary evil of a balance between the competing values of liberty and security. Rather, they reveal the inherent subordination of individual liberty to state interests, defined as security, which is inherent in liberal democracies. Liberal democratic states have frequently invoked prerogative or special powers to override civil liberties to deal with 'states of emergency'. Such measures are justified on the grounds that they are temporary, but they easily become entrenched and permanent. Security, he concludes, has always been the 'political trumps' for liberals – rather than rights, as Dworkin has argued (Dworkin, 1978). This approach suggests that although security is invoked to mean the safety of citizens, it refers in reality to the protection and preservation of the state.

Box 9.2 Restricting civil liberties to combat terrorism: competing norms and values

The debate around civil liberties and anti-terrorism measures centres around competing interpretations and values assigned to liberty, security and the role of the state, and equality:

• Liberty

Those who defend restricting civil liberties to combat terrorism argue that liberties can only be exercised when people do not fear for their lives and safety. Liberty has no value if security cannot be assured.

Critics of restricting civil liberties counter that even large-scale terrorist attacks do not constitute the fundamental breakdown in law and order that makes freedom impossible to exercise. Some make the stronger case that individual liberties are fundamentally constitutive of what it means to be a person, and cannot be abrogated.

• Security and the state

Supporters of restrictions argue that protecting the security of citizens is the most essential duty of the state, and anti-terrorist measures are designed to preserve the safety of individuals, including members of minority groups targeted by restrictions.

Critics counter that anti-terrorist measures exceed what is required to protect the safety of citizens, and are designed, instead, to reinforce the power of the state. Their aim is state security, rather than the security of individuals.

• Equality

Many supporters of anti-terrorist measures are not unsympathetic to the argument that these measures have an unequal impact on minorities. They point out, however, that members of minority groups also benefit from improved security.

Opponents of anti-terrorist measures claim that they are unequal in their application and impact. Members of particular minorities are much more likely to be targeted and to have their civil liberties reduced.

Conclusion

There is more general agreement among political philosophers on the importance of preserving civil liberties in anti-terrorist legislation than might first
appear. Even those, such as Barber and Elshtain, who are uncomfortable
with criticism of the measures introduced by the United States and other
countries to counter terrorism, focus more on what they see as the unpatri-
otic rhetoric of critics, than on their substantial arguments. All agree that
civil liberties are valuable, and that they should not be sacrificed except
where there is a clear and imminent threat of terrorist violence – and then not
without careful assessment of the benefits that sacrificing them brings, and
the burden that sacrifice places on individuals and groups.

These provisos require us to focus on the way in which decisions about the
extent of individual rights are made in democratic societies. They are particularly important, given that the threat of the mass destruction caused by
terrorism is a powerful inducement to think in consequentialist terms, and to
regard the consequences of terrorist violence as outweighing everything else.
As American historian Alan Brinkley has noted, public support for protecting basic freedoms is highly contingent and can easily evaporate, as it has
historically during wartime (Brinkley, 2007). Public fear of mass violence
might easily be manipulated by governments in the interests of extending
executive power. The debate about civil liberties reminds us of the dangers
and difficulties involved in making simple consequentialist arguments in
politics. Not only can this blind us to the ease with which fundamental rights
and liberties are sacrificed for consequences that are threatened, but cannot
be calculated, but also, the consequences of government policies are never
simple. Measures introduced to protect the security of people against each
other and against foreigners can ultimately result in increasing the power of
the state to exert control over its own citizens in ways that can very
concretely be measured.

Chapter 10

Should Rich Countries Give More Foreign Aid?

There are all too many ways of measuring the enormous inequalities between rich and poor on a global scale. United Nations figures show that 40 per cent of the world's population lives on less than US$2 a day, while 15 per cent lives on less than US$1 (UNDP, 2007/8). The gross domestic product (GDP) of the world's 41 poorest countries is less, in total, than the wealth of the world's seven richest individuals combined (Kroll and Fass, 2007; World Bank, 2007). The poorest 40 per cent of the world's population accounts for 5 per cent of total income, while the richest 20 per cent accounts for 75 per cent of global income (UNDP, 2007/8). According to UNICEF: more than a quarter of all the children in developing countries are underweight or stunted in their growth; one billion children, or one in every two in the world, live in poverty; 640 million children live without adequate shelter; and 400 million children have no access to safe water. UNICEF estimates that over 26,000 children died every day in 2006 – a total of 9.7 million deaths. The over-whelming majority of these deaths are in the 60 countries of the developing world, and are from preventable causes. As Nelson Mandela said in 2005: 'Massive poverty and obscene inequality are such scourges of our times – times in which the world boasts such breathtaking advances in science, technology, industry and wealth accumulation – that they have to rank alongside slavery and apartheid as social evils' (UNDP, 2005).

These statistics focus on relative inequalities across the global population, rather than between countries. But, if we look at overall national wealth and wealth per capita, we see that the world's wealthy and developed countries enjoy considerably higher levels of income and wealth than poorer nations. Table 10.1, based on figures from the World Bank, shows countries' gross national income per capita in 2007.

However, poverty is not confined to underdeveloped countries. Some of the world's most developed countries, with high levels of overall wealth and GDP per capita, have sectors of the population living if not in absolute poverty by global standards, then with insufficient material means to function fully in society. A 2007 study by the US Census Bureau found that 12.3 per cent of Americans, and 17.4 per cent of American children, lived in poverty (De-Navas Walt *et al.*, 2006). In the UK, where poverty is defined as falling below 60 per cent of median income, the government's Households

Table 10.1   *Gross National Income per capita of
selected countries in US$, 2007*

Norway	76,450
Switzerland	59,880
United States	46,040
United Kingdom	42,740
Canada	39,420
Australia	35,960
China	2,360
India	950
Bangladesh	470
Tanzania	400
Uganda	340
Ethiopia	220
Liberia	150
Burundi	110

Source: data from World Bank (2008).

Below Average Income data shows that 21.6 per cent of the population lived in poverty in 2006, a proportion higher than all but five other European Union countries. Amongst developed countries, the income gap between richest and poorest is highest in the United States, but more than 80 per cent of the world's population lives in countries where the income gap is growing (UNDP, 2005).

Redistributing existing resources in the world could dramatically reduce extreme poverty. The United Nations Development Programme estimates that it would cost US$300 billion to lift one billion people over the US$1 a day line. This amount represents 1.6 per cent of the income of the world's richest 10 per cent (UNDP, 2005). International institutions and non-governmental organizations (NGOs) have called for increased aid to reduce inequalities for over four decades. In a 1970 United Nations General Assembly (UNGA) Resolution, developed nations committed to spending 0.7 per cent of gross national product (GNP) on overseas aid by the middle of the decade. The General Assembly resolved that aid was to be untied – or not linked to requirements imposed by the donor country about how it was to be spent – both continuous, and long-term. It should take the form of financial and technical assistance aimed at improving the economic progress of the recipient country, and should not be designed to benefit the donor countries.

Box 10.1 The Millennium Development goals

The UN General Assembly Millennium Declaration of 2000 committed UN member states to eight development goals to be achieved by 2015, including halving the 1990 rate of extreme poverty (an income of US$1 per day or less), achieving universal primary education and reducing child mortality by two thirds of the 1990 figures (that is, to fewer than 5 million child deaths a year). In 2005, at the Gleneagles Summit, the G8 countries, along with the World Bank and the IMF, agreed to a package of multilateral debt relief. This was designed to help achieve the millennium goals by freeing up debtor country resources to be used in reducing poverty and improving health and education for their citizens.

- The goals focused not only on transferring wealth, but also on changing the rules of the international economy to remove structural inequalities. One of the goals was to develop a 'global partnership for development', including an open trading and financial system that is rule-based, predictable and non-discriminatory.
- Donor governments also reinforced the importance of economic and political reform within recipient countries. The High Level Panel for Financing for Development, which was charged with exploring financing for the millennium goals, recommended in its 2002 report that every developing country 'needs to set its economic fundamentals in order', by building sound economic institutions, as well as political institutions based on popular participation in government and the rule of law. Developing nations are required to commit to combating corruption and protecting education, health, the status of women and the rural sector (Zedillo, 2001).
- Progress in achieving the goals has been uneven. A 2008 progress report found that in some areas – including primary education, AIDS treatment and access to safe drinking water – substantial progress has been made. Poverty has been reduced in China and India, but in sub-Saharan African countries it has been reduced by about only 1 per cent, and these countries appear unlikely to meet the goals by 2015. Developed countries had reduced their aid in 2007 and 2008, and the stalling of international trade negotiations meant that reforms required for equitable development were very unlikely to be made.

Even though these targets and agendas have been set, year after year since 1970, and developed countries have recently committed to halving extreme poverty by 2015 (see Box 10.1) almost all rich nations have constantly failed to reach their agreed obligations of the 0.7 per cent target. Instead, the proportion of income given in aid has been around 0.2 to 0.4 per cent, some US$100 billion short. Moreover, as many critics have pointed out, what aid has been delivered has not been given on the terms required by the UNGA

Resolution. A good deal of assistance is designed to serve the strategic and economic objectives of the donor country, or powerful interest groups within that country. Much aid is in the form of technical assistance, which is exempt from the requirement that it not be tied. Furthermore, aid tends to be targeted not necessarily to the areas of greatest need, but to areas of the world where the donor country has a strategic or historical interest. Israel and Egypt account for more than half of all United States development assistance – although Israel is classified as a high-income economy by the World Bank. Since the terrorist attacks of 2001, much of the increase in United States aid has gone to countries that have assisted the United States in anti-terrorist operations. In fact, a 2002 Senate Resolution directed that US aid should play an increased role in supporting American foreign policy objectives, particularly in the 'war against terror' (Hirvonen, 2005).

A study of poverty over the period 1981 to 2004 found that poverty in the developing world had declined, but the decline was uneven (Chen and Ravallion, 2007). Poverty measured in headcounts had declined by 0.8 per cent a year over this period. But, even with this rate of decline, there would still be over 800 million people living on less than US$1 a day by 2015. (We should note that many critics consider US$1 a day to be far too low a measure of extreme poverty.) There is no consistent decline in people living at under US$2 per day, and there would be a projected 2.8 billion people living at this level by 2015. In any case, these figures include China: if it is excluded, there is no decline in the number of people living below US$1 a day, and an increase in people living at below US$2 per day. There are sharply falling numbers of the poor in East Asia, but rising numbers of the poor in Eastern Europe and Central Asia in this period. There are rising numbers but falling percentages of the poor in Latin America, the Middle East and North Africa, and poverty continues to increase in sub-Saharan Africa.

These figures reflect the continuing trend in low levels of aid given by wealthy countries. While some rich nations do give quite high dollar amounts of aid, their percentages of gross national income (GNI) are still small – the United States and Japan, the world's two largest donor countries, fall into this category. The percentage of GNI in aid given by the OECD Development Assistance Committee, the largest donor countries, declined from a high of 0.33 per cent in 1990 to a low of 0.22 per cent in 1997. It has risen overall since 2001, but much of this is due to debt relief rather than direct assistance (OECD, 2007). In 2007, aid figures were down again, reflecting the end of high levels of debt relief for Iraq and Nigeria, and a small increase in other forms of aid. The OECD announced that donor countries would have to make unprecedented increases in the amount of foreign aid they gave in order to meet targets set by the G8 for 2010 (OECD, 2008). Table 10.2 shows overseas development aid as a percentage of GNI in 2007. (These figures include debt and emergency relief, but not the charitable

Table 10.2 *Aid as a percentage of Gross National Income for selected countries, 2007*

	%
Norway	0.95
Sweden	0.93
Luxembourg	0.91
Denmark	0.81
The Netherlands	0.81
France	0.38
Germany	0.37
UK	0.36
Australia	0.32
Canada	0.29
Japan	0.17
United States	0.16

Source: data from the OECD Development Co-operation Directorate, 2008.

contributions made by individuals.) Only the first five countries met or exceeded the target of 0.7 per cent of gross national income in aid.

In 2007, total aid given by OECD donor countries was 0.28 per cent of GNI, or around US$103 billion. To put these figures in context, UNDP figures show that rich countries spend just under US$1 billion each year on domestic agricultural subsidies – about the same amount that is spent on agricultural aid to poor nations (UNDP, 2005).

Philosophers have addressed the problem of global poverty in two ways. Some have approached the issue in terms of need, asking whether or not we, as individuals, have moral duties to relieve the acute suffering of people in other countries with whom we do not share citizenship in common. As we shall see, ethicists generally agree that if we can save someone's life, or relieve their serious suffering without experiencing any important loss ourselves, we ought to do so. For some, this means that, as individuals, we have a moral duty to contribute wealth to the needy – whether at home or abroad – through private charity. Philosophers who take this approach generally (though not always) agree that governments should also provide assistance to the needy through foreign aid. The second way of framing the issue is by concentrating on the relative inequalities between nations, and on the duties of governments to reduce these by transferring wealth. We will begin by considering some of the ethical arguments based on need, and will then turn to those that also consider questions of relative inequality.

Philosophical arguments alone cannot fully answer the question as to whether wealthy states should provide more aid. Practical issues are also involved: while everyone agrees that global poverty should be relieved, there is considerable debate not only among political philosophers, but also among economists and development workers about the most effective way of going about it. Some economists argue that the best way to relieve poverty in developing nations is not to transfer resources through direct assistance but, rather, to eliminate barriers to trade (Bauer, 2001). This would address the problem of trade subsidies in the developed world, and the costs they impose on poorer nations. Some maintain that the key strategy should be to establish and maintain political institutions that protect private property rights (Leeson, 2008). Some emphasize the need for developing countries to rectify intra-country inequalities, arguing that unequal distribution within countries is a major contributing factor for extreme poverty (Sen, 1981). The importance of both internal and external factors is reflected in donor countries' exhortations to recipients in the report on the Millennium Development Goals (see Box 10.1).

Ethical arguments for redistribution to the world's poor

Perhaps the most influential ethical argument in favour of transferring wealth to the poor and needy has been made by the utilitarian philosopher Peter Singer. In his essay 'Famine, Affluence and Morality', written during the 1971 famine in Bengal, Singer examines the assumption that we do not have moral duties to help people in need with whom we are not in any particular relationship. He does so by drawing an analogy: if we are walking past a shallow pond and see a drowning child, whom we can save without risk to ourselves, are we morally obliged to jump in and save the child, even if we have no prior connection to, or responsibility for, him or her? The answer is clearly 'yes': the basic humanitarian duty of mutual aid means that we have a moral duty to help the child. It makes no difference to our moral obligation whether she lives next door, or is a visitor from thousands of miles away. Neither does it matter from a moral point of view if there are other passers-by who could also have jumped in to save the child: we still have a duty to do so. The global poor might be physically further away from us than the drowning child, but this is irrelevant from an ethical perspective as long as we are actually capable of helping them without great sacrifice ourselves (Singer, 1972). Singer concludes that we should be giving much more aid on both an individual and a governmental basis. Peter Unger argues similarly that we are morally obliged to help those in need, and we only fail to recognize our obligations when the needy are physically removed because of psychological intuitions that are irrelevant to the moral views that we hold (Unger, 1996).

There has been considerable debate among moral philosophers about these claims – which apply also to our duties to transfer wealth to poor citizens in our own countries. David Miller points to some problems with the analogy Singer draws between the drowning child and the global poor: it presupposes that there is only one child drowning, and only one potential rescuer. What if there are many children, and many possible rescuers? Whom do we rescue first, and how should we decide who is responsible, or most responsible, for undertaking the rescue? Also, when a child is rescued, we might assume that he or she is returned to his or her parents, and goes back to a safe and secure life, without needing further assistance from the rescuer. Global poverty is not like this; it is chronic and continuing, and cannot be solved by one humanitarian intervention. Finally, casting the victim as a child reinforces this idea that the global poor are helpless victims rather than autonomous actors (Miller, 2007). Singer is not primarily concerned with attributing blame for global poverty; this means that he does not factor in the way political corruption and mismanagement in poor countries might contribute to it, but he also does not insist (as we shall see later, some philosophers do) that wealthy nations are responsible for the situation of the poor.

Singer's approach is utilitarian, but parallel arguments for the duty to assist the needy can also be made on the deontological grounds of basic rights. As we saw in Chapter 2, Martha Nussbaum and Amartya Sen argue that human beings have basic, essential capabilities that are entitled to protection in all societies (Nussbaum, 1999; Sen, 1992). This means not only requiring that human rights be respected, but also transferring resources necessary to ensure that the poor can exercise their basic capabilities. Henry Shue contends similarly that everyone is entitled to basic rights – the generic conditions for living an acceptable life, and for being able to exercise other rights (Shue, 1980). These include the right to bodily integrity and personal freedom, and to a minimum level of resources required for subsistence. Shue's argument provides more scope for considering the role of governments in poor countries in contributing to the plight of their citizens. As these different definitions demonstrate, the concept of basic rights can be elastic: Simon Caney argues that universal basic rights of individuals include equality of opportunity – no one should miss any opportunities because of their nationality (Caney, 2005). In any case, commitment to basic rights imposes a duty on wealthy countries to transfer aid to the most needy, but also to cease supporting governments in poor countries that deprive citizens of their basic rights. As we shall see later in this chapter, several philosophers accept the argument that wealthy nations have a duty to provide basic subsistence to the very poor, but go on to reject more extensive duties of justice.

Needs-based arguments make an ethical claim on individuals and governments. Their focus is on meeting the absolute needs of the poor, rather than on altering the relative positions of rich and poor nations. The philosophers we consider next see the problem of global poverty in more explicitly political terms – grappling with the relationship between the duties we owe the global poor as fellow human beings, and the duties we owe to fellow citizens. Following John Rawls in the tradition of social contract thinking, they approach the problem by asking what people would or should agree to with respect to global inequality. From this perspective, the question is whether the same principles of social justice that apply within the state should also apply across national borders. As we shall see, those who argue that domestic principles should apply globally have come up with different concrete proposals. Some suggest redistributive payments based on resources; some, different types of taxes; and some, simple transfers. We will take as our chief argument against redistribution that advanced by Rawls, which distinguishes between principles of justice to be applied within states, and those humanitarian principles that operate between states. We shall also explore other philosophical defences of the position that our duties to redistribute wealth to fellow citizens are stronger than our duties to send aid abroad. We will then consider various arguments against these positions and in favour of international redistribution. Lastly, we will look briefly at arguments against all governmental aid.

Social cooperation and the limits of justice

In Chapter 2, we examined Rawls' argument that society, as a system of fair cooperation, should be regulated by principles of justice to which all citizens can agree. As we saw, Rawls argued that two fundamental principles of justice, designed to regulate the basic structure of society, would be selected if parties were choosing under fair conditions (the 'original position'). These are, first, that basic liberties be equally available to all citizens, and, second, that inequalities in resources should be acceptable only insofar as they are attached to positions open to all under conditions of fair equality of opportunity, and only if they result in the position of the worst-off group in society being as high as it can be (Rawls, 1971, 1993).

There are three important points to emphasize before we discuss whether or not Rawls' principles are applicable at the global level:

1 This is not a purely egalitarian approach to justice: inequalities are justified if they maximize the position of the worst-off group.
2 The purpose of maximizing resources to the least well-off is to enable them to live free and autonomous lives, governed by their own choices and values.
3 These principles must be acceptable to all reasonable citizens.

As we saw in Chapter 2, Rawls argues that his principles would be chosen in a situation (the original position) constructed so that people would not know anything about their particular situations in life, and so were unable to choose principles that would particularly benefit themselves. All people should know, when they decide on principles of justice, is that they are members of a shared scheme of social cooperation, which has a basic institutional structure that exercises determining influence over the shape of everyone's lives. Even when, in his later work, he moved away from justifying his principles as they would be chosen in the original position, Rawls retained the idea that those agreeing to the principles should regard themselves as having shared fates – as being bound together by some degree of interdependence. Society is a 'fair system of cooperation' (Rawls, 1993), or a cooperative venture for mutual advantage.

These three points are key to understanding why Rawls makes a fundamental distinction between the principles of justice that apply in the domestic sphere, and those that regulate relations between countries. But he also distinguishes between societies that are poor and those that are 'burdened' by unfavourable conditions. Burdened societies are not necessarily – or only – poor; they have weak political and cultural traditions, insufficient human capital and know-how, and, often, insufficient material and technological resources to be well-ordered (Rawls, 1999). A society will only be burdened by poverty if it lacks the resources – material, political and cultural – that it needs to order itself. If a poor society can nevertheless order itself according to its own political and cultural goals and traditions, it is not burdened. As Rawls puts it, 'a society with few natural resources and little wealth can be well-ordered if its political traditions, law and property and class structure with their underlying religious and moral beliefs and culture are such as to sustain a liberal or decent society' (Rawls, 1999: 106).

Rawls argues that the goal of justice between peoples (or global justice) is not to achieve equality between peoples or nations, or to justify and regulate inequalities between them. Rather, it is to establish and maintain a world society of well-ordered nations. Such nations need not be liberal democracies, although they must be peaceful and non-aggressive. Societies that are not liberal, and are, for example, hierarchical are considered 'decent', as long as they respect basic human rights – the right to life, to liberty, and to property – and as long as they ensure that justice takes into account the interests of everyone in society (Rawls, 1999). Given this goal, the two principles of justice, which regulate social and economic inequalities, are not appropriate between nations. Rawls suggests that a second original position be introduced, in which the representatives of liberal and decent peoples choose principles of justice. Here, they are not deciding how to regulate a basic structure because, Rawls argues, none exists in global society. The principles they would choose are those of 'the law of peoples': respecting the freedom and independence of peoples, observing treaties, non-intervention, self-defence, human rights, respecting the laws concerning warfare and, finally, assisting burdened peoples who live in conditions that make it impossible for them to have a liberal or decent social system.

Well-ordered peoples thus have a duty to assist burdened societies, but not necessarily to relieve their poverty, unless their poverty makes it impossible for them to function as decent or liberal societies. After all, just as the purpose of the domestic principles of justice is to provide to the worst-off the resources that they need in order to shape and carry out their own plans in life, the purpose of the global principles is to allow nations to build institutions and structures that reflect their own culture and values. Rawls argues that a major problem with applying egalitarian redistribution at the global level is that there is no cut-off point at which the principles will cease to apply. If a well-ordered and unburdened society decides that the accumulation of wealth is not that important, continual transfers of wealth from richer nations cannot be justified. Rawls identifies three basic guidelines for assisting burdened societies:

1 The goal is not necessarily to make them wealthy.
2 They must change their social and political culture to respect basic human rights.
3 The aim of assistance must be to help societies to become well ordered.

Respect for the particular political culture of each burdened society is key to these principles. What most clearly distinguishes Rawls from most of his critics is his assumption that it is the political culture – as well as the religious, moral and philosophical grounds that underpin it – that most fundamentally determines whether or not a state is wealthy. In practical terms, it is each country's political virtues, its structures of civil society, its population policy (grounded, often, in religious ideas) that determines how much each society values the accumulation of material wealth, or other activities, such as religious piety or environmental sustainability. Rawls reminds us of Sen's findings that famine is caused not by lack of food but, rather, by the failures of governments to distribute to those in need (Sen, 1981). We might also cite statistics about relative inequalities within wealthy nations. Respect for human rights, freedom of expression and the rights of women are essential to solving the problem of extreme poverty, and these can be solved not by transferring resources, but by reforms within recipient countries. This does not mean, however, that Rawls advocates imposing free-market economic policies on poor countries. The aim of aid should be to allow a nation to be self-determining within its own social and political culture. Rawls' approach focuses clearly on the claims of national societies, and this marks it out from the cosmopolitan views of Singer, as well as from the global egalitarian thinkers we consider later in this chapter.

Nationality and particular obligations

As does Rawls, Thomas Nagel distinguishes between our duty to provide assistance to relieve those radical inequalities that make it impossible for the world's poorest people to subsist, and a more general duty to correct inequalities. Nagel argues that wealthy nations are morally required to relieve extreme poverty through aid, whether or not they have contributed to causing it. But these humanitarian duties do not amount to the requirements of justice. They apply because of absolute need, while justice is concerned with relative need (Nagel, 2005).

Justice, Nagel suggests, is inextricably tied to sovereignty. As the seventeenth-century English political philosopher Hobbes argued, it is only in the context of civil society, guaranteed by the sovereign state, that moral principles can be developed (Hobbes, 1962 [1651]). The concepts of justice and obligation depend on the existence of a state, with shared political institutions. According to this view, there can be no global justice without world government to ensure that states meet their obligations and act reciprocally. While Hobbes is well known for emphasizing ultimate state power, it is important to note that the purpose of such power is to enable coordinated action by large numbers of people, acting in mutual self-interest. Rawls' theory, Nagel contends, is consistent with this political approach to justice; it springs from our association as citizens together in society (Nagel, 2005).

This helps us to flesh out the objection to cosmopolitanism: we owe special duties to our fellow countrymen, but the reason we owe such duties is because of our political association in the state, and the obligations this imposes on us. Nagel argues that society is more than a scheme for mutual advantage: it is a political association with a strong non-voluntary component. Citizens are joint authors of the system, and they are subject to its norms, and it is this, Nagel suggests, that creates a presumption against arbitrary domestic inequalities. Citizens are responsible for the acts of the society made in their name and, therefore, they take responsibility for the institutions that create and distribute benefits and disadvantages. As Nagel points out, this political conception of justice is consistent with that defended by Ronald Dworkin: the law must express equal concern for all citizens, and treat them all objectively and impartially. All citizens must participate in making the law with this in mind (Dworkin, 2000). In short, justice is what Nagel refers to as an associative obligation: we owe it to each other because we are citizens living and deliberating together. International society has not yet reached the level of generating associative obligations. There undoubtedly exists considerable economic interdependence and institutional cooperation across the globe, but this does not mean that there is political cooperation. Consequently, we are not obliged to redistribute resources to people beyond our national borders according to principles of justice.

Samuel Freeman argues similarly that, while a kind of society exists at the global level, it is not a political society in which people deliberate about a common good (Freeman, 2006). Nations retain their sovereign rights in a way that citizens do not in civil society and, thus, there can be no guarantee of reciprocity. Any political power granted at the global level can be withdrawn. Freeman points out that Rawls' difference principle was not intended to stand alone; rather, it was part of a particular social and economic structure (the basic structure). As such, it is part of the larger question of how to structure relations between individuals who have mutual social, economic and property relations. Citizens caught up in this network of relations must be able to deliberate democratically about how to share social goods – and no structures exist to ensure such deliberation across national borders (with some exceptions, such as the EU).

Miller makes perhaps the most comprehensive defence of the claim that national borders are relevant to thinking about justice, and that there can be no principle of economic equality among nations (Miller, 2000, 2007). As does Nagel, he cautions that this does not mean that wealthy nations do not have a duty to provide the global poor with the minimum that they need for subsistence. Neither does it mean that inequalities in power and influence between rich and poor countries are acceptable in their interactions. A wealthy country should not be able to dictate terms of trade to a poorer one. But these concerns, Miller argues, are with the effects of economic inequality, rather than inequality itself. The aim of assistance should not be to achieve distributive equality, or even equal opportunity. In fact, global justice should be restricted to three duties:

1 Respecting basic human rights world-wide.
2 Refraining from exploiting vulnerable human beings and communities.
3 The obligation to provide all communities with the opportunity to achieve self-determination and social justice.

Miller's reason for limiting global justice is that, despite globalization, national membership is still morally significant (Miller, 2000, 2007). The great majority of people still identify with their national community; most significant decisions are still made at the national level; and nations constitute themselves as mutual benefit schemes. As such, nation-states and their citizens must bear responsibility for the gains and losses that they create and from which they benefit. Moreover, even if we were to start from equality, the decisions that national governments make reflecting particular cultural and political differences would not maintain it. This argument recalls Rawls' focus on the role played by a country's political, cultural and social values in determining whether it becomes wealthy. But it also resembles Robert

Nozick's argument against egalitarianism in domestic justice, which we discussed in Chapter 2 (Nozick, 1974).

Arguments against international aid

We turn briefly here to arguments against all international aid provided by states. This position has relatively few defenders among political philosophers, although it raises arguments similar to those we have already considered for limiting international transfers. The strongest position against global redistribution follows from the libertarian defence of a limited state. In Chapter 2, we considered arguments for and against redistributing wealth domestically, through tax and welfare, and, as we saw, Nozick argued that such redistribution is beyond the role of the state (Nozick, 1974). Individuals are entitled to their earnings, and should only be required to return them to the state to pay for its protection of our rights. Nozick opposes all patterned theories of justice similar to egalitarian theories, on the grounds that they interfere with the freedom of individuals to hold or transfer their own property as they wish. Moreover, it is impossible to maintain patterns, because people's freedoms will interfere with them. Nozick was referring to justice within states, but as we have seen, his objections are echoed by Rawls and by other theorists who oppose applying principles of justice globally. Of course, Nozick's entitlement theory rests on the assumption that the original acquisition of resources was legitimate, in that it left enough for others. As we shall see later in this chapter, the rejection of this assumption underpins Thomas Pogge's proposals for redistribution.

Chandran Kukathas contends that justice should not be pursued as a goal in international affairs, because there is no consensus on what it involves (Kukathas, 2006). Our understandings of justice and of what is valuable in society are diverse and contentious. It follows that institutions designed to pursue and establish justice will ultimately impose the meanings held by powerful states and coalitions. Moreover, distributing resources has negative consequences for poor peoples: it encourages recipient states to become dependent on aid, rather than to achieve their own economic development. It also reinforces the power of corrupt elites in recipient states, and contributes to widening inequality within the recipient state. Kukathas suggests that the better course of action is for individuals to contribute more to international relief – particularly through collective and voluntary action with NGOs. In addition, poor countries should be encouraged to institute economic and political reforms that will free up resources internally (Kukathas, 2006). This brings us back to the argument that poverty and hunger are produced by government policies, rather than insufficient resources.

Justice and obligation between nations

While the arguments we considered in the previous section reject all redistribution in the name of justice, defenders of aid tend to position themselves
against those who defend egalitarian redistribution in the domestic sphere,
but deny that it applies globally. As we have seen, Rawls argues that there is
a fundamental difference between our obligation to redistribute resources at
the domestic level, where our lives are regulated by the basic structure of the
social scheme in which we cooperate, and our lesser obligations across
national borders. Nagel and Miller agree, asserting that nationality imposes
particular duties on citizens that cannot be transferred across national
borders. Several political philosophers who share Rawls' basic commitment
to redistribution at the domestic level reject this distinction. They argue that
the impact of the international system on poor nations means that we should
regulate the inequalities it produces in the same way as the basic structure is
regulated. Or, to put it in terms of the duties of nations: as members in a
global system, wealthy nations have obligations based on reciprocity. In an
early and influential argument along these lines, Charles Beitz applies Rawls'
arguments for his domestic principles of justice to the global level, concluding that justice, and not merely mutual aid, requires us to transfer wealth
across national borders to the needy (Beitz, 1979). In order to make this case,
he contends that:

1 Nations are joined together in a network of interdependence that has the
  same effect as a shared scheme of social cooperation.
2 Natural resources, which are undeserved like natural talents, generate
  benefits in this shared scheme that should be shared by all.

Beitz argues that people are linked together meaningfully across national
borders, whether or not they are actively cooperating together in a shared
scheme of social cooperation. We should not interpret Rawls' requirement
that such a scheme exists too literally; the fact is that states are no longer self-
sufficient cooperative systems. They are linked together in a complex pattern
of social interactions: trade, travel, foreign investment, aid and communications. The appropriate definition of social cooperation that attracts the
requirements of justice occurs when 'social activity produces relative or
absolute benefits or burdens that would not exist if the social activity did not
take place' (Beitz, 1979: 131). This definition of social cooperation does not
restrict it to national borders – even Rawls imagines a certain degree of interdependence, so that parties representing nations would choose the familiar
principles of international law to regulate their interactions. The most
important feature of this interdependence with respect to questions of
justice, Beitz argues, is the volume of international investment and trade.

Corporate investment is increasingly international, the market is global, and corporations are multinational. We might also note that Beitz was writing in 1979 – there has since been even more growth in international economic interdependence.

Moreover, the economic interactions between countries produce substantial economic benefits that are unevenly distributed (see Table 10.1, p. 190). Beitz points out that interdependence widens the gap between rich and poor nations, even though it produces absolute benefits for all nations. Nations have different resources and levels of technology, and multinational corporations can shift investment around to the most productive and lowest cost nations, thus exacerbating economic inequality. Countries are unequal in their ability to secure the gains of international trade, as this depends on the ability of domestic governments to maintain control over domestic, but largely multinational, corporations. Some nations are asymmetrically vulnerable if they rely on concentrated exports in a few products. Also, governments find it hard to control domestic economies as they are so dependent on economic developments elsewhere.

Globalization has only exacerbated this loss of national control, and it is uncontroversial now to claim that nations are not self-sufficient and that social cooperation is not contained by national borders. There is a complex pattern of social interactions that produces benefits and burdens that would not otherwise exist. This is what Rawls identifies as crucial in his discussion of the application of principles of justice to domestic societies. Allen Buchanan defines the global basic structure as a set of economic and political institutions that have 'profound and enduring effects' on the distribution of goods and burdens among people throughout the world (Buchanan, 2000).

But there is also another feature of the global situation that strengthens the analogy to the domestic, and this is the role played by natural resources in generating wealth. Beitz argues that natural resources make a crucial contribution to the material advancement of societies. Parties in the original position would view the distribution of resources in much the same way as they view the distribution of natural talents – namely, as unearned. In fact, Beitz argues that we can make an even stronger argument for natural resources than we can for natural talents – they are not an inextricable part of a human self and human personality. Given that there is social cooperation at the global level, the unequal benefits that come from appropriating natural resources should be regulated by principles of justice.

Beitz concludes that if Rawls' two principles can be justified at the domestic level, they must also be justified at the global level. There is no reason to think that parties in the original position should know what nation they belong to – the 'veil of ignorance' that prevents parties from knowing facts about their own identities and places in the world must also apply to citizenship. Parties in the original position will choose to maximize the position of the worst-off group of people in the world. As he points out, this will not necessarily consist of people within one particular state: what matters here is interpersonal inequalities, rather than international. Beitz's position is cosmopolitan, in that he thinks the principles of justice must apply to everyone, irrespective of national membership, but we should note that this does not mean that he sees states as irrelevant. State borders are not morally significant, but they are practically important, as states are in the best position to carry out redistributive responsibilities.

In response to Beitz, Rawls insists that we cannot draw an analogy between natural talents and natural resources, because the latter can be distinguished from the country's political and civic culture, which determines how resources shall be used. Moreover, while people are engaged in social cooperation at the global level, this cooperation does not require regulation by principles of justice, because it does not take place within a basic structure (Rawls, 1999). Beitz has maintained, however, that global society has a basic structure – the economic, political and legal institutions and practices within which people and states interact. In his later work, he has moved away from arguing that aid payments – large-scale transfers of resources between countries – are the most effective means of achieving global justice (Beitz, 2005). He argues now that reorganizing the basic structure of global society to make sure that its institutions and practices do not reproduce and exacerbate inequality is the most important task. This encompasses regulating private capital flows, trade, and international property rights.

As does Beitz, Thomas Pogge takes a cosmopolitan view, arguing that principles of justice apply to global society (Pogge, 2002). But where Beitz asserts a positive duty to redistribute wealth, Pogge bases his argument on the negative duty states have *not* to contribute to the life-threatening poverty of others. Given that global poverty and need, and radical inequality are facts, what are the duties of wealthy nations? Pogge accepts that we have a positive duty to aid those in distress. But, as we saw in Miller's critique of Singer, acknowledging this does not tell us whom to help. Rather than providing foreign aid, we could argue for redistributing resources within the country. Pogge argues that the duty to redistribute wealth abroad depends on a negative duty not to profit from or contribute to the impoverishment of others. This negative duty depends on establishing three factors relating to the situation of the worst-off:

1 Shared social institutions must contribute to global inequality, and must be imposed on the worst-off.
2 The worst-off must be excluded from the benefits of natural resources, without compensation.
3 The relative positions of the worst-off must be caused by a historical process involving violence and repression.

Pogge argues that each of these conditions is satisfied. In the case of the first, global institutions around trade and foreign investment at least contribute to global inequality, although Pogge leaves open the idea that corruption and poor policy decisions in impoverished countries also play a role. Investments, loans, trade, bribes, military aid and sex tourism (and this is not an exhaustive list) all maintain and exacerbate the condition of the global poor. Local decisions and cultural factors in poor countries also have an influence, but Pogge points out that these are not independent factors – they are influenced by the existing global order. We might, for instance, look at the relationship between the international arms trade and violence and civil war in developing countries, or between the exploitation and oppression of women and girls, and international sex tourism. Affluent countries and their citizens have used their power to shape the rules of the world economy, and this affects the fate of all who participate in it.

The second condition is easy to establish – countries that happen to have no natural resources in their territory are not compensated for the fact that they derive no benefit from them. As does Beitz, Pogge assumes that natural resources are not morally deserved by nations. This strand of his argument appeals to the argument of seventeenth-century British philosopher John Locke, that the appropriation of property and its benefits is legitimate as long as enough and as good is left for others (Locke, 1988 [1690]). (We discussed this with respect to domestic justice in Chapter 2.) Enough and as good has clearly not been left for countries without natural resources.

In the case of the third condition, colonialism and foreign intervention by developed states incorporated violence and repression. Wealthy and poor countries have a common and violent history, which has led to current inequalities. In sum: people in wealthy countries, by shaping and enforcing the global conditions that cause the suffering of global poverty, are actively harming the global poor – in a way comparable to the mass sufferings inflicted by dictators such as Hitler and Stalin (Pogge, 2005).

Pogge's proposed solution focuses on the second condition – the exclusion of poor countries from the benefits of resources. He begins from the premises that the world's resources are held in common, and that, if they were properly distributed, would be enough to meet everyone's basic needs. He argues that states should not have full property rights over the resources in their territories, but should be required to share a small part of the resources they decide to use or sell (Pogge, 1998, 2004). The proceeds from this should be used to make a payment – the global resources dividend (GRD), which would be redistributed to poor countries. The point of the GRD is to ensure that all human beings can meet their basic needs with dignity – to make it possible for them to defend their basic interests. Pogge estimates that it could comfortably raise 1 per cent of global social product, which could be redistributed for the eradication of poverty. These funds could also be spent so as

Box 10.2 Global redistribution: competing norms and values

The debate over redistributing resources globally turns on competing interpretations of justice and rights, and their relationship to the nation-state, as well as property rights.

• Justice

Supporters of global redistribution argue that justice requires that all human beings have, at least, a basic level of resources necessary to live a decent life. Principles of justice are not limited by national borders: human beings are all morally equal, and we owe duties to each other – at least, to provide for basic needs – on the basis of shared humanity, rather than fellow-citizenship.

Opponents counter that justice depends on the existence of a shared social contract, or shared participation in a political process, or overarching state sovereignty. In any case, the principles of justice cannot apply at the global level in the absence of these. Some supporters of redistribution counter this by pointing out that there is substantial interdependence between nations, and that states participate in international social and economic institutions (see the section on private property, in this box).

• Rights

Supporters of redistribution argue that all human beings have, at least, basic rights – defined usually as the right to freedom from violence and material want. These rights are independent of nationality. Those with sufficient resources have a duty to ensure that others can exercise their basic rights.

Many critics accept a right to basic subsistence, but criticize more extensive redistribution, on the grounds that all but the most basic rights are dependent on common membership in a shared project such as the nation-state.

• Private property

Supporters of redistribution argue here, as in the domestic case (see Chapter 2), that property rights are subordinate to the requirements of justice. Even in the absence of a world state, there is sufficient cooperation and interdependence between nations to conclude that property is produced as a result of social interaction, and should be distributed socially.

According to the strongest argument against this, made by libertarians, states are not entitled to demand the property of some in order to redistribute it to others.

Some critics argue that even if redistribution can be defended at the domestic level, social cooperation and interdependence at the international level does not constitute participation in a shared social and economic project analogous to the state.

to encourage less corrupt government in recipient countries. The GRD would raise about US$320 billion annually – or about 86 times the amount all wealthy countries are currently spending on basic social services in the developing world (Pogge, 2005).

It is important to note Pogge's claim that the GRD is not aid; neither is it the transfer of what rightfully belongs to wealthy countries (Pogge, 2005). Rather, it reflects Locke's view that everyone should be entitled to a proportional share of the world's natural resources – that those who appropriate and benefit from them must ensure that enough and as good are left for others. Wealthy nations never had the right to all the profits they made from using or selling their natural resources. The GRD is designed to undo an unfair historical process, and to provide a share (not necessarily an equal one) of those resources to which all countries were originally entitled. Pogge means this to be consistent with historical entitlement arguments for private property, such as that made by Robert Nozick. But, as with the basic income proposals we discussed in Chapter 2, the GRD also incorporates a libertarian concern that the poor (in this case, poor nations) be provided with the resources they were originally entitled to, in order to make their own free and autonomous decisions about development. In this way, the GRD is an alternative to conventional development assistance: it cannot be tied, and it empowers poor countries to make their own decisions about development. We might note that this is consistent with Rawls' concern that countries be able to determine their own levels of material wealth, in line with their political, social and cultural values.

Conclusion

It would be easy to see arguments that justice requires increased international distribution by means of foreign aid as an unqualified endorsement of transferring more wealth to poor nations. The reality is much more complex. As we noted at the beginning of this chapter, wealthy countries have been attacked not only for the shortfall in the amount of resources that they give, especially compared with internationally agreed goals, but also for the type of aid that is given, and to whom it is directed. A disproportionate amount of assistance is given to strategic allies of the donor countries, rather than to the world's most needy, and much of it is tied. All this means that aid tends to be designed to benefit the donor country as well as the recipient – and, if we accept the conventional realist understanding of international relations as being driven by national interest, this is no surprise. But, given these constraints on aid, it is also not surprising that global poverty continues to exist. This is sometimes forgotten in the public debate in wealthy countries about whether or not aid works. Opponents point to continuing extreme poverty in parts of the world such as sub-Saharan Africa, and argue, as Kukathas does, that aid has reinforced corruption in recipient countries, and dissuaded them from assuming responsibility for their own development. As supporters of aid point out, however, there have been important successes in the areas of child health and mortality, and increased agricultural production in China, India and South East Asia (Sachs, 2005).

Almost all of the philosophical arguments we have considered offer some grounds on which to criticize the way aid is given, and suggest ways that it could be improved. Arguments for humanitarian assistance to relieve extreme poverty are made by philosophers across the spectrum, from Singer's utilitarian case, to Rawls' more cautious contractarian approach. All agree that the world's wealthy states are morally obliged, at least, to provide the resources needed by the world's poor for subsistence. Above and beyond this, philosophers who defend applying egalitarian principles to international distribution (such as Beitz) emphasize the importance of improving the position of the worst-off group. While Rawls argues against global egalitarianism, his focus on the importance of preserving the political culture, and the social, cultural and religious values of well-ordered societies, reminds us of the dangers of imposing social and economic policies on recipient countries. This does not mean that mismanagement and corruption in recipient countries can be excused on the grounds of cultural difference. Rawls emphasizes that societies must be well-ordered, whether liberal or decent, and this is reflected in the findings of the World Bank, that aid is most likely to be effective when recipient countries recognize the rule of law and human rights, and are free of corruption (Dollar and Pritchett, 1998).

Pogges's GRD embodies a different approach to transferring resources, in that it understands the resources transferred to be the legitimate property of recipient countries. As we have seen, the dividend is compensation for their share of property that was appropriated by other states in the form of natural resources. As such, it allows recipient countries maximum freedom in deciding what to do with their resources, according to their own political, cultural and moral lights. This is in line with recommendations by NGOs concerned with aid that recipient countries must be involved in deciding how funds are used. But cultural values and national autonomy must not be allowed to cloak corruption and exploitation. In the case of corrupt governments that prefer to spend the GRD on elites rather than on their poor and needy, Pogge suggests that the funds could be paid directly to the needy through the United Nations or NGOs. If it were impossible for the GRD to go to the people in a particular nation that needed it most, the dividend should not be paid to that nation at all (Pogge, 2004). The challenge that aid raises for both philosophers and practitioners is to balance universalist concern with human needs, on the one hand, with respect for national autonomy and self-determination of developing countries, on the other.

Chapter 11

Can Military Intervention in Other Countries be Justified on Humanitarian Grounds?

The question as to whether states have the right to intervene to prevent the tyrannical abuse of people in other countries has been debated since nation-states and the law of nations emerged in the seventeenth century. Intervention can take many forms, including the imposition of sanctions and diplomatic pressure, but the use of armed force is particularly controversial. The dilemma intervention poses can be considered in legal, political and moral terms: as we shall see, international law recognizes intervention as a very limited exception to state sovereignty. But the political and moral dimensions of intervention are more complex and difficult to evaluate. As both historical and contemporary cases demonstrate, intervention has often been justified on moral grounds, but carried out, in large part, to advance the self-interest of the intervening power. Western imperial expansion in Asia and Africa in the nineteenth century was justified in moral terms by the claim that indigenous people required protection from local tyrants (an argument supported, as we shall see, by the one of the founders of modern liberalism, John Stuart Mill). In 1938, Adolf Hitler tried to justify his invasion of Czechoslovakia on the grounds of protecting the German minority in the Sudetenland from human rights abuses. The 2003 invasion of Iraq by the United States and its allies was publicly justified, at least in part, on the grounds that it would liberate the Iraqi people from the tyrannical rule of Saddam Hussein. Humanitarian intervention has also been opposed on the grounds of political interest: in the early twentieth century, Turkish massacres of Armenians prompted international calls for humanitarian intervention – which United States President Woodrow Wilson ignored, out of concern not to jeopardize diplomatic relations with Turkey.

Humanitarian intervention has become a particularly pressing issue since the 1990s; many commentators argue that whether to intervene to help victims of human-engineered catastrophes was the most important and diffi-cult issue facing the world from the end of the Cold War until September 2001 (ICISS, 2001). Conflicts in this period in Europe and Africa have involved serious violations of human rights, and international media cover-age has made these more immediate and visible to the public in western nations, resulting in increased pressure on governments to act. But there continues to be widespread global debate over whether military intervention in other countries is a just course of action, and under what circumstances. A closer look at recent cases in which humanitarian intervention was undertaken illustrates the complexities of this issue.

On 24 March 1999, NATO launched Operation *Allied Force,* a programme of aerial bombing in the Yugoslav province of Kosovo, with the aim of preventing the practice of ethnic cleansing – forced expulsion of the ethnic Albanian population of the province. A civil war was then in progress between the Serb-led Yugoslav forces, and the ethnic Albanian Kosovo Liberation Army, over independence for Kosovo. The displacement of thousands of people in the conflict prompted relief organizations such as Oxfam to support intervention. NATO's action, led by the United States, was not authorized by the United Nations Security Council; the Security Council had not even considered a resolution authorizing the use of force, as Russia, a permanent member and a long-time ally of Serbia, had vowed to veto any such resolution. The US government claimed that NATO was acting to save lives – that Yugoslav forces had 'crossed a line' with ethnic cleansing, and were contravening the core norms of human rights. They declared their intentions to minimize civilian casualties but, nevertheless, most of the bombs and missiles struck Serbia and its infrastructure, rather than the Serbian military, paramilitary and police in Kosovo (Shue, 2003). Many observers commented that the bombing targets suggested that punishment was the real aim, rather than ending ethnic cleansing. Moreover, there were several mistaken targets. In May, for example, the Chinese Embassy in Belgrade was hit in error, and three Chinese journalists were killed.

Irrespective of justification, the immediate results of the action were challenging for its defenders. Before it took place, 230,000 people had been displaced in Kosovo, and 2,500 killed. Afterwards, 1.4 million had been forced to flee their homes, and 10,000 people were killed during the bombardment (although these were mainly ethnic Albanians killed by Serbs in retaliation) (Mandelbaum, 1999). The bombing ended when Yugoslav President Slobodan Milosevic agreed to accept UN Security Council Resolution 1244, which authorized an international civilian and military force in Kosovo, to administer the province and conduct peacekeeping operations. In terms of ending ethnic cleansing, the operation might be judged a success. But, in terms of reducing suffering in the short term, it clearly was not successful. Neither did it create a society in which members of warring groups could live together and respect each other's human rights (Booth, 2001). Moreover, western critics also claimed that it alienated Russia and China from western nations on the Security Council, with long-term consequences for the ability of the Council to work together on other issues (Mandelbaum, 1999).

Much of the global debate about the intervention in Kosovo concerned not the importance of alleviating human rights abuses there; rather, it dealt with the way in which ends and means should be balanced. Intervention had to be weighed in terms of both its immediate and long-term effects for those suffering, as well as its effects on others, and the importance of moral versus other motives in justifying military action. Unsurprisingly, given the complexities of this issue, the decision not to intervene has also been controversial. In the 1990s, conflict escalated in the central African state of Rwanda between ethnic Hutu and Tutsi groups, who had competed for power in the country since independence in 1959. UN peacekeepers arrived in 1993 but, in April 1994, Hutu militias, with the support of the Hutu-led Rwandan government, launched a campaign of genocide against the Tutsi. The attacks were ruthless, bloody and effective – over 250,000 Tutsi were murdered in two weeks, half a million by the end of the genocide in July 1994.

The scale of the genocide became known only gradually to international observers in Rwanda. Belgian peacekeepers installed in 1993 withdrew after 10 were killed by Hutu extremists, and the Security Council cut the peace-keeping forces to a skeleton staff. As international outcry mounted from late April, the UN reversed its decision, announcing that it would increase the numbers of peacekeepers there. But the UN was unable to persuade members to commit substantial extra troops or equipment. The United States was reluctant to act in the wake of the disastrous intervention in Somalia in 1993 (see below and p. 212). Eventually, the UN authorized France to carry out its own intervention in late June, by which time most Tutsi victims were long dead (Kuperman, 2000). There was evidence that the Hutu held back from mass killings in sites where there were western observers, but it is impossible to tell whether intervention would have prevented the genocide, or accelerated it. Some critics have argued that 5,000 well-armed interveners could have prevented the genocide if deployed immediately at the outbreak of violence. In reality, immediate deployment of large numbers of personnel is hardly ever possible. As critics point out, if foreign intervention is seen as likely, the danger is that the militarily weaker force will be bolstered. This can lead them to escalate fighting in the expectation of helpful foreign intervention (Kuperman, 2000).

Other high profile cases in which intervention has occurred on the grounds of preventing human rights abuses include Somalia in 1993 and the Bosnian conflict during the early 1990s. In 1992, UN Security Council Resolution 724 authorized intervention in Somalia, to stem the human rights abuses resulting from the collapse of the state. The Secretary General justified the intervention under Chapter VII of the UN Charter, on the grounds that the strife in Somalia was a threat to international peace and security (for more on this, see page 214). But humanitarian concerns were a major factor, as the damage resulting from the civil war and the plight of thousands of refugees were exacerbated by drought-caused famine. The United States took a more active role in peacekeeping in 1993, and several American soldiers were killed in fighting, resulting in a public relations disaster for the Clinton Administration. The United States announced immediate plans to withdraw its forces.

In another product of the break-up of Yugoslavia, civil war broke out in Bosnia in 1992, after Bosnian Serbs resisted a move towards independence. Serb-led forces shelled Muslim Bosnians, and thousands of Muslim Bosnians were driven from their homes. In addition, Serb forces carried out torture, rape and ethnic cleansing, in actions determined later by the International Court of Justice to be crimes against humanity. Western governments imposed sanctions on Serb-dominated Yugoslavia, and the UN deployed peacekeepers that were required to remain neutral in the conflict. In 1995, Bosnian Serbs massacred nearly 8,000 Bosnian Muslims in the town of Srebrenica, a UN-declared safe haven, while UN peacekeepers stood by. Shortly after this, the United States led a massive NATO bombing campaign against the Serbs, and sent 20,000 American troops as part of the contingent of NATO-led peacekeepers. President Clinton's decision was opposed by the foreign policy elite and much of Congress, and supported by only 36 per cent of the American population. Richard Holbrooke, who was Clinton's envoy in the Balkans through the conflict, claimed later that, if the intervention had not taken place, Bosnia would not have survived; there would have been 2 million Bosnian refugees displaced in Europe, and militant Islamic terrorist cells would have become established in the region (Holbrooke, 2005).

Shifts in international political attitudes towards humanitarian intervention

The attitudes of national governments and international institutions towards intervention have shifted and evolved in response to these humanitarian crises. In April 1992, in the midst of the war in Kosovo, British Prime Minister Tony Blair formulated a new 'doctrine of the international community', or what came to be called the Blair Doctrine: nations should go to war not for reasons of territorial interest, but to protect people threatened by humanitarian disasters. Humanitarian considerations have been invoked by the British government in every international intervention since then, including Afghanistan in 2001 and Iraq. The Blair doctrine is based on the long-standing tradition of Just War theory, which we examine in detail later in this chapter. It lists five questions that must be answered before humanitarian intervention is undertaken:

Box 11.1 Human rights abuses in Sudan

Perhaps the most widely supported – and unsuccessful – recent demand for humanitarian intervention relates to the Darfur region in Sudan. The Sudanese government and the militias it supports launched a brutal campaign of mass killings and ethnic cleansing after an uprising in Darfur in 2003. Due to the conflict, an estimated 500,000 people have died as a result of violence, starvation or disease. In 2005, a Commission of Inquiry created by the UN Security Council concluded that, while the Sudanese government did not have a policy of genocide, it was involved in numerous war crimes and crimes against humanity. Despite numerous condemnations by western states and the Security Council, UN member states have refused to intervene. There has been much debate over who is responsible for protecting the citizens of Darfur (see the discussion of the 'responsibility to protect' on p. 214).

- Opponents of intervention argue that the Sudanese government must be made to fulfil its responsibility to protect its citizens. UN Security Council members China, Russia and Pakistan have invoked arguments about state sovereignty to oppose intervention.
- Some have suggested that the African Union, as the regional organization, has prime responsibility for dealing with the situation in Sudan. African Union peacekeepers were sent to the region in 2004, but the force was small and ineffective in preventing human rights abuses. African Union peacekeepers were incorporated into a larger UN/African Union mission in 2000.
- Even some of the strongest academic critics of the Sudanese regime have argued that a large-scale UN intervention is unlikely to be effective, as the struggle is grounded in long-standing historical and ethnic conflicts in the region. These can be addressed and resolved only by the Sudanese people themselves (Prunier, 2005).

1 Are we sure of our case?
2 Have we exhausted all diplomatic options?
3 Are there military operations than can prudently be undertaken?
4 Are we prepared for the long term?
5 Are national interests at stake?

The doctrine addresses both moral and pragmatic considerations; the final question sets clear national interest limits on humanitarian considerations, and perhaps explains why no action has been taken in Darfur.

The UN Secretary General Kofi Annan raised the issue of humanitarian intervention in speeches to the General Assembly in 1999 and 2000, asking member nations to come to consensus on how to approach this issue, and agree to basic principles. In response, the Canadian government established the International Commission on Intervention and State Sovereignty (ICISS) in 2000. The ICISS published its findings in 2001 in a report entitled *The Responsibility to Protect* (ICISS, 2001). The report redefines state sovereignty, asserting that it carries with it two fundamental responsibilities: to the citizens of the state concerned, and also to the international community. States become accountable to the global community for the ways in which they treat their citizens and, where a population is suffering serious harm and a government is unwilling or unable to prevent this, then sovereignty must be yielded, and the international community should take over the responsibility to protect citizens. The ICISS listed four requirements for legitimate intervention, again reflecting Just War criteria:

1 The intention must be to protect.
2 Intervention must be a last resort.
3 Intervention must be proportional.
4 Intervention must have reasonable prospects of success.

The Report concluded that the UN Security Council was the appropriate body to authorize interventions, and that it should adopt a set of guidelines for such cases, based on principles 1–4 (ICISS, 2001). Although the findings of the ICISS were largely overshadowed by the events of September 11, 2001, the UN General Assembly did accept the responsibility to protect at the World Summit in 2005. It has been invoked against Sudan, but no intervention has yet taken place.

Intervention and international law

These changes in the way international institutions and some governments perceive humanitarian intervention must be viewed in the context of prevailing international law. The UN Charter makes it clear that the sovereignty of states and their rights to freedom from outside interference are paramount. The Charter authorizes the use of force against another nation in very limited circumstances: self-defence under Article 51 of the Charter, or 'to maintain or restore international peace and order' under Chapter VII. The principle of the sovereign equality of states is enshrined in Article 2.1 of the UN Charter. Article 2.4 requires member states to 'refrain in their international relations from the threat or use of force against the territorial integrity or political independence of any state'. Article 2.7 specifies that nothing in the Charter authorizes the UN 'to intervene in matters which are essentially within the domestic jurisdiction of any state'.

The assumption that sovereignty could be challenged only when a state posed a threat to the international order reflects the origins of the UN in the aftermath of World War II. State sovereignty in this conventional sense is still dominant in international legal argument. But the sources of violence and threat in the world have changed in the past sixty years: most conflicts are now intra-, rather than interstate. In addition, the proportion of civilians to military personnel killed in these conflicts has risen from 1 in 10, at the beginning of the twentieth century, to 9 in 10 by the end (Evans, 2004). As we shall see, state sovereignty continues to be a crucial value in political and moral debates about intervention. But the way in which sovereignty is defined, and the moral challenges to it, reflect these postwar changes in global conflict and threat.

The controversy in political philosophy over intervention reflects a fundamental conflict between absolute state sovereignty and cosmopolitan arguments for the moral primacy of individual human rights – arguments we discussed with respect to redistribution of resources in Chapter 10. This is sometimes expressed as a conflict between state and human security (Kaldor, 2007). It gives rise to two questions:

- Do the human rights of individuals trump the rights of states to exercise control within their territorial borders?
- If they do, who should act to protect them?

We can also understand this debate in terms of different conceptions of sovereignty. On the one hand, the sovereignty of states in the international system has been viewed as being independent of the actions of government within the state. More recently, however, some theorists have argued that sovereignty is dependent on states fulfilling their responsibilities to protect the basic human rights of citizens. As we have seen, this second view has gained some international support, and is expressed in the recent ICISS report.

Political philosophers usually address these issues in the deontological terms in which they are framed here; that is, as questions of moral principle. But, as we can see from the Blair doctrine and the ICISS report, considerations of cost and consequence are never absent from political debate around intervention. There is more concern about the consequences of principled action with respect to this issue than any others we have considered in this book. Utilitarians, of course, assess humanitarian interventions – either each, in itself, or allowing them as a rule – in terms of their consequences. But all theorists agree that even grave human rights abuses cannot justify military intervention that is unlikely to be successful, and that will involve significant loss of human life. And, even if action is judged likely to prevent human rights abuses, the costs of it in terms of lives and damage, including to the intervening forces, must be weighed up against the good it might do.

We begin by examining ideas about state sovereignty, and the case against intervention. We then turn to related arguments against intervention that emphasize not the sovereign rights of the state as an absolute good but, rather, the value of the intact political community as the context in which political values and actions have meaning. These are often described as communitarian arguments against intervention but, as we shall see, they also rely on fundamental values liberals attach to free and autonomous human action. From this perspective, intervention is wrong not because it undermines sovereignty, but because it prevents people from acting freely to make their own political decisions when constructing their own political institutions. It is important to note that most arguments on any of these lines against intervention make exceptions for cases where the human rights abuses are particularly egregious – such as genocide and enslavement. This also reflects international law: the 1948 Genocide Convention requires states to prevent genocide.

Turning to arguments in favour of humanitarian intervention, we examine, first, those theorists who accept the value of community membership, but reject the identification of the nation-state with that community. We then turn to Just War theory. This framework draws on a natural law tradition to argue for values that override the security of the state, and from which state security arguments derive their own legitimation. Just War has traditionally been used to evaluate warfare in moral terms, but its principles have recently been influential in the special case of humanitarian intervention. From there we move to cosmopolitan arguments for universal human rights. Cosmopolitanism, which here takes the form of universalist liberalism, has developed on a separate historical trajectory from Just War theory, although, as we shall see, there is some overlap in the criteria on which these traditions rely to justify military intervention. Finally, we explore a contractarian cosmopolitan case for regulating intervention. In all of these perspectives, consequentialist concerns constrain arguments from moral principle.

State sovereignty

The argument from state sovereignty asserts that, by their very definition, states have exclusive control over all their own affairs, and that they co-exist in an international society in which all recognize this right in each other. We should note at the beginning that although this 'statist' position is well grounded in the history of western political thought, it is not widely supported among contemporary political philosophers. Even those who invoke it tend to argue that sovereignty should have some limits in terms of how states treat their citizens, as we discuss in greater detail later in this chapter (Cohen, 2005).

The idea that each state has an exclusive right to territorial integrity against other states developed relatively recently, along with the concept of government as the single sovereign authority within the state. Once the institutions of government were established as the legitimate central authority within the state, particularly as against the Church, it followed that governments asserted their independence not only against religious authorities outside their borders – the Pope – but also against other states. The system of sovereign states emerged with the Peace of Westphalia in 1648, which ended the Thirty Years War in Europe, and allowed princes the right to determine Christian worship in their own states, free from the control of the Holy Roman Empire. Sovereignty was established as the supreme authority – legitimate power – within the territory of the state. The earlier antecedents of the concept can be found in Renaissance political philosophy: in the early sixteenth century, in *The Prince*, the Italian diplomat and political philosopher Niccolo Machiavelli advised on how to maintain supreme control over territory, independent of the authority of the Church and natural law (Machiavelli, 1988 [1532]). At around the same time, Protestant reformer Martin Luther insisted that the spiritual realm and the realm of secular society were distinct, and the Church must not compete with temporal and secular authority (Figgis, 1931).

The early modern political philosophers Jean Bodin and Thomas Hobbes further developed the concept of the sovereignty of government within the state, establishing its central importance in western political thinking. Bodin's *Six Books of the Commonwealth* was written in 1576, when France was beset by religious civil war. He argued that social unity could be achieved only under the aegis of a single and unitary political body, one that was above human law and was the source of such law (Bodin, 1992 [1576]). Sovereignty must be absolute and perpetual, and the sovereign state was not subject to any civil law in either its domestic or its foreign actions. But it was subject to divine law and natural law – God's direct law, and his law as revealed in nature. It follows that the state could not act tyrannically against its own citizens, in contravention of natural law.

The most absolute defence of state sovereignty was made by Thomas Hobbes, writing also in the context of civil and religious war, this time in England. Hobbes' argument is contractarian – he defends state sovereignty on the grounds that it is part of a basic contract between citizens. In *Leviathan*, Hobbes argued that human beings existed originally in a state of nature, in which there was no civil authority (Hobbes, 1962 [1651]). Human life was characterized by constant and unavoidable insecurity and, as a result, individuals had no choice but to agree to form a contract to establish an overarching authority – the state. They transferred to the state all of the powers they had by nature, so that it could ensure them protection. The social contract formed was not between people and the state but, rather, between people to set up the state. The purpose of the state was to provide security, and this took precedence over all else. Consequently, it had absolute authority over citizens, who were obliged to obey all of its commands except those that would result in self-destruction. Sovereignty was to be absolute and indivisible, as for Bodin; but, unlike Bodin, Hobbes did not see it as subordinate to natural law. Once the state was in existence, neither citizens nor foreigners could justify their disobedience or interference by invoking natural or God's law. There could be no substantive law or justice outside the state, because the state was the source of all law and morality.

We might see Hobbes and Bodin as the respective points of origin of two currents of thinking about sovereignty:

1 On the one hand, sovereignty is absolute, and cannot be challenged by moral arguments.
2 On the other, it is absolute against all civil law, both domestic and foreign, but is subject to the fundamental principles of natural law.

Both Hobbes and Bodin were primarily concerned with internal sovereignty: the absolute authority of government within the state. Most political philosophers – and liberal democracies – now no longer accept their view that governmental power must be single, centralized and above the law. But these two currents of thinking continue to inform our thinking about external state sovereignty in the international system. If we take a Hobbesian approach to cases where states act tyrannically, for example, practising genocide on their own citizens, we cannot invoke natural law, or any moral arguments to defend intervention. From Bodin's perspective, however, events such as the genocide in Rwanda, which might be characterized as abuses of natural law, could justify foreign intervention.

External sovereignty produces a system composed of states which are not subject to a common authority or overarching law, but which interact with each other in conditions of anarchy. Some contemporary political philosophers who defend the sovereignty of states against each other invoke this interaction under anarchy to defend non-intervention. Terry Nardin argues that we should respect the sovereignty and political independence of states, because an international system that practises non-intervention would exhibit the virtues of mutual restraint and toleration of diversity (Nardin, 1983). The stability of the society of states is key here, and it is only when that is under threat due to human rights abuses that intervention can be justified. Armed intervention to protect human rights is permitted to take place under four conditions:

1 It must be a last resort, after other less drastic remedies have failed.
2 It must be likely to end the abuse of human rights.

3 The human rights abuses must be sufficiently serious to merit the loss of human life that would inevitably occur as a result of armed intervention.
4 The disruptive effects of armed intervention on international stability must be minimal (Nardin and Slater, 1986).

As critics have pointed out, arguments on the basis of state sovereignty and the stability of the international order assume that order is the primary social value, both within the state and between states. They assume, as does Hobbes, that justice cannot flourish without order. Many philosophers argue on the contrary that order only has value if it is just. Not all who take this view are cosmopolitans: John Rawls, notably, allows only limited exceptions for intervention. As we saw in Chapter 10, Rawls argues that justice requires a society of well-ordered nations (Rawls, 1999). People's primary duties in terms of sharing wealth are owed to their fellow citizens, rather than to others in the global community. However, the 'law of peoples' that governs states' relations entails that liberal and decent societies do not tolerate outlaw states that systematically abuse the rights of their citizens. Sanctions and non-violent means of persuasion must be applied first but, if all else fails, forcible intervention might be justifiable.

Community membership and external assistance

Hobbes' contractarian argument assumes that state sovereignty is legitimate because citizens consent to it – or can be assumed to do so – and valuable because it ensures security, civil society, justice and morality. An important strand of thinking critical of intervention is based on the view that, in challenging state sovereignty, even well-meaning intervention challenges people's right to establish their own political institutions. This position depends on the fundamental liberal principle that all peoples have the right to determine and consent to the political system under which they live. As liberal philosopher John Stuart Mill argues in his 1859 essay *A Few Words on Non-intervention*, foreign military intervention alone cannot bring about the liberation of an oppressed people. Mill's argument relies less on the value of sovereignty in itself, and more on the importance of political participation: 'The only test possessing any real value, of a people's having become fit for popular institutions, is that they, or a sufficient portion of them to prevail in the contest, are willing to brave labour and danger for their liberation' (Mill, 1984 [1859]: 122). Liberation has a participatory dimension, and a people cannot benefit from outside help unless they are willing to take up their own cause.

This suggests that there is an important difference between intervening from the outside out of moral concern, and intervening at the request or plea of the subordinated, who are already doing what they can to resist, or who are prevented from resisting. It is only in the latter case that intervention can actually bring about its moral goals, because those moral goals must include not only the elimination of tyranny, but also the restoration of freedom and autonomy. Mill continues: 'I know it may be urged that the virtues of freemen cannot be learnt in the school of slavery, and that if a people are not fit for freedom, to have any chance of becoming so, they must first be free. And this would be conclusive, if the intervention recommended would really give them freedom. But the evil is, that if they have not sufficient love of liberty to be able to wrest it from merely domestic oppressors, the liberty which is bestowed on them by other hands than their own, will have nothing real, nothing permanent' (Mill, 1984 [1859]: 122).

A more recent argument along these lines is made by Michael Walzer, who appeals not to the issue of whether people can be liberated or must liberate themselves but, rather, to the value of the state as 'the arena in which self-determination is to be worked out' (Walzer, 1980). The national community – if not the state, and this is an important distinction – is the context in which social meaning and value are embedded. If we compare this to Mill, Walzer might seem to be more dedicated to preserving the community than individual freedom. But this is because Walzer understands individual freedom not as abstract and unchangeable across cultures but, rather, as located within a particular communal context. Walzer contends that the relationship between a community and a state emerges in a specific historical context, and that community and state are mutually intertwined in a way that outsiders cannot judge or even truly know (Walzer, 2004).

As with most theorists who defend the rights of states, however, Walzer is not absolutely opposed to intervention in all circumstances. He suggests, rather, that a presumption be accepted that intervention is wrong, because it interferes with self-determination. That presumption could be overridden, when the threat to human rights is sufficiently serious. This might include cases in which the social instability caused by persecution or genocide can spread and cause wider political instability, threatening the self-determination of people in neighbouring countries. (We might note that this echoes Nardin's final criterion for legitimate intervention.) Intervention could not be justified in the name of principles such as democracy, or property rights, or freedom of association. But it would be legitimate if it aimed to put a stop to actions that 'shock the conscience of mankind'. Also, it should be carried out by neighbouring countries, who have a stake in regional security, and who have a better understanding of the political culture of the offending state (Walzer, 2004). This covers, in Walzer's view: India's military intervention in East Pakistan (present-day Bangladesh) in 1971, to stop the mass murder of Hindus; Tanzania's action in Uganda in 1979 (which was justified in terms of self-defence, rather than humanitarian intervention); and Vietnam's military intervention in Cambodia in 1972, to stop the genocidal killings by the Khmer Rouge. In terms of the cases we discussed at the beginning of this chapter, Walzer's approach supports the adequate funding of African Union troops in Darfur, and European humanitarian intervention in the Balkans.

As do most philosophers who support the rights of states against intervention, in all but exceptional circumstances, Walzer insists that such interventions should be endorsed by multilateral or unilateral institutions. This provides a means of controlling the self-aggrandizing tendencies of states to use the pretext of humanitarian concerns to advance their own national interests. Here, the country intervening must be acting as the 'agent of last resort'. Finally, one test of a genuinely humanitarian intervention is that the intervening forces are quickly in and out quickly – so that intervention does not become occupation. This would clearly rule out intervention in the case of Iraq. The 'politics of rescue', Walzer concludes, are certain to be complex and messy (Walzer, 2004). In practice, it is often difficult to identify a single human-rights abuser, and to distinguish the victimizers and the victims. In the case of Bosnia, for example, both Serbs and Bosnian Muslims committed atrocities. Moreover, in some cases, the objectionable policies or actions were supported by local cultural and social structures. This was particularly relevant in Kosovo, where the Serbs argued that the ethnic cleansing of Albanians was justified because the area was historically, culturally and religiously Serbian.

As with other critics who allow for exceptions to a general presumption in favour of non-intervention – Rawls, for example – Walzer does not offer any clear criteria for determining whether human rights abuses are serious enough for armed intervention. Human sacrifice, slavery and genocide are often mentioned as the kind of state actions that would qualify and, indeed, the logic of Walzer's argument is that only behaviour that was widely agreed to be abhorrent across cultural and national borders could justify intervention. In cases where there is widespread international condemnation of human rights abuses, it is least likely that the intervention will entail imposing alien ideas and values. The requirement that intervention be multilateral or authorized by the UN reflects the same concern: international bodies are assumed to represent general interests, or what eighteenth-century philosopher Rousseau referred to as the General Will – uncontaminated by particular interests (Rousseau, 1973 [1762]). In practice, Walzer's opposition to intervention has so many qualifiers that it is difficult to distinguish his position from that of supporters who base their case on quite different cosmopolitan arguments.

Community membership and the case for intervention

Many critics have accused Walzer of romanticizing the nation-state – assuming, mistakenly, that it embodies communal values and meanings to citizens (Luban, 1980). It is one thing to protect the independence and self-determination of communities in which people are embedded, and that give their lives meaning, and quite another to assume that those communities are the same as nation-states. Charles Beitz argues that the 'fit' Walzer assumes between nation-states and communities frequently does not exist (Beitz, 1980). The fact that a government exists and manages the institutions of state power does not necessarily mean that it constitutes the cultural and historical representative of a people. Beitz points out that, if a government is not democratically grounded, we cannot assume that it represents its people.

In a related argument, Bhikhu Parekh suggests that Walzer and other communitarians are right to see individuals as embedded in their social and cultural communities, but wrong to see those communities in unitary terms (Parekh, 1997). In fact, individuals are members of a range of communities within their nation-state. They are shaped by all of these affiliations, but not determined by any single one. The identities of human beings are socially constructed from a range of affiliations and memberships, and individuals can use this complex range to reflect on different aspects of their social membership, from their different communal viewpoints. States are, thus, characterized by irreducible diversity. We might note that intervention is frequently demanded in order to protect this diversity, as human rights abuses often target minority groups (Caney, 1997). Neta Crawford argues further that the multiplicity of identities within nation-states makes it possible for leaders to invoke, create and manipulate different identities in order to legitimize intervention (Crawford, 2002).

As Parekh argues, membership in the nation-state is important, but it does not transcend the obligations that people owe to each other as human beings. The autonomy of states is conditional on them meeting basic moral standards, and other states are obliged to help non-citizens in need. However, they are not the only organizations with a responsibility to act. Other groups, religious associations and non-governmental organizations, representative of the diverse groups that express human social identity, also have a moral and social responsibility to reduce and prevent conflict (Parekh, 1997).

Just War

Running through Walzer's defence of intervention in limited circumstances, as well as the ICISS principles we discussed above, are the principles of the

Just War tradition – a set of norms and conventions institutionalized in western thought, in the medieval period that established principles governing the waging of war. Traditional Just War theory depends on the concept of natural law: the idea that there exist principles of justice, originally established by divine authority, and accessible to people through nature and reason, that take ultimate precedence over human law. (We discussed the concept of natural law in relation to moral issues such as abortion and euthanasia in Chapter 7.) The Roman politician and philosopher Cicero argued, in the first century BCE, that there must be legal and ethical constraints on states' decisions to wage war, and how to conduct those wars (Cicero, 1991 [44 BCE]). The fourth-century Christian philosopher Augustine of Hippo argued that some wars could be waged with justice if there were a just cause, such as the conversion of infidels, or the protection of Christians (Augustine, 1931 [426 CE]). Later, medieval Christian philosopher Aquinas codified Just War into three principles governing both the grounds for going to war, and the way in which it could be waged. With respect to the first of these principles, three requirements must be satisfied in order for war to be just:

1 It must be waged by a legitimate authority.
2 It must be waged for just cause.
3 It must be waged with rightful intention (Aquinas, 1952 [written 1265–74]).

Just War was incorporated into international law in the seventeenth century by Dutch jurist Hugo Grotius, who argued that intervention by force was justified against states that had contravened natural law (Grotius, 2004 [1625]).

The rules of Just War continue to be the official teaching of the Roman Catholic Church, and have enjoyed a resurgence of interest since the 1970s, when Walzer published an influential book on the subject shortly after the Vietnam War (Walzer, 2006 [1977]). As we have already seen, these principles form the basis of current political arguments defending military intervention to protect human rights. Some political philosophers, however, have relied more on the broader traditions of cosmopolitanism and universal human rights, and it is to these that we now turn.

Justifying intervention: the cosmopolitan argument

Cosmopolitanism is based on the principle that all human beings have universal rights and interests, irrespective of national membership, and that states must respect those rights and interests of citizens and non-citizens alike. As Simon Caney points out, intervention cannot be considered separately from the question of whether universal human rights exist (Caney, 2005). There would be no reason to intervene in the internal affairs of another state if its citizens did not possess rights above and beyond those they acquired through citizenship. The idea of a universal human community dates back to the ancient world: in the early modern period, when Hobbes and Bodin were justifying state sovereignty, Spanish philosophers Vitoria and Suarez argued that both states themselves and the society of states were grounded in, and derived their moral value from, that broader universal community (Parekh, 1997). As a political issue, however, this is relatively recent; it is only in the post-World War II period that we have seen states agree to put limits on their sovereignty, beginning with the UN Declaration of Human Rights (1948), which guarantees respect for the fundamental rights of individuals.

Cosmopolitan defenders of intervention start from Immanuel Kant's premise fundamental to modern liberalism: that all individuals have inherent moral value and are deserving of equal respect (Kant, 1993 [1785]). The moral value of individuals does not depend on their national membership, so our duties to each other are also not dependent on nationality. We discussed this with respect to redistribution in Chapter 10. The universal moral status of individuals gives rise to universal human rights that are entitled to protection (the question of who is obliged to protect them is a further issue). While people might disagree over the extent of these, it is clear that some basic rights are recognized across cultures; for example, the right to subsistence, and the right not to be killed or tortured. These apply across cultures. Those who take this position argue that any rights that states have to sovereignty (understood as immunity from external interference) derive from the fact that they protect and preserve the human rights of citizens. This means that state sovereignty has conditional, rather than absolute, value. We have seen this view reflected in the ICISS report on the responsibility to protect.

This does not mean that cosmopolitans advocate humanitarian intervention in all circumstances where human rights are under threat. As with philosophers who make a more limited defence of intervention, they argue for a balancing of factors and consequences, along the familiar lines of the Just War tradition. Legal philosopher Fernando Teson has set out the moral basis of humanitarian intervention in an influential argument that draws on cosmopolitan principles and natural law (Teson, 2006). First, sovereignty has instrumental value – as we have seen, governments derive their legitimacy from the fact that they protect the human rights and basic interests of their citizens. Tyrannical governments who threaten or fail to protect those rights forfeit their right to non-interference: they forfeit the protection of international law. Further, the fact that all people have basic rights means that governments have duties to protect those human rights at home, and to protect the human rights of other people if they can do so with minimum cost to themselves. This is part of a wider moral duty to assist others in need. But the costs of assisting always need to be weighed up in the decision. We might interpret this as the unavoidability of consequentialist factors in moral decision-making on this issue. Teson follows the natural law tradition in arguing that, as long as any bad consequences are unintended, and as long as the good consequences for intervention outweigh the bad, intervention is justified. But, as he points out, we could also think of weighing the costs of intervening as a Kantian objection. Kant argues that we must see people as ends in themselves, not means to the ends of others – and, if we are willing to sacrifice people to assist others, there is always the possibility that we are using them as a means to others' ends (Teson, 2006).

Also following natural law theory, Teson argues that a justifiable intervention must be intended to end the human rights abuses. It does not matter on cosmopolitan grounds if the intervening state also has other motives, as long as these were not the real intent of the intervention. In practice, these are often not easy to disentangle. The United States claimed that its intent in invading Iraq was to rid the Iraqi people of a tyrannical regime, but it clearly also had other motives (Roth, 2004). In order to test this, Teson suggests that we examine the consequences of the action:

- If it results in occupation – clearly, not part of ending human rights abuses – then we might conclude that other and less selfless motives were the real intent of the action.
- In addition, and in accordance with Mill's concerns, the intervention must be approved and requested by the people suffering themselves.
- The final cosmopolitan criterion Teson lists is that the intervention must be supported by the community of democratic states. This reminds us that what appear to be moral reasons for intervention on the part of western states can look like neo-imperialism to states in the developing world (Caney, 1997).

Universal principles are vulnerable to criticism that they are the reflection of particular interests, masquerading as universal (a point made in a more general context by Marx) (Marx and Engels, 1978 [1848]). In response to criticism, cosmopolitans point out that there is global agreement on some political and moral values – as we see from the widespread agreement to international conventions on human rights. Moreover, as Caney reminds us, cosmopolitanism does not require that there be general agreement on all questions of human rights, but only that certain basic rights be accepted (Caney, 1997).

As with sovereignty arguments that allow intervention in exceptional cases, cosmopolitanism offers no clear and single test for determining when intervention is justified. No matter what the theoretical justification for the action is, practical considerations concerning its likely effectiveness, how it will be interpreted, and the costs for those intervening are always relevant – and often determining – factors. And, as Beitz concludes, when there is no moral reason against intervention in cases of human rights abuses, the only reason not to intervene might be that the effects of intervention are unknown, and there is a possibility that the costs in terms of bloodshed might be greater than the benefits of ending human rights abuses (Beitz, 1980).

The final cosmopolitan argument we consider justifies humanitarian intervention on the basis of contractual agreement. So far, the contractarian theories we have considered have supported state sovereignty. As we have seen in this chapter and Chapter 10, John Rawls maintains that the parties who decide in the original position upon principles of justice at the global level are representatives of peoples, rather than individuals, and the principles of justice upon which they agree are more limited than those that regulate domestic society. Philosopher Gillian Brock develops an original position argument for global justice in which the parties to agreement would legitimize international intervention in specific circumstances (Brock, 2006). Brock asks us to imagine a thought experiment such as the one Rawls describes in *A Theory of Justice* (Rawls, 1971). A global conference has been set up, the aim of which is to choose the rules by which the world's people will live and interact. None of the delegates present know the information about demographics that would help them estimate the chances of them belonging to any particular group or nation. However, they do know about global collective problems. This includes the existence of threats to peace and security, information about history and how brutal dictators have sometimes oppressed people, and about how states have caused damage by intervening with good intentions.

What basic guidelines would delegates to the conference agree on? Brock argues that people would choose institutions that would protect their basic freedoms and fulfil their basic needs, because they would realize that this is essential to ensuring that they can enjoy the prospects of a decent life. Delegates would wish to allow intervention to help those suffering from tyranny and cruelty on the same grounds, but would want to ensure that it could not be abused by the powerful. The principles of Just War might serve as a useful guide to the delegates deciding on the rules for intervention. First, there must be just cause: severe suffering that the domestic government causes or cannot prevent. Then, delegates would wish to make sure that the intentions of the intervening state were good – that they were not acting in pursuit of ulterior motives. One means by which to ensure this would be to require that the intervention be authorized or justified by an international organization in which a range of nations was represented. Delegates might

Box 11.2 Humanitarian intervention: competing norms and values

The philosophical debate over humanitarian intervention centres on different interpretations of state sovereignty, national community, the social contract, justice and rights.

- State sovereignty

Those supporting intervention argue that sovereignty is conditional upon a state discharging its duty to protect citizens, and when states fail to do this, it is legitimate for others in the international community to step in.

Those opposing intervention rely on the definition of state sovereignty enshrined in international law: states have full control over all affairs within their own territory.

- Community

Supporters argue that the state, as a set of institutions to regulate and control life, is not the same as a meaningful community. In fact, intervention might sometimes be required to protect minority communities. Cosmopolitans maintain that the only morally important community is the universal community of humanity.

Those opposing intervention argue that the national community is the forum and context in which citizens express their cultural and social values, and participate in establishing their political institutions. Outsiders can never really understand those values from the inside. Democratic institutions will not be legitimate if they are imposed from the outside.

- Justice and rights

Supporters argue that justice requires the recognition of universal human rights, independent of national membership.

Opponents of intervention claim that it is not legitimate to cite principles of justice or human rights against a state, because justice and rights cannot exist outside the context of state-established order.

- The social contract

Supporters argue that we can imply a social contract between all human beings, in which they determine the principles that govern life both within the state and amongst states.

Opponents of intervention counter that the state sovereignty (see the section on state sovereignty in this box) is established by an implied social contract between the members of a nation-state. There is no global social contract in which people agree to intervene to protect non-citizens.

also plausibly insist that intervention only take place when other peaceful and less costly alternatives have been ruled out. And, finally, delegates would require proportionality, so that only the amount of force necessary to relieve suffering would be used (Brock, 2006).

Conclusion

What is striking about the various positions we have considered on the issue of humanitarian intervention is how similar their conclusions are in practice. Most theorists agree that interventions must be judged on a case-by-case basis. The same abuses of human rights might justify intervention in one case (where, say, the costs are relatively low and the prospects of success great), and not justify intervention in another (where the costs of action would be high and the chances of success slim). And most agree on the criteria by which interventions should be judged: the seriousness of the suffering, the motives of those intervening, the likely costs and the prospects of success. These are the principles of the Just War tradition.

In some ways, it might seem that there is little difference between allowing intervention as an exception to state sovereignty arguments, on the one hand, and allowing it for cosmopolitan reasons, though in circumstances limited by practical considerations, on the other. But, as defenders of cosmopolitanism argue, it provides a more morally consistent position, by giving primary value to justice and morality, rather than the preservation of the state (Caney, 1997). Even for those who insist on the value of state sovereignty, the debate over intervention has forced us to reconsider and re-evaluate the purpose of sovereignty. The case for a responsibility to protect reminds us that states are not inherently valuable in the same way as human beings, and that any value they have must come from their value to their citizens. These debates play out the historical logic that led to the formation of the UN: the UN Charter was agreed in the aftermath of a war marked not only by attempts at foreign conquest, but also by systematic genocide on the part of Germany against its own Jewish citizens.

Most of the theoretical arguments we have examined here agree that intervention is justified in cases where the local government is promoting, or failing to prevent, systematic and extreme abuses of human rights. Why is it, then, that the international community has not intervened in a case such as Darfur, given universal condemnation of human rights abuses and the global publicity afforded to human suffering there? The UN and individual states have condemned the failure of the Sudanese government to protect its citizens, and yet no effective intervention has occurred. Of course, there are practical factors that might explain the reluctance of western nations to act, particularly the fact that the US and its allies already have substantial military commitments in Iraq and, to a lesser extent, Afghanistan. We might conclude also, however, that the weighing up of consequences has been crucial here. States appear to have decided that intervention might not be successful, and that too many intervening soldiers might die in the course of it. In practice, every decision to intervene is made in political contexts that are both global and domestic, and nations that have sustained high losses in previous interventions find it more difficult to justify further risk to the lives of their soldiers and citizens. Walzer has criticized this focus on the costs of intervention, arguing that it should be subordinate to acting effectively on the international stage (Walzer, 2004). But it remains a powerful consideration, not only politically for governments, but also morally, given that humanitarian intervention means sacrificing the lives of some in order to save others.

Chapter 12

Should the Natural Environment be Protected for Future Generations?

Western political theory is based on the assumption that political communities extend backwards into the past and forwards into the future. Almost all political and social thinkers since the Enlightenment have assumed that those communities and their economies would continue to grow and develop, sustained by natural resources and the increasing stores of wealth that their exploitation produces. Philosophers and politicians have recognized that resources were scarce and the subject of constant competition. That is why principles of justice must be developed to regulate their distribution. But most have believed that there existed, and would continue to exist, sufficient resources to sustain economic growth and development into the foreseeable future. This assumption that economies must and would expand, constantly searching out new resources (and markets), is an essential aspect of capitalism. However, Marxists have also assumed the potential for unlimited economic growth.

This is not to say that there have not been critics of economic and industrial development and its relentless exploitation of natural resources. The Romantic thinkers of the early nineteenth century condemned the destructive impact of industry (the 'dark satanic mills' of William Blake's poem 'Jerusalem') on both the natural landscape and human community. John Stuart Mill argued that economic growth should pause, so that natural resources could be conserved, and social and moral progress would catch up (Mill, 1965 [1848]). Nineteenth-century American conservationists such as Henry David Thoreau argued for the preservation of natural landscapes; indeed, legislation was passed in the United States to establish national parks in the late nineteenth century, and other western countries soon followed suit. But it is only since the 1970s that scientists have warned that natural resources are not unlimited, and are being depleted and destroyed – with potentially disastrous consequences for human civilization. There were, in the words of an influential report at the time, 'limits to growth' (Meadows *et al.*, 1972). The damaging effects of industrial development on air, water and the natural environment were reported by scientists such as Rachel Carson, who warned in 1962 that pesticides were destroying bird species (Carson,

1962). Carson's influential book *Silent Spring* mobilized popular opinion and the environmentalist movement was born.

Environmentalism's concern with protecting and preserving the natural world has many aspects, ranging from protecting individual species of animals, to preventing damage to natural resources such as air and waterways, to conserving natural and non-renewable resources used by humans. Perhaps its most pressing current concern is to preserve the atmosphere and climate: fundamental natural resources that make human life not only meaningful and enriching, but actually possible. Because a thriving natural environment is – at least at this point – necessary to human society, the conservation of natural resources has become since the 1980s a matter of concern for political philosophers. There had been considerable discussion before this among philosophers about our duties to future generations; much of this initially concerned our duties to save and pass on wealth, but the debate increasingly focuses on protecting non-renewable resources. We will concentrate in this chapter on philosophical arguments around the protection for the future of non-renewable natural resources, and the earth's atmosphere and climate.

The global nature of threats to the environment, and the necessity of international cooperation, were first recognized in the UN's Conference on the Human Environment held in Stockholm in 1972. The Stockholm Declaration issued by the conference recognized the right to a healthy environment, on the part of both present and future generations, and called for countries to preserve non-renewable resources and to prevent damage to ecosystems and to the earth's atmosphere. Following the conference, UN member states set up the UN Environment Programme, and many national governments established ministries for the environment. In 1982, the World Charter for Nature, agreed by all UN members except the United States, recognized that people must use natural resources in such a way as to ensure the preservation of species and ecosystems for the benefit of present and future generations. The United States' chief objection concerned the costs that would be imposed on the agricultural and mining sectors – the same grounds on which Congress has refused to ratify the Convention on Biological Diversity adopted in 1992 at the Earth Summit.

Since the 1980s, the international community has adopted the concept of sustainability to describe a balance between the need for economic development and the protection of resources for future generations. The energy crisis of the 1970s forcibly reminded developed countries of their heavy dependence on non-renewable sources of energy. At the same time, public concern grew over global population growth, increased consumption, and the impact of industrial production on the atmosphere. In 1987, the Brundtland Report 'Our Common Future' was published by the UN's World Commission on Environment and Development. The Commission argued that, in a world of limited resources, countries should be able to develop theirs only to the extent that the world's total stock of resources is not diminished. In practice, this meant cooperation between developed and developing nations, so that the needs of the world's poor are met, both currently and in the future. Sustainable development was defined as that which 'meets the needs of the present, without compromising the ability of future generations to meet their own needs'. As we shall see, questions of current distribution and saving for the future are closely related in much contemporary political theory concerning the environment. In accordance with sustainability, many nations introduced policies for the conservation of resources, such as recycling, and began to explore renewable energy sources as alternatives to fossil fuels. However, some radical environmentalists have expressed scepticism about the concept, arguing that it cannot be defined clearly, and that the structures of the world economy, and cultural attitudes towards the use of nature, mean that further development will inevitably compromise the needs of future generations (Redclift, 1987).

A global campaign to ban chlorofluorocarbons (CFCs) was launched in the 1980s, intensifying in 1985, when scientists discovered a large hole in the ozone layer over Antarctica. The Vienna Convention for the Protection of the Ozone Layer was agreed in 1985, and the 1987 Montreal Protocol to the Convention established legally binding reduction goals for the use of CFCs. As a result of the Protocol, there has been a 95 per cent drop in the presence of ozone depleting substances in the atmosphere and, by the year 2010, CFCs are scheduled to be banned from all countries. UN Secretary General Kofi Annan called this the most successful international agreement ever. It is important to note that the Montreal Protocol treated developed and developing nations differently: under Article 5, developing nations were permitted to postpone their commitments under the agreement for up to ten years, during which time they could increase their production of ozone depleting substances (which, comparatively, were very low). This was agreed so that developing countries could reap some of the economic advantages of development.

The issue of CFCs was distinctive in that it dealt with a global problem that could be resolved only by countries acting together. Anthropogenic warming (that caused by human activity) is similarly international in scope, and has become increasingly urgent since the 1990s. Scientists have recorded increases in the earth's temperature over the course of the twentieth century, with most of the rise dating from the mid-century and post-World War II increases in industrial development. There is still some disagreement from individual scientists about global warming, but a consensus now exists among the world's major scientific establishments that human activity is causing accelerated increases in temperature. Climate model projections predict that the temperature of the earth will increase by between 1.1 to 6.4

degrees Celsius over the course of the twenty-first century. As a result, the earth's oceans will rise, and there will be an increase in warm spells, heat waves and heavy rainfall. In 1988, the international Intergovernmental Panel on Climate Change (IPCC) was established to evaluate the risk of climate change caused by human activity. It has published a series of assessment reports, which confirm that climate change is a fact and that it is likely to have devastating consequences for human societies.

The poorest people in the world, in Africa and Asia, will be disproportionately affected by global warming, because of the impact of droughts and floods caused by rising sea levels. The Stern Review on the Economics of Climate Change, commissioned in 2006 by the British government, reported that climate change was already a grave threat to the developing world, and an obstacle to poverty reduction. Developing countries already have warm climates and variable rainfalls. Moreover, they are often highly dependent on agriculture, which will be affected by global warming. Agricultural yields will decline by an estimated 15–35 per cent in Africa, and Zambia, Niger and Chad are predicted to lose their entire farming sectors by 2100. Up to a further 80 million people are likely to become at risk from malaria in Africa. In the event of a one-metre rise in sea levels, possible by the end of this century, more than one fifth of Bangladesh could be under water. In addition to all this, because land and resources will become scarcer, ethnic and national conflicts are likely to become worse (Stern, 2006).

The UN Framework Convention on Climate Change, signed at the Earth Summit of 1992, was designed to stabilize greenhouse gas emissions in the atmosphere, in an attempt to arrest global warming. It provides that countries party to it 'should protect the climate system for the benefit of present and future generations of humankind, on the basis of equity and in accordance with their common but differentiated responsibilities and respective capabilities' (Article 3.1). The claim that, because of uneven rates of development, states have different responsibilities for climate change, and varying capacities to pay for remedies, has played a crucial and controversial role in the international negotiations about how to deal with the problem. Some developed countries, particularly the United States, have complained that they are being asked to shoulder all the responsibility for reducing emissions, while developing countries are not required to cut their own. Developing countries respond that wealthy nations have the resources necessary to make changes and, in addition, that they have benefited from unrestricted emissions in the past, in the process of development and modernization. It would be unfair, developing countries claim, to prevent them from reaching comparable levels of affluence and modernization. In the final Declaration, it was agreed that poorer nations could be rewarded for protecting their forests. But richer nations could earn carbon credits by supporting forest development in poorer countries.

The Kyoto Protocol to the Convention, signed in 1997, set legally binding targets for the reduction of specified greenhouse gases produced by developed countries, and provided for emissions trading. Levels in these 36 countries were to drop to 5 per cent below 1990 levels by 2008–12. The Protocol encouraged developing countries to reduce greenhouse gas emissions, but no targets were set. In addition, a multilateral fund was set up to assist developing countries in offsetting the costs involved in phasing out ozone depleting substances. As of 2008, 183 countries have ratified the Protocol. The Bush administration in the United States refused to ratify, claiming that, because the Protocol did not require developing countries to reduce their emissions, it was not only unfair, but also likely to be ineffectual.

While some countries (including the United Kingdom) have decreased their greenhouse gas emissions, it is clear that not enough progress has been made. When developed nations met in 2007 to consider successor strategies to the Kyoto Protocol, the UN reported that the negative effects of climate change were already being felt. The rate of warming of the Arctic was accelerating, and there were adverse effects on human activities and the sources of human food. UN Secretary General Ban Ki Moon said: 'We cannot go on this way for long. We cannot continue with business as usual. The time has come for decisive action on a global scale.' One group of nations, led by the EU, urged countries to commit to reducing greenhouse gases by 40 per cent. An opposing camp, led by the United States and supported by Japan, Canada and Australia wanted a two-year timetable for a successor to the Kyoto Agreement, but no set numbers. Negotiations continue, and a new international agreement is expected to be signed in 2009 to negotiate further reductions. It is likely that China and India will demand that rich countries increase financial support to help poor countries to pay for cleaner technology, and to cover the economic impact of climate change.

Table 12.1 lists the most recent figures available for carbon dioxide emissions per capita in a range of countries. (It does not include some small economies that score very high in per capita figures, but low in terms of their overall contribution, such as the oil-producing states of the Gulf region.) We should note that the levels of greenhouse gas emissions in rapidly developing countries, particularly India and China, have substantially increased since 2004.

The political debates over international treaties on the environment raise some underlying normative questions:

- Should we protect the environment for the benefit of future generations?
- If we have such a duty, is it a moral obligation, or one of justice?
- Who is responsible for paying for the cost of environmental protection?
- How should we balance our responsibilities here to future generations with the moral and political responsibility to supply the basic needs of the global population (issues that we considered in Chapters 2 and 10)?

Table 12.1   *Carbon dioxide emissions of selected countries, per capita in metric tons, 2004*

Chad	0.0127
Afghanistan	0.0288
Bangladesh	0.2469
Sudan	0.2870
India	1.2023
Brazil	1.8001
China	3.8393
Sweden	5.8940
United Kingdom	9.7934
Japan	9.8434
Russia	10.5393
Australia	16.2720
Canada	20.0095
United States	20.3792

Source: data supplied by the Carbon Dioxide Information Analysis Center for the UN.

• How far into the future – for how many future generations – should resources be protected? What we should do for the benefit of our children and grandchildren might well be different from any duties we owe to our descendants a thousand years from now.

In this chapter we will examine arguments that we are obliged to protect resources from a utilitarian perspective based on the consequences for individuals and then from the perspective of equality. We will also consider the specific question of whether future persons have rights. We then examine the communitarian case for protecting resources and, finally, a libertarian argument for conservation. We then consider arguments from an egalitarian perspective that are sceptical of the claim that justice requires saving natural resources for the future. We conclude with the libertarian case against mandated conservation, on the grounds of property rights.

As we shall see, most political theorists accept the need for some protection of the natural environment for future generations. The key points on which they differ are the grounds for any obligation we have, and its nature: whether this is an obligation of justice, similar to the requirement of just distribution to the current population, or whether it is a weaker ethical duty.

Several philosophers argue that, while justice does not oblige us to protect resources for people who do not yet exist, we should acknowledge moral obligations – as peoples as well as individuals – to ensure that human societies can continue. The issue of environmental protection tests the boundaries and limits of justice and rights, by raising the issue of who counts in making claims for justice. In this, it is similar to the case of abortion (see Chapter 7) and to the debate on whether we owe justice to people in other countries (see Chapter 10).

Before considering these arguments, however, we examine the claim that the natural environment should be protected not for the benefit of future human beings, but for its own sake. Radical environmentalists argue that the natural world is morally worthwhile in itself, and should be protected for itself rather than for human use or enjoyment. We discuss this argument briefly, as well as the related ecofeminist case for valuing nature. We conclude our examination of the inherent rights and value of the non-human world in Box 12.1 on animal rights.

Nature as an intrinsic good

According to 'deep ecologists', nature and the natural environment are goods in themselves, with inherent value and worth. They should not be seen as valuable and deserving of protection because of their usefulness to human beings. Deep ecologists criticize the 'anthropocentric' view of the world that puts humans at the centre and considers all other living things from the point of the view of their worth to humans. The ecological philosopher Val Plumwood, for example, argues that anthropocentrism leads us not only to exploit nature, but also to lose touch with ourselves as natural beings, deeply embedded in our natural environment and ecosystem. It justifies a rationalizing and instrumental approach to the world, which encourages the domination of nature in the name of capitalist development (Plumwood, 2002). To speak of protecting 'natural resources' already sees nature in terms of potential uses to humans. From the deep ecology perspective, ecosystems – and the whole ecosphere – must be preserved because they are inherently worthwhile, and human beings have no right to affect them to any extent greater than is required to protect their vital needs.

'Ecocentric' philosophers also argue that the anthropocentric approach establishes the model for relations of dominance and subordination within human societies. They reject the 'human chauvinism' of anthropocentrism, which they compare to other forms of prejudice. Treating human beings as the standard of value in relation to which all else is measured is thus comparable to racism, sexism or heterosexism (Eckersley, 1993). It is not clear, however, how an ecocentric approach could be actually applied in politics.

John Dryzek suggests that we should move beyond the opposition between ecocentric and anthropocentric thinking, to establish a model of 'ecological democracy' in which humans learn from, and interact and communicate with the natural world. Rather than trying to control nature, we should treat its signs and signals with respect, and respond to them as we would respond in rational deliberation to human communication (Dryzek, 2000).

Ecofeminism

The nature-centric approach of deep ecology underlies ecofeminism, a form of radical feminism that sees the domination of nature, and its instrumental status as a resource to be used and exploited, as deeply linked to the male exploitation of women (Plumwood, 1993). It is not accidental, ecofeminists argue, that nature is often referred to as female. Women have been understood throughout the recorded history of western societies as being closer to nature and natural processes and rhythms than men, because of their involvement in reproductive processes. This has been construed by a long tradition of patriarchal (male-dominated) political philosophy to exclude women from public life and politics, on the grounds that they are allegedly irrational, unpredictable and potentially uncontrollable, as is a 'force of nature'. Ecofeminists argue, however, that both men and women are embedded in the natural world. As with other forms of deep ecologism, ecofeminism advocates a radically new way of seeing the relationship between human beings and nature, denying the opposition between them and rejecting relationships of domination, control and exploitation between men and nature. There is no doubt that the natural environment should be preserved – not for the use of future generations, but in acknowledgement of the relationship between those future generations and the natural world of which they are a part. Many ecofeminists are influenced by the feminist ethics of care approach, which asserts that we should replace the concept of justice as a relationship between separate and self-interested individuals with an ethic that recognizes people's connectedness with and dependence on others for care (Mies and Shiva, 1993).

Most political theorists writing on the environment accept the anthropocentric view – as all social sciences, politics deals fundamentally with human beings and human societies. But understanding the value of nature in terms of people's relationship to it to it does not mean focusing only on its material and economic uses. We can also see nature as valuable to people because it is beautiful, awe-inspiring and enriching; something that is greater and older than ourselves, a focus for appreciation, and a source of belonging and self-respect. This way of valuing nature is particularly important to communitarian environmentalist theories, as we shall see. Moreover, some critics claim that the problem of exploitation of nature is caused not by the

Box 12.1 Animal rights

Most western philosophers have proceeded on the assumption that human beings are inherently more morally worthy than animals. Aristotle argued, in the fourth century BCE, that animals were created in order to be used by man, and this view was generally shared in the Judeo-Christian tradition. For Enlightenment philosophers, it was the human ability to reason that guaranteed their superiority to animals. Those such as Immanuel Kant and John Locke who opposed cruelty to animals did so because they believed that mistreating animals taught habits of brutality that were damaging to human social relations (Kant, 1993 [1785]; Locke, 1996 [1693]). In the eighteenth century, however, Jeremy Bentham first made the case for animal rights that is still influential today. Bentham argued that we have moral obligations to all creatures that can feel pleasure and pain, including animals. In deciding whether something should be the subject of moral consideration, we should ask, not 'Can they reason? nor Can they talk? but Can they suffer?' (Bentham, 1988 [1789]). Bentham compared mistreatment of animals to racial discrimination and slavery.

There was a flurry of popular concern over animal welfare in western countries during the nineteenth century – associations to protect animals were formed and legislation was passed against cruelty. But the animal rights movement only emerged in the 1960s, with a critique of 'speciesism' – the assumption that the human species is superior. Radical animal liberation groups were formed in the 1970s, and some have engaged in direct action to damage research facilities that use animals. In the early twenty-first century, western countries have passed a raft of animal welfare measures, and Germany was the first to enshrine protection of animal rights in its constitution in 2002.

- The most influential case for the equal moral value of animals is made by philosopher Peter Singer (Singer, 1975). As a utilitarian, Singer relies on welfare rather than rights, and argues that we should give equal consideration

human exercise of rationality over it but, rather, by a failure of rationality. Recent critics of Marx argue, for example, that he believed that people must learn to conform to the rational laws of nature, rather than attempting to exert dominance and control over it (Burkett, 1999; Foster, 2000). Overcoming alienation meant reconciling people to their natural environments, as well as to their true nature as humans.

The utilitarian case for conserving resources

The most straightforward argument for saving resources for the future is

→

to the interests of all sentient beings – those who have the capacity to feel enjoyment and to suffer.

- An alternative, rights-based approach is taken by Tom Regan. He argues that we cannot restrict rights to rational creatures, as neither infant nor senile human beings are rational, and yet we recognize that they have moral rights. Any creature that experiences its life, or is the 'subject-of-a-life', and for whom life can become better or worse, is inherently valuable. Thus, they possess moral rights, including the right to be treated with respect, and not to be harmed (Regan, 1983).

- Many philosophers have insisted that animals cannot be said to have rights or to be the subjects of justice. This does not mean, however, that we have no moral obligations or duties in how we treat them. They remind us that justice does not cover all of our moral obligations (although it does embrace our political obligations). Brian Barry and John Rawls both argue that justice applies only between creatures who are moral equals (Barry, 1999; Rawls, 1993). Animals are not the moral equals of humans and, therefore, we are not bound by principles of justice to them. We do have moral duties to treat them well – however this may be defined – but these are duties we owe to our fellow citizens, rather than to animals themselves.

- We might also argue that animals cannot be the subject of justice, because justice applies only to creatures that are in a reciprocal relationship with each other. The imbalance in power between animals and humans means that they cannot affect us as we can affect them (see the discussion of David Hume on p. 246).

- The arguments for animal rights share some of the critiques of anthropocentrism made by deep ecologists. But some ecocentric philosophers have been critical of Singer and Regan for assuming that non-sentient beings do not have morally relevant interests. They have also criticized the animal rights movement for focusing on individual animals, rather than the entire ecological context (Plumwood, 1993).

utilitarian: we should maximize the welfare of people. But this only holds as long as we accept that the welfare of future generations must be counted with that of people now alive. If we accept this premise, then there is no doubt that natural resources should be saved: future generations are so numerous (in fact, potentially limitless) that their welfare will always exceed that which is reduced now as a result of having to conserve resources – say, to pay for expensive clean technology, or to forgo a higher material standard of living. The sheer numbers of future people pose a potential concern: as John Rawls suggests, utilitarianism might call for heavy sacrifices from current poor generations for the sake of advantages to those in the future (Rawls, 1971). Economists deal with this by applying a discount rate to future goods, so that they are not worth the same as present goods. But, as Singer points out, this is only relevant if we are considering relative rates of the value of money (Singer, 1993). Some environmental goods cannot be replaced by any money; for example, virgin forest. We might include non-renewable resources; the earth's atmosphere, which is (at least, now) essential to life; and the wide range of natural features that will be affected by global warming. Are these still vulnerable to Rawls' criticism? Some might argue that future generations will be wealthier and better able to deal with the challenges posed by global warming, but the consensus among scientists now is that the damage being done is irreversible. It seems clear that current generations can afford environmental protection for the benefit of those in the future. Perhaps human welfare might be satisfied in the future by an entirely artificial environment, created by advanced science. Robert Goodin addresses this possibility in his utilitarian case for environmental protection. Goodin argues that it is valuable to human beings to be connected to the natural world because it is natural, and that cannot be replicated by artificial means (Goodin, 1992).

On the controversial question of who should pay now for environmental protection, a utilitarian approach suggests that we look to the distribution of costs that would maximize welfare among the world's people. Who has historical responsibility for polluting is not a relevant factor here, but we could assume that wealthy countries now should bear the burden, as the cost in welfare to those in poorer countries would be considerable. This is reflected in the fund established by the Kyoto Protocol to meet the costs of offsetting global warming.

Egalitarian arguments for conservation

The utilitarian case for conservation appeals to concerns about the consequences of environmental damage on the welfare of future people. But we can also make an argument based on the principle of equality, and following the same lines as egalitarian theories that deal with current generations. Brian Barry suggests that we see environmental protection in distributive terms, and that we should think about justice between generations as being guided by the same principles as justice within a generation (Barry, 1999). Barry identifies four premises implied in equality and, as we shall see, these are consistent with other egalitarian arguments:

1 All individuals have equal moral worth, and deserve equal rights.
2 As long as we have fair equality of opportunity, we should take responsibility for our free choices, but not for the negative things that happen to us beyond our control. (This is the same key distinction as Dworkin made between option and brute bad luck, which we discussed in Chapter 2.).

3 We have vital interests or basic needs, and we are equally entitled to have these satisfied. (We discussed the basic needs argument in Chapter 2, and in Chapter 10 on foreign aid.)

4 Any departures from equality must be on agreed to on the basis that they are to the mutual advantage of those involved. (This is consistent with Rawls' difference principle, discussed in Chapter 2.)

We can apply these principles to assess equality within our own time framework. But do they justify protecting natural resources for future generations? As Barry argues, we cannot ensure that people have equal rights across generations – for one thing, we have more rights now than did people in the past. But we might agree that we have an obligation to ensure that members of a subsequent generation can have equal rights with respect to each other. (As we shall see later in this chapter, Rawls concedes that those in the original position would want to pass on a just society with just institutions to later generations.) On the issue of responsibility, it is clear that members of future generations who have to live with a substantially damaged environment and depleted resources did not choose this situation, and should not have to bear its costs. They are, however, responsible for the size of their population, and for the impact that this has on their ability to survive given the resources they have inherited. On the criterion of equally satisfying vital interests, global warming is clearly likely to have an impact on the outlook of future generations. And, finally, those in future generations obviously cannot have agreed that it is to their mutual advantage to be unequal.

The role that environmental protection plays in ensuring the equality of future generations is recognized, as we have seen in the Brundtland Report, in the concept of sustainability. Barry suggests that sustainability requires that people across generations should have equal opportunities, which they may use as they wish. There must be available a range of possible ways of living a good life and, at the minimum, people's basic and vital needs must be satisfied. People both in the present and in the future must have sufficient resources to lead a basically decent life, in which they exercise their innately human characteristic. But those in the future retain some responsibility for their own fates: if future generations continue to expand their populations at the current rate, they must take responsibility for the impact of this on their need for natural resources.

Equality arguments remind us that intra-generational and inter-generational inequalities are closely related, and that the latter cannot be achieved without the former. As we have seen, the Stern Review emphasized the disproportional burdens that global warming imposed on developing societies. Kristin Shrader-Frechette has shown that many other cases of environmental degradation have a heavy impact on poor communities. In the United States, for example, minority communities 'have been forced to trade unemployment for environmental pollution, to exchange a shrinking local tax base for toxic dumps, to trade no bread for a bloody half loaf' (Shrader-Frechette, 2002). She argues, as do other leftist critics such as Avner de-Shalit, that current and future inequalities must be dealt with together by measures to prevent environmental degradation and arrest global warming. As we shall see in a later section, however, some egalitarian critics think that the focus must be on present, rather than future, inequalities.

How are we to ensure that the interests of people not yet alive are taken into account in decision-making about natural resources? It seems we must rely on people now alive to recognize their obligations of justice, but we cannot see the effects of our decisions on future generations, as we can see them on the poor in our own society and, thanks to electronic media, in the remotest corners of the world. Andrew Dobson has made the controversial argument that we must nominate people today to represent the interests of future generations (Dobson, 1997). In order to ensure that they really do care about subsequent generations, Dobson suggests choosing environmentalists to be these representatives, as they avowedly do care for the future. But, as many critics have pointed out, this assumes that environmentalists will represent the interests of others rather than their own, and it opens the door to demands for representation to many other groups who claim to be concerned about the future.

Future generations and rights

A recurring question in considering arguments in favour of saving resources for future generations is whether future generations (generations as yet unborn) have rights. If they do, it is commonly agreed that someone has an obligation to satisfy those rights, and, in the case of the right of future generations to necessary natural and non-renewable resources, the onus would clearly fall on present generations. Some philosophers insist that, no matter how we define rights, those who do not exist cannot possibly be said to have them (Beckerman and Pasek, 2001). It is not as if, after all, future people do in some way exist, and are merely waiting to be born. 'They' are indeterminate – we have no way of knowing who and how numerous 'they' will be. As Hillel Steiner says, 'it seems mistaken to think of future persons as being already out there, anxiously awaiting either victimization by our self-indulgent prodigality or salvation through present self-denial' (Steiner, 1983: 159). Non-existent people cannot exercise choices, which is one definition of what is required for someone to have rights. Neither, according to critics, can they be said to have interests. This commonly agreed interpretation of rights has been famously described by Joel Feinberg: in order to possess a right, one must have an interest that can be represented (Feinberg, 1974).

We might argue further that the problem is not even that we cannot know the identities of future generations but, rather, that their identities depend on our choices. Derek Parfit formulates this as the 'non-identity problem' (Parfit, 1984). The case for preserving natural resources for future generations is that, if we do not do so, we will make life worse for members of a subsequent generation. However, the identity of members of the subsequent generation – who they are, as individuals – is dependent on the choices that we make now, including our choice to save or to deplete resources. So, we cannot compare the situation of future generations based on which policy we adopt, because their very identity will change, depending on which policy is adopted (Parfit, 1984).

But does it matter that 'future persons' have no determinate identities? Even though we cannot identify the specific people who will be in future generations, we can identify that there will be people. As Feinberg puts it: 'Any given one of them will have an interest in living space, fertile soil, fresh air and the like, but that arbitrarily selected one has no other qualities we can presently envision very clearly' (Feinberg, 1974). We know that there will be human beings, and that they will have interests that we can affect right now – so, it does not matter that we do not know who they will be. Similarly, the non-identity problem assumes that moral duties relate to the particular – in this case, relative – identity of people in the future. We might respond that we have duties not because we can compare the fate of indeterminate people in the future if we do not act to conserve resources with those who might exist if we did but, rather, because some people in the future will suffer if we do not act. This response might, however, be easier to defend from the position that we have moral obligations to people in the future, but not duties of justice towards them (see the discussion of Rawls, pp. 246–7).

Natural environments and communities

Egalitarian arguments consider nature as a resource to be used by human beings, to be possessed and enjoyed. But we might, instead, see it as part of the context, the environment, both social and natural, that shapes our identities, our sense of who we are. As we have seen with respect to other social issues, communitarians see individuals not as separate and atomistic but, rather, as embedded in context (see Chapter 2). We have focused on social context, but some philosophers have asserted that our connection to particular natural landscapes and places is also a deep and constitutive part of our sense of who we are. A similar argument is often made by nationalists, who emphasize the importance of particular territory and land to national identity.

Goodin argues along these lines that people want to see some sense or pattern to their lives, and that this requires that their lives be set in a larger context. Natural processes, unaffected by human hands, provide that larger context (Goodin, 1992). It is also important that context, both natural and social, extends both backwards and forwards in time. Communitarians see human communities as larger than their present members – they are shaped by their histories and their plans and hopes for the future (Walzer, 1983). We might note that this view of human community across time was explicitly set out by the eighteenth-century conservative thinker and politician Edmund Burke. He described society as: 'a partnership in all science, a partnership in all art; a partnership in every virtue and in all perfection ... As the ends of such a partnership cannot be obtained in many generations, it becomes a partnership between ... those who are living, those who are dead and those who are yet to be born' (Burke, 1955 [1790]).

Communitarianism, with its focus on context and historical continuity, does appear to be, as Robyn Eckersley claims, amenable to ecological concerns; moreover, it explains why we might be motivated to protect the environment for future people we cannot know (Eckersley, 2006). But it has limits: if there is a conflict between the needs of a social community that subsists on the exploitation of natural resources and preservation of a natural environment, there is no reason why the latter will take precedence. This has been particularly evident in controversies in many countries over logging, where a local community with a history of working in the timber industry resists the attempts of environmentalists to stop logging and preserve trees. As Cecile Fabre points out, the concept of a transgenerational community tells us only that we have communal obligations to future generations – not the nature of the specific obligations that we owe (Fabre, 2007). Those must be worked out as part of democratic debate. A communitarian approach to environmental conservation emphasizes the importance of including ethical questions, such as our obligations to future generations, in political debates and deliberation (de-Shalit, 2004). This is more consistent with Michael Sandel's communitarian argument for the place of ethical commitments in politics (Sandel, 1982). It also allows us to avoid the problem of reciprocity between current generations and those not yet existing (see p. 246).

Finally, we might also argue that our commitments to future community members will be much stronger for close or overlapping generations. Communities change a great deal over time, and we might not think of ourselves as particularly close to those a long way in the future. Neither might we feel our identities to be closely bound to future generations in other countries. Environmental problems such as global warming and the exhaustion of non-renewable resources are not local, and require international solutions that require us to recognize commitments to people beyond our communities. A more cosmopolitan approach helps us to see the relationship between those who create ecological risks, and those who experience them (Eckersley, 2006). This is certainly apparent in the current debates over whether developed nations should bear more of a cost for dealing with climate change, given that they have polluted in the past. Andrew Dobson has argued for a 'thick cosmopolitanism' that grounds norms of environmental justice recognizing the unequal burdens of environmental degradation (Dobson, 2006).

Private property and leaving 'enough' for others

We conclude our discussion of arguments in political theory in favour of saving natural resources for the future by considering a libertarian defence. This might seem an unlikely argument: libertarian theories such as that of Robert Nozick are strongly in favour of private property rights, and opposed to state-mandated redistributions. We might expect that they would be even more sceptical of demands that we redistribute resources to future generations. As we saw in Chapter 2, Nozick argues that individuals who hold property to which they are entitled are not obliged to transfer or spend it in any way other than how they please. Those in the future would appear to have no right to require the present owners of resources to save them, or to pay for their protection. It is important to remember, though, that the initial appropriation of property, on which all subsequent transfers depend for legitimacy, must leave, as Locke puts it, 'enough and as good for others' (Locke, 1988 [1690]). Unlimited appropriation that leaves nothing for others is not legitimate. Nozick takes this to mean that appropriation must leave enough for others to be able to improve their situation, as they would have been able in a state of nature. Robert Elliot suggests that we can conclude from this that people have rights of some kind to resources that were available to them in the state of nature (Elliot, 1986). This covers, at least, resources such as clean air, water and an atmosphere, and, as a result, we might argue that present generations are required to conserve these for the future. But there is no reason, according to the libertarian perspective, why rich nations should pay more for the cleaning up of the environment.

Egalitarianism and the limits of justice

As we have seen, we can make an egalitarian case for conserving resources for future generations. But there is no consensus among liberal egalitarians on this issue; many argue that while we are morally obliged to consider the needs of people in the future, and should make some effort to protect natural resources, we have no obligations of justice towards them. One important reason often cited for this is that people in the future cannot be in a reciprocal relationship with those existing now. Justice is often seen as depending on the social fact that we can affect and be affected by the actions of others. The eighteenth-century philosopher David Hume expressed this fundamental idea when he argued that justice (the 'jealous virtue') is a matter of convention – it is not natural, but arises because it is useful, given the common interest that individuals have in ensuring the stability of their possessions, and their ability to interfere with each others' interests (Hume, 1983 [1751]). As we saw in Box 12.1, the lack of reciprocity in the relationship between humans and animals is cited by some philosophers as a reason why that relationship should not be understood as one of justice.

According to this approach, justice and principles such as equality cannot apply between people of different generations. Rawls expresses this in the terms of contractual agreement, by which he establishes his principles of justice: people of different generations cannot be parties to the same agreement in the original position (see Chapter 2 for a detailed discussion of Rawls' principles of justice). We owe no duties of justice to subsequent generations, because 'we can do something for posterity but it can do nothing for us' (Rawls, 1971: 271). Consequently, the difference principle, which regulates inequalities to ensure that they are only allowed if they maximize the position of the worst-off in society, does not apply across generational lines. The parties in the original position do not know to which generation they belong, but they do know they all belong to the same one. This does not mean, however, that those in the original position will be unconcerned about the fate and prosperity of future generations. By definition, human societies will be recognized as schemes of understanding that extend over historical time. Thus, there must be an understanding between generations that each must carry their fair share of the burdens of 'realizing and preserving a just society' (Rawls, 1971: 289). In *Theory of Justice*, Rawls stipulates that the parties in the original position will care, at least, about their own close descendants, and so should be regarded as representing family lines, with ties of sentiment between succeeding generations (Rawls, 1971).

Under these circumstances, Rawls argues, the parties would recognize their obligation to save for the future, and would agree to a principle of 'just savings' as a constraint on distributive justice. The purpose of saving would not be to equalize wealth between generations but, rather, to provide the resources necessary for a just society to maintain itself into the future: 'Each generation must not only preserve the gains of culture and civilization, and maintain intact those institutions that have been established, but it must also put aside in each period of time a suitable amount of real capital accumulation' (Rawls, 1971: 285). Writing in the early 1970s, Rawls envisaged saving as taking the form of investing in technology and education. But, although he did not envisage the natural environment as a primary good, we could easily extend his argument to saving natural resources. Rawls does not explore this himself, and comments that the question of human duties to nature and animals is ethical, rather than political (Rawls, 1993). Nevertheless, the purpose of saving is to preserve just institutions, and this obviously includes, at a minimum, the preservation of natural resources essential to human life.

The just savings principle clearly limits the amount of sacrifice required of people for those in the future. How much would be required? Rawls suggests in his later *Political Liberalism* that, because the parties in the original position would not know to which generation they belonged, they would have to ask themselves how much they would be prepared to save, on the basis that the previous generation will have saved at the same rate (Rawls, 1993). This removes the need for contracting parties to identify with the interests of subsequent generations.

Looking at liberalism more broadly, we might conclude that its conception of justice as the distribution of primary goods means that it has limited applicability to environmental conservation. As David Miller points out, we can define environmental goods as primary goods in only the few (although crucial) cases of basic resources essential to human life. In these cases, the protection of natural resources such as the earth's atmosphere and climate will be prior to any social cooperation being possible. Ensuring them is not a matter of justice but, rather, a pre-condition for it (Miller, 1999). This is similar to the way that security is often viewed as the essential basis for justice, as we saw in Chapter 9. Some radical survivalists in the green movement have argued that the need for human survival outweighs all other moral and justice-related considerations. In 1972, economist Robert Heilbroner asserted that human beings are fundamentally motivated to act selfishly and, thus, would be unable to come together and cooperate to save the natural resources necessary for continued human life. He concluded that the only solution to the unsustainability of growth was to expand the authority of the state to force people to change their behaviour. This meant state regulation of consumption patterns, family size, and the nature and composition of industrial production (Heilbroner, 1972).

From a liberal perspective, however, we might argue that environmental degradation must be controlled because of the impact it has on the distribution of other goods. This is particularly clear in the case of global warming, which has already had a substantial impact on the world's poor. Saving non-renewable resources for future generations is often spoken of as if it were indistinguishable from mitigating inequalities among people alive now (see the section on equality and conservation, pp. 240–2). In practice, however, the relationship between the two is not always so clear. Consider the case of bio-fuels, for example. As corn-based ethanol became popular as an alternative (and

Box 12.2   Protecting the natural environment for the future: competing norms and values

The philosophical debate over saving the environment for the future turns on different (although not always opposing) interpretations of justice, rights and community:

- **Justice**

Some who support protection of the environment argue that we have obligations of justice to people in future generations. They have rights (see the section on rights, in this box) to be treated equally, according to much the same criteria that we would apply to justice between people alive today.

Others argue that justice applies only to those in a reciprocal relationship, which cannot include people who do not yet exist. While we have moral obligations to save some resources for the future, these are not the same as the duties of justice we owe to those alive now.

- **Rights**

Some philosophers argue that people not yet alive can be said to have rights – in this case to the natural resources necessary to a good life – or, at least, to what is essential for life. It does not matter that we do not know the identities of those in the future, as long as we are satisfied that there will be people with interests that will suffer if we do not act to preserve resources now.

Others maintain that future generations do not yet exist, and thus cannot be said to have rights.

- **Community**

Some philosophers argue that the natural environment in which a social community lives forms part of the context that shapes individual identity and moral obligation. We should – and will be motivated to – protect our environment for future community members, because it is deeply linked to who we are.

Some critics point out, however, that while this might reinforce environmentalism at a local level, there could be conflicts between the economic needs of a social community and environmental conservation. Moreover, it cannot deal with the crucial issues that are global in scope, and that require us to identify with people – both present and future – in different communities than our own.

renewable) fuel in the United States and Europe, the price of corn surged. This affected not only corn-based cereals, but also other grains, stock feed and the price of meat. In just one of many worldwide consequences, Mexican corn was diverted into the United States to take advantage of the high prices, and as a result, the price of corn products such as tortillas, a staple food of Mexico's poor, sky-rocketed.

In the light of such cases, a few critics argue that we should focus on addressing inequalities now. Wilfred Beckerman and Joanna Pasek assert, as we have seen, that members of future generations cannot be said to have rights. Our priority should be to ensure that people across the world now have access to just institutions that ensure basic liberties, and a decent society that protects people who are not members (Beckerman and Pasek, 2001). As we saw in Chapter 10, we are very far from meeting the basic needs, let alone providing the conditions for equality and autonomy among the world's poor. It is an added advantage that these policies are likely to reduce future inequality. For example, exploitative industries often treat marginalized people badly, as well as destroying the environment. Ensuring women's equality is necessary to limit population growth – one of the ways in which, we remember, Barry argued that future generations must take responsibility for their own situation.

Conclusion

The issue of protecting the environment for the future, more than any of the others we have considered in this book, requires us to explore the extent and limits of justice. In Chapters 3 and 4, we considered the claims of members of ethnic and racial minorities within countries to equal treatment and, in Chapter 7, the claims of foetuses yet to be born. In Chapters 10 and 11, we explored duties to people in other countries. Environmental protection requires us to examine our obligations not only to people in other communities and nations, but also to those in future generations. In posing the question: To whom do we owe duties of justice, we also ask: What is the extent of politics? Where do our political obligations end, leaving us with moral duties as the only checks on our behaviour?

This is increasingly the case, given the effects of climate change, but it applies more broadly because of the fact that natural resources extend beyond national boundaries. Some environmental issues are predominantly local, such as the preservation of local animal species, or woodlands or waterways, and can be dealt with at the local or national level, but even these relate to the broader concern of preserving the earth's biodiversity. Threats to the earth's atmosphere and climate, however, require coordinated global action. But, because of differences in industrial and technological development, the impact of climate change on national populations varies. As the Stern Report recognizes, advanced industrial development offers a temporary cushion against the worst effects of climate change, while its consequences are more urgently felt in many developing countries. At the same time, industrial development offers immediate and medium-term economic benefits to poorer countries. Achieving coordinated international action under these circumstances has proved to be very difficult. Protecting the environment is a collective action problem: it requires all to act together for a common benefit, although it might be in the short-term interest of each individual party to act selfishly.

From the perspective of normative political theory, however, the problem of achieving joint action to protect the environment is not one of strategy but, rather, is one of justice. The need to conserve resources for the benefit of all the world's people in the future must be balanced with the existing needs of poor populations. Resources are scarce, and if we are going to argue that justice requires us to provide at least the basic requirements for a decent life for future generations, it seems essential that this be tied to efforts to supply the basic requirements of a decent life to those existing in the world now. We can understand this, as we have seen in Chapters 2 and 10, in terms of the satisfaction of basic needs, or the provision of equality – however that is defined. The relationship between future needs and current poverty was first recognized in the Brundtland Report in 1982, and recently in the UN Development Programme's Human Development Report for 2007/8, entitled *Fighting Climate Change: Human Solidarity in a Divided World*. As a result of climate change, the boundaries of justice are extended not only to all people (and, some argue, to nature itself), but also to the protection of people, societies and the conditions of political life in the future.

List of Cases

Bibliography

Ackerman, B. (2006) *Before the Next Attack: Preserving Civil Liberties in an Age of Terrorism* (New Haven, CT: Yale University Press).

Ackerman, B. and Alstott, A. (1999) *The Stakeholder Society* (New Haven: Yale University Press).

Altman, A. (2005) 'The Right to Get Turned On: Pornography, Autonomy, Equality', in Cohen, A.I. and Wellman, C.H. (eds), *Contemporary Debates in Applied Ethics* (Oxford: Blackwell).

Anderson, E. (1993) *Values in Ethics and Economics* (Cambridge, MA: Harvard University Press).

Anderson, E. (1999) 'What is the Point of Equality?', *Ethics*, 99, 287–337.

Anderson, E. (2002) 'Integration, Affirmative Action and Strict Scrutiny', *New York University Law Review*, 77, 1195–271.

Associated Press (2006) 'Blair Toughens Stance on Religious Tolerance and Cultural Assimilation', *International Herald Tribune*, 8 December.

Appiah, K.A. (1996) 'Race, Culture, Identity: Misunderstood Connections', in Appiah, K.A. and Gutmann, A. (eds), *Color Conscious: The Political Morality of Race* (Princeton: Princeton University Press).

Aquinas, St Thomas (1952 [1265–74]) *Summa Theologica* (Chicago: Encyclopaedia Britannica).

Aristotle (1981 [Third century BCE]) *The Politics* (London: Penguin).

Augustine of Hippo (1931 [426 CE]) *The City of God* (London).

Ball, C.A. (2003) *The Morality of Gay Rights* (New York: Routledge).

Barber, B. (2003) *Fear's Empire: War, Terrorism and Democracy* (New York: Norton).

Barry, B. (1999) 'Sustainability and Intergenerational Justice', in Dobson, A. (ed.), *Fairness and Futurity* (Oxford: Oxford University Press).

Barry, B. (2001) *Culture and Equality: An Egalitarian Critique of Multiculturalism* (Cambridge: Polity Press).

Barry, K. (1984) *Female Sexual Slavery* (New York: New York University Press).

Barry, K. (1996) *The Prostitution of Sexuality* (New York: New York University Press).

Bauer, P.T. (2001) *From Subsistence to Exchange and Other Essays* (Princeton: Princeton University Press).

Beauchamp, T. (1996) 'The Justification of Physician-Assisted Suicide', *Indiana Law Review*, 29, 1173–200.

Beckerman, W. (1999) 'Sustainability and Our Obligations to Future Generations', in Dobson, A. (ed.), *Fairness and Futurity* (Oxford: Oxford University Press).

Beckerman, W. and Pasek, J. (2001) *Justice, Posterity and the Environment* (Oxford: Oxford University Press).

253

Beckwith, F.J. (1998) 'Arguments from Bodily Rights: A Critical Analysis', in Pojman, L.P. and Beckwith, F.J. (eds), *The Abortion Controversy: 25 Years After Roe v. Wade, A Reader*, 2nd edn (Belmont, CA: Wadsworth).

Beckwith, F.J. (1999) 'The "No One Deserves His or Her Talents" Argument for Affirmative Action: A Critical Analysis', *Social Theory and Practice*, 25, 53–60.

Beitz, C.R. (1979) *Political Theory and International Relations* (Princeton: Princeton University Press).

Beitz, C.R. (1980) 'Nonintervention and Communal Integrity', *Philosophy and Public Affairs*, 9, 385–91.

Beitz, C.R. (2005) 'Cosmopolitanism and Global Justice', in Brock, G. and Moellendorf, D. (eds), *Current Debates in Global Justice* (Dordrecht: Springer).

Bellah, R., Madsen, R., Sullivan, W., Swidler, A. and Tipton, S. (1985) *Habits of the Heart* (Berkeley, CA: University of California Press).

Bentham, J. (1824) *The Book of Fallacies: From Unfinished Papers by Jeremy Bentham* (London: J. and H.L. Hunt).

Bentham, J. (1931 [1802]) *Theory of Legislation* (Buffalo, NY: Hein).

Bentham, J. (1988 [1789]) *An Introduction to the Principles of Morals and Legislation* (Amherst, NY: Prometheus).

Bentham, J. (1988 [1756]) *A Fragment on Government* (Cambridge: Cambridge University Press).

Berlin, I. (1969) 'Two Concepts of Liberty', in *Four Essays on Liberty* (Oxford: Oxford University Press).

Blumstein, P. and Schwartz, P. (1983) *American Couples: Money, Work, Sex* (New York: Morrow).

Bodin, J. (1992 [1576]) *On Sovereignty: Four Chapters from the Six Books of the Commonwealth* (Cambridge: Cambridge University Press).

Booth, K. (ed.) (2001) *The Kosovo Tragedy: The Human Rights Dimensions* (London: Routledge).

Bowen, W.G. and Bok, D. (1998) *The Shape of the River: Long-term Consequences of Considering Race in College and University Admissions* (Princeton: Princeton University Press).

Brinkley, A. (2007) 'Past as Prologue?', in Leone, R.C. and Anrig, G. (eds) *Liberty under Attack: Reclaiming our Freedoms in an Age of Terror* (New York: Century Foundation).

Brock, G. (2006) 'Humanitarian Intervention: Closing the Gap between Theory and Practice', *Journal of Applied Philosophy*, 23, 277–91.

Buchanan, A. (2000) 'Rawls' Law of Peoples: Rules for a Vanished Westphalian World', *Ethics*, 110, 697–721.

Burke, E. (1955 [1790]) *Reflections on the Revolution in France* (New York: Macmillan).

Burkett, P. (1999) *Marx and Nature* (New York: St Martin's Press).

Calhoun, C. (2000) *Feminism, the Family and the Politics of the Closet: Lesbian and Gay Displacement* (New York: Oxford University Press).

Caney, S. (1997) 'Human Rights and the Rights of States: Terry Nardin on Nonintervention', *International Political Science Review*, 18, 2–37.

Caney, S. (2005) *Justice Beyond Borders: A Global Political Theory* (Oxford: Oxford University Press).

Capotorti, F. (1979) 'Study on the Rights of Persons Belonging to Ethnic, Religious and Linguistic Minorities', U.N. Doc.E/CN.4/Sub.2/384/Rev.1. (New York: UN).

Card, C. (1996) 'Against Marriage and Motherhood', *Hypatia*, 11, 1–23.

Carens, J.H. (2003) 'An Interpretation and Defense of the Socialist Principle of Redistribution', *Social Philosophy and Policy*, 20, 145–77.

Carson, R. (1962) *Silent Spring* (Boston: Houghton Mifflin).

Carter, J. (2007) 'Subsidies: Harvest of Misery', *Washington Post*, 10 December, A19.

Chambers, S. (2003) 'Deliberative Democratic Theory', *Annual Review of Political Science*, 6, 307–26.

Chen, S. and Ravallion, M. (2007) 'Absolute Poverty Measures for the Developing World, 1981–2004', Development Research Group (Washington, DC: World Bank).

Cicero (1991 [44 BCE]) *On Duties* (Cambridge: Cambridge University Press).

Cohen, C. and Sterba, J.P. (2003) *Affirmative Action and Racial Preference: A Debate* (Oxford: Oxford University Press).

Cohen, G.A. (1989) 'On the Currency of Egalitarian Justice', *Ethics*, 99, 906–44.

Cohen, G.A. (2004) 'Expensive Taste Rides Again', in Burley, J. (ed.), *Dworkin and his Critics, With Replies by Dworkin* (Oxford: Blackwell).

Cohen, J. (1989) 'Deliberation and Democratic Legitimacy', in Goodin, R. and Pettit, P. (eds), *Contemporary Political Philosophy: An Anthology* (Oxford: Blackwell).

Cohen, J. (1996) 'Freedom, Equality, Pornography', in Sarat, A. and Kearns, T.R. (eds), *Justice and Injustice in Law and Legal Theory* (Ann Arbor: University of Michigan Press).

Cohen, J.L. (2005) 'Whose Sovereignty? Empire v. International Law', in Barry, C. and Pogge, T. (eds), *Global Institutions and Responsibilities: Achieving Global Justice* (Oxford: Blackwell).

Cornell, D. (1995) *The Imaginary Domain: Abortion, Pornography and Sexual Harassment* (New York: Routledge).

Crawford, N. (2002) *Argument and Change in World Politics: Ethics, Decolonization and Humanitarian Intervention* (Cambridge: Cambridge University Press).

Davis, D.S. (1998) 'Why Suicide is Like Contraception', in Battin, M.P., Rhodes, R. and Silvers, A. (eds), *Physician Assisted Suicide* (New York: Routledge).

D'Emilio, J. (1998) *Sexual Politics, Sexual Communities: The Making of a Homosexual Minority in the United States, 1940–1970* (Chicago: University of Chicago Press).

De-Navas Walt, C., Proctor, B.D. and Smith, J. (2006) 'Income, Poverty and Health Insurance Coverage in the United States: 2006 Report' (Washington, DC: US Census Bureau).

Dershowitz, A.M. (2002) *Shouting Fire: Civil Liberties in a Turbulent Age* (New York: Little Brown).

De-Shalit A. (2004) *The Environment Between Theory and Practice* (Oxford: Oxford University Press).

De-Shalit, A. (2006) 'Nationalism', in Dobson, A. and Eckersley, R. (eds), *Political Theory and the Ecological Challenge* (Cambridge: Cambridge University Press).

Devlin, P. (1959) *The Enforcement of Morals* (London: Oxford University Press).

Dobson, A. (1997) 'Representative Democracy and the Environment', in Meadowcraft, J. (ed.), *Democracy and the Environment* (Cheltenham: Edward Elgar) 121–41.

Dobson, A. (2003) *Citizenship and the Environment* (Oxford: OUP).

Dobson, A. (2006) 'Thick Cosmopolitanism', *Political Studies*, 54, 165–84.

Dollar, D. and Pritchett, L. (1998) 'Assessing Aid: What Works, What Doesn't, and Why' (Washington, DC: World Bank).

Donceel, J.F. (1970) 'A Liberal Catholic's View', in Hall, R.E. (ed.), *Abortion in a Changing World, Volume I* (New York: Columbia University Press).

Downs, D.A. (2005) *Restoring Free Speech and Liberty on Campus* (Cambridge: Cambridge University Press).

Dryzek, J. (2000) *Deliberative Democracy and Beyond: Liberals, Critics, Contestations* (Oxford: Oxford University Press).

Dworkin, A. (1981) *Pornography: Men Possessing Women* (London: Women's Press).

Dworkin, A. (1985) 'Against the Male Flood: Censorship, Pornography and Equality', *Harvard Women's Law Journal*, 8.

Dworkin, R. (1978) *Taking Rights Seriously* (London: Duckworth).

Dworkin, R. (1984) 'Rights as Trumps', in Waldron, J. (ed.), *Theories of Rights* (Oxford: Oxford University Press).

Dworkin, R. (1986) *A Matter of Principle* (Oxford: Clarendon Press).

Dworkin, R. (1991) 'Liberty and Pornography', *New York Review of Books*, 38, 14, 15 August.

Dworkin, R. (1993) *Life's Dominion* (New York: Knopf).

Dworkin, R. (1996) *Freedom's Law: The Moral Reading of the American Constitution* (Cambridge, MA: Harvard University Press).

Dworkin, R. (2000) *Sovereign Virtue: The Theory and Practice of Equality* (Cambridge, MA: Harvard University Press).

Dworkin, R. (2002) 'The Threat to Patriotism', *New York Review of Books*, 49, 3, 28 February.

Dworkin, R. (2003) 'Terror and the Attack on Civil Liberties', *New York Review of Books*, 50, 17, 6 November.

Dworkin, R. (2006) 'The Right to Ridicule', *New York Review of Books*, 53, 5, 23 March.

Dworkin, R., Nagel, T., Nozick, R., Rawls, J., Scanlon, T.M. and Thomson, J.J. (1997) 'Assisted Suicide: The Philosophers' Brief', *New York Review of Books*, 44, 5, 27 March.

Dyzenhaus, D. (1992) 'John Stuart Mill and the Harm of Pornography', *Ethics*, 102, 534–51.

Eagleton, T. (1991) *Ideology* (London: Verso).

Eckersley, R. (1993) *Environmentalism and Political Theory: Towards an Ecocentric Approach* (Albany: State University of New York Press).

Eckersley, R. (2006) 'Communitarianism', in Dobson, A. and Eckersley, R. (eds), *Political Theory and the Ecological Challenge* (Cambridge: Cambridge University Press).

Elliot, R. (1986) 'Future Generations, Locke's Proviso and Libertarian Justice', *Journal of Applied Philosophy*, 3 (2), 217–27.

Elshtain, J.B. (1981) *Public Man, Private Woman: Women in Social and Political Thought* (Princeton: Princeton University Press).

Elshtain, J.B. (1995) *Democracy on Trial* (New York: Basic Books).

Elshtain, J.B. (2003) *Just War Against Terror: The Burden of American Power in a Violent World* (New York: Basic Books).

Engels, F. (1948 [1884]) *The Origin of the Family, Private Property and the State* (Moscow: Foreign Languages Publishing House).

English, J. (1974) 'Abortion and the Concept of a Person', *Canadian Journal of Philosophy*, 5, 233–43.

Ericsson, L.O. (1980) 'Charges Against Prostitution: An Attempt at a Philosophical Assessment', *Ethics*, 90, 335–66.

Eskridge, W.N. (2002) *Equality Practice: Civil Unions and the Future of Gay Rights* (New York: Routledge).

Evans, G. (2004) 'The Responsibility to Protect: Rethinking Humanitarian Intervention', American Society of International Law, 98th Meeting, Washington, DC.

Fabre, C. (2007) *Justice in a Changing World* (Cambridge: Polity).

Feinberg, J. (1974) 'The Rights of Animals and Unborn Generations', in Blackstone, W. (ed.), *Philosophy and Environmental Crisis* (Atlanta: University of Georgia Press).

Feinberg, J. (1985) *Offense to Others: The Moral Limits of the Criminal Law* (New York: Oxford University Press).

Figgis, J.N. (1931) *Studies of Political Thought from Gerson to Grotius, 1414–1625,* (Cambridge: Cambridge University Press).

Finnis, J. (1980) *Natural Law and Natural Rights* (Oxford: Clarendon Press).

Finnis, J. (1995) 'A Philosophical Case Against Euthanasia', in Keown, J. (ed.), *Euthanasia Examined: Ethical, Clinical and Legal Perspectives* (Cambridge: Cambridge University Press).

Finnis, J. (1997) 'The Good of Marriage and the Morality of Sexual Relations: Some Philosophical and Historical Observations', *American Journal of Jurisprudence*, 42, 97–134.

Fischer, C. (1996) *Inequality by Design: Cracking the Bell Curve Myth* (Princeton, NJ: Princeton University Press).

Fish, S. (1994) *There's No Such Thing As Free Speech, And It's a Good Thing, Too* (New York: Oxford University Press).

Fiss, O.M. (1996) *Liberalism Divided: Freedom of Speech and the Many Uses of State Power* (Boulder, CO: Westview Press).

Foster, J.B (2000) *Marx's Ecology* (New York: Monthly Review Press).

France, A. (1910) *The Red Lily* (London: Bodley Head).

Fraser, N. (1995) 'From Redistribution to Recognition? Dilemmas of Justice in a "Post-Socialist" Age', *New Left Review*, 212, 68–93.

Freeman, S. (2006) 'The Law of Peoples, Social Cooperation, Human Rights and Distributive Justice', in Paul, E.F., Miller Jr, F.D. and Paul, J. (eds), *Justice and Global Politics* (Cambridge: Cambridge University Press).

Gates Jr, H.L., Griffin, A.P., Lively, D.E., Post, R.C., Rubenstein, W.B. and Strossen, N. (1994) *Speaking of Race, Speaking of Sex: Hate Speech, Civil Rights, and Civil Liberties* (New York: New York University Press).

George, R.P. (2003) 'Neutrality, Equality and "Same-Sex Marriage"', in Wardle, L.D., Strasser, M., Duncan, W.C. and Coolidge, D.O. (eds), *Marriage and Same-Sex Unions: A Debate* (Westport, CT: Praeger).

Gilligan, C. (1982) *In a Different Voice: Psychological Theory and Women's Development* (Cambridge, MA: Harvard University Press).

Gitlin, T. (1995) *The Twilight of Common Dreams: Why America is Wracked by Culture Wars* (New York: Henry Holt & Co).

Glendon, M.A. (1987) *Abortion and Divorce in Western Law* (Cambridge, MA; Harvard University Press).

Godfrey, C. (2002) 'Oxfam Briefing Paper no. 31: Stop the Dumping! How EU Agricultural Subsidies are Damaging Livelihoods in the Developing World' (Oxford: OXFAM).

Goldman, A. (1976) 'Affirmative Action', *Philosophy and Public Affairs*, 5, 178–95.

Goldman, A. (1979) *Justice and Reverse Discrimination* (Princeton: Princeton University Press).

Goodin, R.E. (1992) *Green Political Theory* (Cambridge: Polity).

Goodin, R.E. (1995) *Utilitarianism as a Public Philosophy* (Cambridge: Cambridge University Press).

Goodin, R.E. (2006) *What's Wrong With Terrorism?* (Cambridge: Polity).

Greenawalt, K. (1995) *Fighting Words: Individuals, Communities, and Liberties of Speech* (Princeton: Princeton University Press).

Grisez, G.G. (1970) *Abortion: The Myths, The Realities and the Arguments* (New York: Corpus Books).

Grotius, H. (2004 [1625]) *On the Law of War and Peace* (London: Kessinger).

Gutmann, A. and Thompson, D. (1996) *Democracy and Disagreement* (Cambridge, MA: Belknap Press).

Habermas, J. (1975) *Legitimation Crisis* (Boston: Beacon Press).

Harris, J. (1995) 'Euthanasia and the Value of Life', in Keown, J. (ed.), *Euthanasia Examined: Ethical, Clinical and Legal Perspectives* (Cambridge: Cambridge University Press).

Hart, H. (1963) *Law, Liberty and Morality* (Stanford: Stanford University Press).

Haubrich, D. (2003) 'September 11, Anti-Terror Laws and Civil Liberties: Britain, France and Germany Compared', *Government and Opposition: An International Journal of Comparative Politics*, 38, 3–28.

Hayek, F.A. von (1960) *The Constitution of Liberty* (Chicago: University of Chicago Press).

Hayek, F.A. von (1962) *The Road to Serfdom* (London: Routledge).

Heilbroner, R. (1972) 'Growth and Survival', *Foreign Affairs*, October.

Herrnstein, R.J. and Murray, C. (1994) *The Bell Curve* (New York: Free Press).

Heywood, A. (2004) *Political Theory: An Introduction* (Basingstoke: Palgrave Macmillan).

Hirst, P. (1994) *Associative Democracy: New Forms of Economic and Social Governance* (Amherst, MA: University of Massachusetts Press).

Hirvonen, P. (2005) 'Stingy Samaritans: Why Recent Increases in Development Aid Fail to Help the Poor' (New York: Global Policy Forum).

Hobbes, T. (1962 [1651]) *Leviathan* (London: Collier Macmillan).

Holbrooke, R. (2005) 'Was Bosnia Worth It?', *Washington Post*.

Holzer, H.J. and Neumark, D. (2000) 'What Does Affirmative Action Do?', *Industrial and Labor Relations Review*, 53, 240–71.

Hume, D. (1983 [1751]) *An Enquiry Concerning the Principles of Morals* (Indianapolis, IN: Hackett).

ICISS (2001) 'The Responsibility to Protect' (Ottawa: International Commission on Intervention and State Sovereignty).

Ignatieff, M. (2004) *The Lesser Evil: Political Ethics in an Age of Terror* (Edinburgh: Edinburgh University Press).

Itzin, C. and Sweet, C. (1993) 'Women's Experience of Pornography: UK Magazine Survey Evidence', in Itzin, C. (ed.), *Pornography: Women, Violence and Civil Liberties* (Oxford: Oxford University Press).

Jeffreys, S. (1997) *The Idea of Prostitution* (North Melbourne, Victoria: Spinifex Press).

Johnson, L.B.J. (1965) 'To Fulfil These Rights', Commencement Address to Howard University.

Kaldor, M. (2007) *Human Security: Reflections on Globalization and Intervention* (Cambridge: Polity).

Kant, I. (1991 [1784]) 'An Answer to the Question: "What is Enlightenment?" ', *Political Writings* (Cambridge: Cambridge University Press).

Kant, I. (1993 [1785]) *Grounding for the Metaphysics of Morals* (Indianapolis, IN: Hackett).

Karst, K. (1990) 'Boundaries and Reasons: Freedom of Expression and the Subordination of Groups', *University of Illinois Law Review*, 95–149.

Kateb, G. (1989) 'The Freedom of Worthless and Harmful Speech', in Yack, B. (ed.), *Liberalism Without Illusions: Essays on Liberal Theory and the Political Vision of Judith N. Sklar* (Chicago: University of Chicago Press).

Keown, J. (1995) 'Euthanasia in the Netherlands: Sliding Down the Slippery Slope?', in Keown, J. (ed.), *Euthanasia Examined: Ethical, Clinical and Legal Perspectives* (Cambridge: Cambridge University Press).

Kristol, I. (2004) 'Pornography, Obscenity and the Case for Censorship', in Stelzer, I. (ed.), *Neoconservatism* (London: Atlantic Books).

Kroll, L. and Fass, A. (2007) 'The World's Richest People', *Forbes*, 8 March.

Kukathas, C. (1992) 'Are There Any Cultural Rights?', *Political Theory*, 20, 105–39.

Kukathas, C. (2006) 'The Mirage of Global Justice', in Paul, E.F., Miller Jr, F.D. and Paul, J. (eds), *Justice and Global Politics* (Cambridge: Cambridge University Press).

Kuperman, A.J. (2000) 'Rwanda in Retrospect', *Foreign Affairs*, 79.

Kymlicka, W. (1995) *Multicultural Citizenship* (Oxford: Oxford University Press).

Kymlicka, W. (1999) 'Liberal Complacencies', in Cohen, J., Howard, M. and Nussbaum, M.C. (eds), *Is Multiculturalism Bad for Women?* (Princeton: Princeton University Press).

Kymlicka, W. (2001) *Politics in the Vernacular: Nationalism, Multiculturalism and Citizenship* (Oxford: Oxford University Press).

Laslett, P. (1956) *Philosophy, Politics and Society*, vol. I (Oxford: Basil Blackwell).

Lee, P. and George, R.P. (2005) 'The Wrong of Abortion', in Cohen, A.I. and Wellman, C.H. (eds), *Contemporary Debates in Applied Ethics* (Oxford: Blackwell).

Leeson, P.T. (2008) 'Escaping Poverty: Foreign Aid, Private Property and Economic Development', *Journal of Private Enterprise*, 23, 2, 39–64.

Leone, R.C. (2003) 'The Quiet Republic: The Missing Debate About Civil Liberties After 9/11', in Leone, R.C. and Anrig, G. (eds), *The War on our Freedoms: Civil Liberties in an Age of Terrorism* (New York: Century Foundation).

Lijphart, A. (1977) *Democracy in Plural Societies: A Comparative Exploration* (New Haven: Yale University Press).

Little, M.O. (2005) 'The Moral Permissibility of Abortion', in Cohen, A.I. and Wellman, C.H. (eds), *Contemporary Debates in Applied Ethics* (Oxford: Blackwell).

Locke, J. (1983 [1689]) *A Letter Concerning Toleration* (Indianapolis: Hackett).

Locke, J. (1988 [1690]) *Two Treatises of Government* (Cambridge: Cambridge University Press).

Locke, J. (1996 [1693]) *Some Thoughts Concerning Education*, Grant, R.W. and Tarcov, N. (eds) (Indianapolis, IN: Hackett).

Luban, D. (1980) 'The Romance of the Nation State', *Philosophy and Public Affairs*, 9, 392–7.

Luban, D. (2005) 'Eight Fallacies about Liberty and Security', in Wilson, R.A. (ed.), *Human Rights in the War on Terror* (Cambridge: Cambridge University Press).

Macedo, S. (2003) 'Homosexuality and the Conservative Mind', in Wardle, L.D., Strasser, M., Duncan, W.C. and Coolidge, D.O. (eds), *Marriage and Same-Sex Unions: A Debate* (Westport, CT: Praeger).

Machiavelli, N. (1988 [1532]) *The Prince* (Cambridge: Cambridge University Press).

MacIntyre, A. (1981) *After Virtue* (London: Duckworth).

MacKinnon, C.A. (1983) 'The Male Ideology of Privacy: A Feminist Perspective on the Right to Abortion', *Radical America*, 17, 23–35.

MacKinnon, C.A. (1985) 'Pornography, Civil Rights and Speech', *Harvard Civil Rights – Civil Liberties Law Review*, 20.

MacKinnon, C.A. (1995) *Only Words* (London: HarperCollins).

MacKinnon, C.A. (2005) *Women's Lives, Men's Laws* (Cambridge, MA: Belknap Press).

Madison, J., Hamilton, A. and Jay, J. (1987 [1788]) *The Federalist Papers* (London: Penguin).

Maine, H.S. (1901) *Ancient Law: Its Connection with the Early History of Society and its Relation to Modern Ideas* (London: John Murray).

Mandelbaum, M. (1999) 'A Perfect Failure: NATO's War Against Yugoslavia', *Foreign Affairs*, September/October.

Margalit, A. and Halbertal, M. (1994) 'Liberalism and the Right to Culture', *Social Research*, 61, 491–510.

Margalit, A. and Raz, J. (1990) 'National Self-Determination', *Journal of Philosophy*, 87, 439–61.

Marquis, D. (1989) 'Why Abortion is Immoral', *Journal of Philosophy*, 86, 183–202.

Marshall, T.H. and Bottomore, T. (1992) *Citizenship and Social Class* (London: Pluto Press).

Marx, K. (1978 [1852]) 'The Eighteenth Brumaire of Louis Bonaparte', in Tucker, R.C. (ed.), *The Marx–Engels Reader*, 2nd edn (New York: Norton).

Marx, K. (1978 [1875]) 'Critique of the Gotha Program', in Tucker, R.C. (ed.), *The Marx–Engels Reader*, 2nd edn (New York: Norton).

Marx, K. (1978 [1843]) 'On the Jewish Question', in Tucker, R.C. (ed.), *The Marx–Engels Reader*, 2nd edn (New York: Norton).

Marx, K. and Engels, F. (1978 [1848]) 'Manifesto of the Communist Party', in Tucker, R.C. (ed.), *The Marx–Engels Reader*, 2nd edn (New York: Norton).

Matsuda, M.J., Lawrence III, C.R., Delgado, R. and Crenshaw, K.W. (1993) *Words That Wound: Critical Race Theory, Assaultive Speech, and the First Amendment* (Boulder, CO: Westview Press).

McConvell, P. and Thieberger, N. (2001) 'State of Indigenous Languages in Australia', *Australian State of the Environment Technical Paper Series* (Canberra, Australia: Department of the Environment and Heritage).

McElroy, W. (1996) *Sexual Correctness: The Gender Feminist Attack on Women* (Jefferson, NC: McFarland).

Meadows, D., Meadows, D., Randers, J. and Behrens III, W. (1972) *The Limits to Growth* (New York: Universe Books).

Meier, D.E., Emmons, C., Wallenstein, S., Quill, T., Morrison, R.S. and Cassel, C.K. (1998) 'A National Survey of Physician-Assisted Suicide and Euthanasia in the United States', *New England Journal of Medicine*, 338, 1193–201.

Meiklejohn, A. (1965) *Political Freedom: The Constitutional Powers of the People* (New York: Oxford University Press).

Meisels, T. (2005) 'How Terrorism Upsets Liberty', *Political Studies*, 53, 162–81.

Mies, M and Shiva, V. (1993) *Ecofeminism* (London: Zed Books).

Mill, J.S. (1965 [1848]) 'Principles of Political Economy', in Robson, J.M. (ed.), *The Collected Works of John Stuart Mill, Vol. II* (Toronto: University of Toronto Press).

Mill, J.S. (1969 [1861]) 'Utilitarianism', in Robson, J.M. (ed.), *The Collected Works of John Stuart Mill, Vol. X* (Toronto: University of Toronto Press).

Mill, J.S. (1984 [1859]) 'A Few Words on Non-Intervention', in Robson, J.M. (ed.), *The Collected Works of John Stuart Mill, Vol. XXI* (Toronto: University of Toronto Press).

Mill, J.S. (1989a [1859]) 'On Liberty', in Collini, S. (ed.), *On Liberty and Other Writings* (Cambridge: Cambridge University Press).

Mill, J.S. (1989b [1869]) 'The Subjection of Women', in Collini, S. (ed.), *On Liberty and Other Writings* (Cambridge: Cambridge University Press).

Miller, D. (1997) *On Nationality* (Oxford: Oxford University Press).

Miller, D. (1999) 'Social Justice and Environmental Goods', in Dobson, A. (ed.), *Fairness and Futurity* (Oxford: Oxford University Press).

Miller, D. (2000) 'National Self-Determination and Global Justice', in Miller, D. (ed.), *Citizenship and National Identity* (Cambridge: Polity Press).

Miller, D. (2006) 'Multiculturalism and the Welfare State: Theoretical Reflections', in Banting, K. and Kymlicka, W. (eds), *Multiculturalism and the Welfare State: Recognition and Redistribution in Contemporary Democracies* (Oxford: Oxford University Press).

Miller, D. (2007) *National Responsibility and Global Justice* (Oxford: Oxford University Press).

Moeckli, D. (2008) *Human Rights and Non-discrimination in the 'War Against Terror'* (Oxford: Oxford University Press).

Morrow, J. (2005) *History of Western Political Thought: A Thematic Introduction* (Basingstoke: Palgrave Macmillan).

Mulvey, L. (1975) 'Visual Pleasure and Narrative Cinema', *Screen*, 16, 6–18.

Nagel, T. (1973) 'Equal Treatment and Compensatory Discrimination', *Philosophy and Public Affairs*, 2, 348–63.

Nagel, T. (2005) 'The Problem of Global Justice', *Philosophy and Public Affairs*, 33, 113–47.

Nagle, J. (1997) *Whores and Other Feminists* (New York: Routledge).

Nardin, T. (1983) *Law, Morality and the Relations of States* (Princeton: Princeton University Press).

Nardin, T. and Slater, J. (1986) 'Nonintervention and Human Rights', *Journal of Politics*, 48, 86–96.

Narveson, J. (1988) *The Libertarian Idea* (Philadelphia, PA: Temple University Press).

Neier, A. (1979) *Defending My Enemy: American Nazis, the Skokie Case, and the Risks of Freedom* (New York: Dutton).

Neocleous, M. (2007) 'Security, Liberty and the Myth of Balance', *Contemporary Political Theory*, 6, 131–49.

Noonan, J.T. (ed.) (1970) *The Morality of Abortion: Legal and Historical Perspectives* (Cambridge, MA: Harvard University Press).

Nozick, R. (1974) *Anarchy, State and Utopia* (New York: Basic Books).

Nussbaum, M.C. (1999) *Sex and Social Justice* (New York: Oxford University Press).

Nussbaum, M.C. (2008) '"Whether from Reason or Prejudice": Taking Money for Bodily Services', in Soble, A. and Power, N. (eds), *The Philosophy of Sex: Contemporary Readings* (Lanham, MD: Rowman & Littlefield).

OECD (2007) *OECD Journal on Development: Development Co-operation Report* (Paris: OECD).

OECD (2008) *Debt Relief is Down, Other ODA Rises Slightly*, OECD Development Co-operation Directorate (Paris: OECD).

Okin, S.M. (1989) *Justice, Gender and the Family* (New York: Basic Books).

Okin, S.M. (1999) 'Is Multiculturalism Bad for Women?', in Cohen, J., Howard, M. and Nussbaum, M.C. (eds), *Is Multiculturalism Bad for Women?* (Princeton: Princeton University Press).

Parekh, B. (1990) 'The Rushdie Affair: Research Agenda for Political Philosophy', *Political Studies*, 38, 695–709.

Parekh, B. (1997) 'Rethinking Humanitarian Intervention', *International Political Science Review*, 18, 49–69.

Parekh, B. (2006) *Rethinking Multiculturalism: Cultural Diversity and Political Theory* (Basingstoke: Palgrave Macmillan).

Parfit, D. (1984) *Reasons and Persons* (Oxford: Oxford University Press).

Pateman, C. (1988) *The Sexual Contract* (Stanford: Stanford University Press).

Phillips, A. (2003) 'When Culture Means Gender: Issues of Cultural Defence in the English Courts', *Modern Law Review*, 66, 510–31.

Plato (1981 [Third century BCE]) *The Republic* (London: Pan).

Plumwood, V. (1993) *Feminism and the Mastery of Nature* (London: Routledge).

Plumwood, V. (2002) *Environmental Culture: The Ecological Crisis of Reason* (London: Routledge).

Pogge, T. (1994) 'An Egalitarian Law of Peoples', *Philosophy and Public Affairs*, 23, 195–224.

Pogge, T. (1998) 'A Global Resources Dividend', in Crocker, D.A. and Linden, T. (eds), *Ethics of Consumption: The Good Life, Justice and Global Stewardship* (Lanham, MD: Rowman & Littlefield).

Pogge, T. (2002) *World Poverty and Human Rights: Cosmopolitan Responsibilities and Reforms* (Cambridge: Polity Press).

Pogge, T. (2004) 'Justice Across Borders: Brief for a Global Resources Dividend', in Clayton, M. and Williams, A. (eds), *Social Justice* (Oxford: Blackwell).

Pogge, T. (2005) 'Real World Justice', *Journal of Ethics*, 9, 29–53.

Pojman, L.P. (1992) 'The Moral Status of Affirmative Action', *Public Affairs Quarterly*, 6, 181–206.

Posner, R. (1997) 'The Economic Approach to Homosexuality', in Estlund, D.M. and Nussbaum, M.C. (eds), *Sex, Preference and Family: Essays on Law and Nature* (New York: Oxford University Press).

Posner, R.A. (2003) 'The Truth About Our Liberties', in Etzioni, A. and Marsh, J.H. (eds), *Rights vs. Public Safety After 9/11: America in the Age of Terrorism* (Lanham, MD: Rowman & Littlefield).

Posner, R.A. (2006) *Not a Suicide Pact: The Constitution in a Time of National Emergency* (Oxford: Oxford University Press).

Post, R.C. (1991) 'Racist Speech, Democracy and the First Amendment', *Wm and Mary Law Review*, 32, 267.

Prunier, G. (2005) *Darfur: The Ambiguous Genocide* (Ithaca, NY: Cornell University Press).

Rachels, J. (1986) *The End of Life: The Morality of Euthanasia* (Oxford: Oxford University Press).

Rauch, J. (2004) *Gay Marriage: Why it is Good for Gays, Good for Straights and Good for America* (New York: Henry Holt).

Rawls, J. (1971) *A Theory of Justice* (Cambridge, MA: Belknap Press).

Rawls, J. (1993) *Political Liberalism* (New York: Columbia University Press).

Rawls, J. (1997) 'The Idea of Public Reason Revisited', *University of Chicago Law Review*, 64, 765–807.

Rawls, J. (1999) *The Law of Peoples* (Cambridge, MA: Harvard University Press).

Raz, J. (1994) 'Multiculturalism: A Liberal Perspective', *Dissent*, winter, 67–79.

Redclift, M. (1987) *Sustainable Development: Exploring the Contradictions* (London: Methuen).

Regan T. (1983) *The Case for Animal Rights* (Berkeley, CA: University of California Press).

Rehnquist, W.H. (1998) *All the Laws but One: Civil Liberties in Wartime* (New York: Alfred A. Knopf).

Renteln, A.D. (2004) *The Cultural Defense* (Oxford: Oxford University Press).

Renzetti, C.M., Edleson, J.L. and Bergen, R.K. (eds) (2001) *Sourcebook on Violence against Women* (Thousand Oaks, CA: Sage).

Rich, A. (1986) *Of Woman Born: Motherhood as Experience and Institution* (New York: Norton).

Rodriguez, R. (1982) *Hunger of Memory: The Education of Richard Rodriguez* (New York: Bantam).

Rosenblum, N.L. (1998) *Membership and Morals: The Personal Uses of Pluralism in America* (Princeton: Princeton University Press).

Roth, K. (2004) 'War in Iraq: Not a Humanitarian Intervention', *Human Rights Watch World Report: Human Rights and Armed Conflict* (New York: Human Rights Watch).

Rothbard, M.N. (1998) *The Ethics of Liberty* (New York: New York University Press).

Rousseau, J.-J. (1973 [1762]) 'The Social Contract', *The Social Contract and Discourses* (London: Everyman).

Rubenstein, W.B. (1994) 'Since When is the Fourteenth Amendment Our Route to Equality? Some Reflections on the Construction of the "Hate-Speech" Debate from a Lesbian/Gay Perspective', in Gates Jr, H.L., Griffin, A.P., Lively, D.E., Post, R.C., Rubenstein, W.B. and Strossen, N. (eds), *Speaking of Race, Speaking of Sex: Hate Speech, Civil Rights and Civil Liberties* (New York: New York University Press).

Russell, D.E.H. (1993) 'Pornography and Rape: A Causal Model', in Itzin, C. (ed.), *Pornography: Women, Violence and Civil Liberties* (Oxford: Oxford University Press).

Sachs, J. (2005) 'Why Aid Does Work?', *BBC News*, Sunday, 11 September.

Sandel, M.J. (1982) *Liberalism and the Limits of Justice* (Cambridge: Cambridge University Press).

Sandel, M.J. (ed.) (1984) *Liberalism and its Critics* (New York: New York University Press).

Sandel, M.J. (1996) *Democracy's Discontent: America in Search of a Public Philosophy* (Cambridge, MA: Harvard University Press).

Sandel, M.J. (2005) *Public Philosophy: Essays on Morality in Politics* (Cambridge, MA: Harvard University Press).

Scanlon, T.M. (1972) 'A Theory of Free Expression', *Philosophy and Public Affairs*, 1, 204–26.

Schneiderman, D. and Cossman, B. (2001) 'Political Association and the Anti-Terrorism Bill', in Daniels, R.J., Macklem, P. and Roach, K. (eds), *The Security of Freedom: Essays on Canada's Anti-Terrorism Bill* (Toronto: University of Toronto Press).

Scruton, R. (1986) *Sexual Desire: A Moral Philosophy of the Erotic* (New York: Free Press).

Sen, A. (1981) *Poverty and Famines: An Essay on Entitlement and Deprivation* (Oxford: Clarendon Press).

Sen, A. (1992) *Inequality Reexamined* (Cambridge, MA: Harvard University Press).

Sher, G. (1975) 'Justifying Reverse Discrimination in Employment', *Philosophy and Public Affairs*, 4, 159–70.

Sher, G. (1979) 'Reverse Discrimination, the Future and the Past', *Ethics*, 90, 81–7.

Shklar, J.N. (1989) 'The Liberalism of Fear', in Rosenblum, N.L. (ed.), *Liberalism and the Moral Life* (Cambridge, MA: Harvard University Press).

Shrader-Frechette, K. (2002) *Environmental Justice: Creating Equality, Reclaiming Democracy* (Oxford: Oxford University Press).

Shrage, L. (1994) *Moral Dilemmas of Feminism: Prostitution, Adultery and Abortion* (New York: Routledge).

Shue, H. (1980) *Basic Rights: Subsistence, Affluence and US Foreign Policy* (Princeton: Princeton University Press).

Shue, H. (2003) 'Bombing to Rescue? NATO's 1999 Bombing of Serbia', in Chatterjee, D.K. and Scheid, D.E. (eds), *Ethics and Foreign Intervention* (Cambridge: Cambridge University Press).

Singer, P. (1972) 'Famine, Affluence and Morality', *Philosophy and Public Affairs*, 1, 229–43.

Singer, P. (1975) *Animal Liberation* (New York: Avon).

Singer, P. (1993) *Practical Ethics* (Cambridge: Cambridge University Press).

Snyder, R.C. (2006) *Gay Marriage and Democracy: Equality for All* (Lanham, MD: Rowman & Littlefield).

Steele, S. (1990) *The Content of our Character: A New Vision of Race in America* (New York: St Martin's Press).

Steiner, H. (1983) 'The Rights of Future Generations', in MacLean, D. and Brown, P. (eds), *Energy and the Future* (Totowa, NJ: Rowman & Littlefield).

Stern, N. (2006) *The Economics of Climate Change: The Stern Review* (London: H.M. Treasury).

Strossen, N. (1994) 'Regulating Racist Speech on Campus: A Modest Proposal?', in Gates Jr, H.L., Griffin, A.P., Lively, D.E., Post, R.C., Rubenstein, W.B. and Strossen, N. (eds), *Speaking of Race, Speaking of Sex: Hate Speech, Civil Rights and Civil Liberties* (New York: New York University Press).

Strossen, N. (1995) *Defending Pornography: Free Speech, Sex and the Fight for Women's Rights* (New York: Scribner).

Sullivan, A. (1995) *Virtually Normal: An Argument about Homosexuality* (New York: Alfred A. Knopf).

Sunstein, C.R. (1995) *Democracy and the Problem of Free Speech* (New York: The Free Press).

Sunstein, C.R. (2003) *Why Democracies Need Dissent* (Cambridge, MA: Harvard University Press).

Sunstein, C.R. (2005) *Laws of Fear: Beyond the Precautionary Principle* (Cambridge: Cambridge University Press).

Swift, A. (2001) *Political Philosophy: A Beginners' Guide for Students and Politicians* (Cambridge: Polity Press).

Tabarrok, A. (2002) 'Abortion and Liberty', in McElroy, W. (ed.), *Liberty for Women: Freedom and Feminism in the Twenty-First Century* (Chicago: Ivan R. Dee and the Independent Institute).

Tamir, Y. (1993) *Liberal Nationalism* (Princeton: Princeton University Press).

Tamir, Y. (1999) 'Siding with the Underdogs', in Cohen, J., Howard, M. and Nussbaum, M.C. (eds), *Is Multiculturalism Bad for Women?* (Princeton: Princeton University Press).

Taylor, C. (1994) 'The Politics of Recognition', in Gutmann, A. (ed.), *Multiculturalism: Examining the Politics of Recognition* (Princeton: Princeton University Press).

Taylor, M.C. (1994) 'Impact of Affirmative Action on Beneficiary Groups: Evidence from the 1990 General Social Survey', *Basic and Applied Social Psychology*, 15, 143–78.

Teson, F.R. (2006) 'The Moral Basis of Humanitarian Intervention', in Tinnevelt, R. and Verschraegen, G. (eds), *Between Cosmopolitan Ideals and State Sovereignty: Studies in Global Justice* (Basingstoke: Palgrave).

Thomson, J.J. (1971) 'A Defense of Abortion', *Philosophy and Public Affairs*, 1, 47–66.

Thomson, J.J. (1973) 'Preferential Hiring', *Philosophy and Public Affairs*, 2, 364–84.

Tomasi, J. (1995) 'Kymlicka, Liberalism, and Respect for Cultural Minorities', *Ethics*, 105, 580–603.

Tooley, M. (1972) 'Abortion and Infanticide', *Philosophy and Public Affairs*, 2, 37–65.

Tronto, J. (1993) *Moral Boundaries: A Political Argument for an Ethic of Care* (New York: Routledge).

Tully, J. (1995) *Strange Multiplicity: Constitutionalism in an Age of Diversity* (Cambridge: Cambridge University Press).

Tully, J. (2000) 'The Struggles of Indigenous Peoples for and of Freedom', in Ivison, D., Patton, P. and Sanders, W. (eds), *Political Theory and the Rights of Indigenous Peoples* (Cambridge: Cambridge University Press).

UN (adopted 19 December 1966; entered into force 23 March 1976) International Covenant on Civil and Political Rights (New York: UN).

UNDP (2005) 'Human Development Report: International Cooperation at a Crossroads: Aid, Trade and Security in an Unequal World' (New York: UNDP).

UNDP (2007/8) 'Fighting Climate Change: Human solidarity in a divided world' (New York: UNDP).

Unger, P. (1996) *Living High and Letting Die: Our Illusion of Innocence* (Oxford: Oxford University Press).

UNICEF (2007) 'The State of the World's Children' (New York, UNICEF).

Valls, A. (1999) 'The Libertarian Case for Affirmative Action', *Social Theory and Practice*, 25, 299–323.

Van Parijs, P. (1991) 'Why Surfers Should Be Fed: The Liberal Case for an Unconditional Basic Income', *Philosophy and Public Affairs*, 20, 101–31.

Van Parijs, P. (1995) *Real Freedom for All* (Oxford: Oxford University Press).

Velleman, J.D. (1992) 'Against the Right to Die', *Journal of Medicine and Philosophy*, 17, 665–81.

Waldron, J. (1992) 'Minority Cultures and the Cosmopolitan Alternative', *University of Michigan Journal of Law Reform*, 25, 751–93.

Waldron, J. (2000) 'What is Cosmopolitan?', *Journal of Political Philosophy*, 8, 227–43.

Waldron, J. (2003) 'Security and Liberty: The Image of Balance', *Journal of Political Philosophy*, 11, 191–210.

Walker, R. (1993/4) 'New Zealand Immigration and the Political Economy', *Social Contract*, 4, 86–95.

Walzer, M. (1980) 'The Moral Standing of States: A Response to Four Critics', *Philosophy and Public Affairs*, 9, 209–29.

Walzer, M. (1983) *Spheres of Justice: A Defense of Pluralism and Equality* (New York: Basic Books).

Walzer, M. (2004) *Arguing About War* (New Haven: Yale University Press).

Walzer, M. (2006 [1977]) *Just and Unjust Wars* (New York: Basic Books).

Warner, M. (1999) *The Trouble with Normal: Sex, Politics and the Ethics of Queer Life* (New York: Free Press).

Warren, M.A. (1997) *Moral Status: Obligations to Persons and Other Living Things* (Oxford: Clarendon).

Wasserstrom, R. (1997) 'A Defense of Programs of Preferential Treatment', in Beckwith, F.J. and Jones, T.E. (eds), *Affirmative Action: Social Justice or Reverse Discrimination?* (Amherst: Prometheus Books).

Weaver, J. (1993) 'The Social Science and Psychological Research Evidence: Perceptual and Behavioural Consequences of Exposure to Pornography', in Itzin, C. (ed.), *Pornography: Women, Violence and Civil Liberties* (Oxford: Oxford University Press).

Weber, M. (1946) *From Max Weber: Essays in Sociology* (New York: Oxford University Press).

West, R. (1998) 'Gay Marriage and Liberal Constitutionalism: Two Mistakes', in Allen, A.L. and Regan, M.C. (eds), *Debating Democracy's Discontent: Essays on American Politics, Law and Public Philosophy* (Oxford: Oxford University Press).

Witte, J. J. (2003) 'Reply to Professor Mark Strasser', in Wardle, L.D., Strasser, M., Duncan, W. C. and Coolidge, D.O. (eds), *Marriage and Same-Sex Unions: A Debate* (Newport, CT: Praeger).

Wolf, S.M. (1996) 'Gender, Feminism and Death: Physician-Assisted Suicide and Euthanasia', in Wolf, S.M. (ed.), *Feminism and Bioethics: Beyond Reproduction* (Oxford: Oxford University Press).

Wollstonecraft, M. (1995 [1792]) *A Vindication of the Rights of Man and a Vindication of the Rights of Woman* (Cambridge: Cambridge University Press).

World Bank (2007) Key Development Data and Statistics (Washington, DC: World Bank).

Young, I.M. (2000) *Inclusion and Democracy* (Oxford: Oxford University Press).

Zedillo, E. (2001) 'Financing for Development' (New York: UN High Level Panel on Financing for Development).

Index